Areas and Municipalities in the U.S.
Open or Closed to Travel by Soviet Official Personnel

Area closed to travel
City closed to travel in open area
River closed to travel
Area open to travel
City open to travel in closed area
Road open to travel in closed area

Note: The state of Hawaii is closed to travel by Soviet official personnel. See large-scale maps of Washington, D.C., New York, Los Angeles, and San Francisco for further travel restrictions.

Source: Note from the Secretary of State to the Ambassador of the Soviet Union dated 16 November 1993

Central New Jersey Area

National Capital Area

Asterisk indicates city has county equivalency.

Scale 1:5,000,000

THE NEW
WIZARD WAR

To Rick,

R S Metcalfe

November
1988

THE NEW
WIZARD WAR

*How the Soviets Steal U.S. High Technology—
And How We Give It Away*

Robyn Shotwell Metcalfe

TEMPUS™

PUBLISHED BY

Tempus Books of Microsoft Press
A Division of Microsoft Corporation
16011 NE 36th Way, Box 97017, Redmond, Washington 98073-9717

Library of Congress Cataloging in Publication Data

Metcalfe, Robyn Shotwell, 1947–
    The new wizard war : how the Soviets steal U.S. high
technology—and how we give it away / Robyn Shotwell
Metcalfe.
        p.   cm.
    Includes index.
    1. Technology transfer—Economic aspects—Soviet
Union.   2. Technology transfer—Economic aspects—United
States.   3. Business intelligence—Soviet Union.   4. Business
intelligence—United States.   5. Soviet Union—Foreign economic
relations—United States.   6. United States—Foreign economic
relations—Soviet Union.   I. Title.
HC340.T4M47   1988   88-19943
338.947'06—dc19   CIP
ISBN 1-55615-016-4

Printed and bound in the United States of America.

1 2 3 4 5 6 7 8 9   HCHC   3 2 1 0 9 8

Distributed to the book trade in the United States by
Harper & Row.

Distributed to the book trade in Canada by
General Publishing Company, Ltd.

Tempus Books and the Tempus logo are trademarks of
Microsoft Press.
Tempus Books is an imprint of Microsoft Press.

Cover art copyright © 1988 by David Shannon.
Inside cover maps courtesy of U.S. State Department, 1983.

Editor: Anne Depue

CONTENTS

Foreword

This book is a timely examination of one of our most pressing national security problems: the Soviet acquisition of U.S. high technology.

Robyn Metcalfe presents vital information for exporters of high technology who are pursuing sales to the Soviet Union and Eastern Europe. Considering the business and patriotic reasons for caution about such exports, she notes the questions of Soviet business reliability in the past and reminds us that the transfer of technology to the Soviet Union could come back to haunt U.S. firms in the future in terms of increased competition. For example, the Soviet Union is taking advantage of the present difficulties in the U.S. and European space programs to campaign for Western customers for Soviet commercial satellite launchings.

Mrs. Metcalfe details the momentum behind the massive Soviet program to acquire advanced Western technology and conjectures that "despite the *glasnost* initiatives it is unlikely that efforts by the Soviet intelligence agencies to steal strategic high technology have ground to a halt." I can confirm that this is correct; these Soviet efforts have not lessened, and nothing indicates that they will. Mrs. Metcalfe also states that the Soviets hope that joint ventures will bring them high technology that is currently prohibited by U.S. export controls. Again, I can confirm her hypothesis. The U.S. government has evidence that the Soviet Union will exploit joint ventures to evade U.S. and allied laws and regulations.

Bringing together information from government documents, newspapers, and trade publications, Mrs. Metcalfe covers the full range of Soviet acquisition programs, from illegal diversion of equipment through scientific exchanges with U.S. universities and research institutes to legal and illegal exploitation of major technical data bases.

The author also reveals the dramatic Soviet campaign to gain technology from the newly industrializing nations, an effort that poses particular problems for Western democracies. Although these nations are challenging the United States, Europe, and Japan commercially, they remain outside our system of alliances.

Mrs. Metcalfe discusses the differences between the Defense and Commerce departments that have existed since our export control system began and that at times have made headlines during the Reagan Administration. I am the first to recognize that these issues are not easy and that serious reporting on export controls must recognize the existence of policy differences; however, a consensus on technology security is now much stronger than it was in the 1970s. In its well-publicized 1987 report on export controls, the National Academy of Sciences stated that "the Department of Defense's determined efforts to reinvigorate the national security export control regime have been useful in raising the general level of awareness of the need for national security export controls among government agencies, high-technology industry, the governments of friendly countries, and world public opinion."

NATIONAL SECURITY AND COMMERCIAL COMPETITIVENESS

Let me now offer some thoughts on two key areas that this book addresses. These thoughts are based on my seven years of experience directing the Defense Department's technology security program.

First, let me answer the charge that is sometimes made that export controls seriously hamper U.S. firms in international competition. I believe that this is not true.

National security export controls are only one of many influences on foreign trade. The Department of Commerce has stated that the major barriers to U.S. exports have included the protectionist trade policies of foreign governments; intense foreign competition for U.S. firms; the overvalued dollar (until mid-1985); heavy offshore production by U.S. manufacturers; and, in the case of computer software, piracy.

We must also remember that the trade deficit is caused much more by an excess of imports than by a shortage of exports. U.S. exports, and in particular exports of high-technology goods, have continued to grow since 1982. For example, U.S. exports in high technology increased from $58 billion in 1982 to $84.1 billion in 1987. The main problem has been on the import side, where foreign competitors are taking an increasing share of the U.S. market. Imports of high technology have jumped from $35 billion in 1982 to $83.5 billion in 1987. According to the Department of Commerce, U.S. companies have contributed significantly to this surge by buying components for their products abroad. Thus, U.S. high-tech firms themselves have had a hand in the deteriorating U.S. position in world trade. Encouragingly, trade figures for April 1988, released by the Commerce Department in June, suggest that our trade balance may have turned a corner.

IMPLICATIONS OF THE TOSHIBA-KONGSBERG SALES

My second point is that the illegal Toshiba-Kongsberg sales, which were made public in 1987, have disturbing implications for the future of U.S.-Soviet trade. These two firms sold the Soviet Navy propeller-manufacturing technology that is helping to make Soviet submarines substantially quieter. The United States will have to spend billions of dollars to counter these improvements.

The Toshiba-Kongsberg sales indicate that the Soviet Union intends, and has the capability, to obtain high technology illegally even from well-known corporations. The firms involved were not back-room operations or mail fronts for technobandits, but solid, established companies that always were assumed to obey the law and to maintain tight internal security. Toshiba Machine is a subsidiary of one of the largest, most technologically advanced and most commercially reputable Japanese corporations. Kongsberg Trading Company was a division of Kongsberg Vaapenfabrikk, which is owned by the Norwegian government. Moreover, as one member of Congress noted, this was not a "rogue operation" but a "conscious corporate decision made at the highest level of these companies."

Recent investigations indicate that more firms than these two were involved. The Norwegian police report on Kongsberg, which was issued in October 1987, stated that machine-tool builders in France, West Germany, and Italy also had shipped goods to the Soviet Union in violation of

Cocom regulations. In April 1988, the government of France announced the arrest of several executives of the Forest Line machine-tool company for illegally selling to the Soviet Union equipment to manufacture turbine blades used in advanced jet engines.

The Toshiba-Kongsberg sales have shaken the Western alliances and the Western trading community more than any export control case in recent memory. All those who wish to encourage legitimate East-West trade must be disturbed by this Soviet penetration of reputable European and Japanese companies. If the Soviets see Western firms as a source of high technology for military purposes, then every corporate executive interested in the Soviet market must concentrate as much on preventing espionage as on promoting trade.

STRENGTHENING EXPORT CONTROLS

The Toshiba case shows where the interests of the U.S. government and U.S. exporters converge strikingly. National security demands tighter technology security throughout the Western alliance. U.S. exporters need a level playing field where their foreign competitors face the same national export controls as do U.S. companies. I believe that we will all gain from both stricter enforcement of export controls within Cocom and greater uniformity in enforcing controls and prosecuting violators.

Cocom member nations vary widely in how they approach both areas. For example, the United States assigns several hundred officials to review license applications and to enforce export control regulations. The U.S. Export Administration Act of 1985 punishes violators of these regulations with prison terms of as much as ten years. The Department of Defense, which has the biggest stake in the success of export controls, plays a vigorous role in U.S. government policy-making. For example, the Department of Defense reviews all proposed sales of export-controlled goods to the Soviet bloc and can raise its objections to the president of the United States.

By contrast, before the Toshiba-Kongsberg case, Japan apparently assigned only 40 full-time officials to export licensing, and the Japanese

Defense Agency played no role whatsoever. In the wake of Toshiba-Kongsberg, Japan and Norway have strengthened their licensing and enforcement systems, but some other governments have moved slowly to investigate the problems revealed by these sales and by the Norwegian police report. Some Cocom governments still have no criminal sanctions for violations of national security that often do more damage than traditional espionage.

To put it bluntly, violators of Cocom rules have operated with impunity for too long in countries that should have acted forcefully to prosecute them. Much national legislation is far too weak and enforced far too haphazardly. Too little information is shared across national boundaries. Most important, violators can far too easily move between countries to avoid prosecution.

We need real reciprocity in Cocom. A technobandit indicted in one Western country should be treated as an outlaw in all. I believe that each Cocom nation should agree to take effective action against any firm—whether foreign or domestic—that illegally exports goods on the control list. This approach will require faster and more systematic sharing of information about potential diversions among customs and law enforcement agencies. It also will require criminal penalties severe enough to deter potential violators. The United States has made it clear that as Cocom governments take such steps the United States will begin to remove the remaining restrictions on the transfer of technology within the West.

The Reagan Administration has moved forcefully to encourage our allies to take necessary steps to stem the tide of illegal high-tech transfers. We successfully pressed for a special Cocom meeting last July, at which member countries agreed to pay greater attention to licensing and enforcement. In January 1988, Cocom governments held a high-level Special Political Meeting, at which the United States delegation was headed by the deputy secretary of state. At that meeting, member nations agreed to share information on potential diversions and to cooperate more effectively to stop them. They also supported selective reductions in the control list, with the stated goal of firmer enforcement of controls on a more limited list of items.

CONCLUSION

Whatever policy decisions the United States and other Cocom governments make, the problems associated with technology security will not go away. Robyn Metcalfe's book will contribute to better-informed public opinion on this subject. It also will be useful for high-tech exporters who need to understand the actions of our Soviet adversaries and the programs that Western governments have mounted in response.

Dr. Stephen D. Bryen
Deputy Under Secretary of Defense
(Trade Security Policy)
and Director
Defense Technology Security Administration
Washington, D.C.
June 1988

Acknowledgments

In 1985 John Walker emerged from obscurity as the owner of a small security firm in Baltimore, Md., to international notoriety as a Soviet agent responsible for delivering billions of dollars' worth of U.S. technology to the Soviet Union. Newspaper headlines delivered the message that he, along with his family and friends, sold U.S. technology secrets to the Soviet Union during a five-year period. Soon thereafter, others, such as James Pelton and Jonathan Pollard, shared Walker's dubious fame as they too succumbed to greed and compromised U.S. national security.

During this same period, Mikhail S. Gorbachev became the new Soviet leader, and in 1986 he presided at the Twenty-Seventh Party Congress, during which the Communist party announced its new Five-Year Plan. The foundation of the plan was a commitment to restructure the Soviet economy in preparation for unprecedented economic growth. Appearing again and again in the long speeches was a strong sentiment that Western technology would be the fuel for economic recovery. To bring a 1950s economy into the 1980s, the Soviets clearly would need Western technical know-how.

The combination of the frequent announcements of spy activities and the proclaimed Soviet drive to acquire U.S. technology made me curious. How long had the Soviets been acquiring our technical know-how? Should U.S. companies sell high technology to the Soviets when they were getting it through clandestine means anyway? Was all the concern expressed by U.S. intelligence agencies about technology espionage overblown? Was the concern based on fact or on propaganda?

The search for answers led me to write this book. It also led me to hundreds of respected authorities on Soviet history, espionage, U.S. government policy, industrial competitiveness, and export control law. I owe gratitude to those who spent countless hours explaining to me the intricacies of U.S.-Soviet relations, the Soviet scientific community, and the frustrations of private industries that struggle to comply with U.S. export controls.

For help in understanding how the U.S. government interrupts illegal exports of high technology to the Soviet Union, I wish to thank Stephen Walton of the U.S. Customs Service's Operation Exodus, and Stephen Dodge, David Hoover, Robert M. Keck, and Chuck McLeod, also of the Customs Service; Paul Freedenberg, undersecretary of commerce for Export Administration; John Black, Anstruther Davidson, Frank Deliberti, Daniel Hoydysh, Brooks Olsen, and Bob Rice, of the Department of Commerce; Sumner Benson, Stephen Bryen, Oles Lomacky, George Menas, and Frank Sobiescyk, of the Department of Defense; Cary Cavenaugh and Tom Robertson of the Department of State; Michael Marks of the Office of Science and Technology Policy; Senator William V. Roth; former Congressman Ed Zschau; Leonard Lederman of the National Science Foundation; and the FBI.

For information about the problems facing private industry, I wish to thank Tom Christiansen, Jan Czekajewski, Bill Fahey, John General, Jeffry Gibson, Guy Palmer, Joseph Russoniello, Morey Schapira, Donald Weadon, and William Zolner.

For a better understanding of the Soviet Union, I wish to thank Lara Baker, Ladislav Bittman, Bob Diorio, Murray Feshbach, Seymour Goodman, Loren Graham, Philip Hanson, Mark Kuchment, Stanislav Levchenko, William McHenry, Scott Norwood, Radio Liberty Research, Henry Rowen, and Charles Vie.

For their patience and willingness to retrieve countless books, articles, and papers, I wish to thank the reference librarians at the Dynamic Information Service, the Hoover Institution, and the Menlo Park Library. Celia Herron Waters spent eighteen months researching and checking facts.

And for turning my research notes into readable prose, I thank Anne Depue, Paul Dreyfus, and Hallberg Hallmundsson. Both Bob and Julia Metcalfe graciously made room for this book in our family.

Introduction

During the early years of World War II, the German air force pounded British cities with bombs dropped from planes directed by radio beams. Winston Churchill, alarmed at the prospect of a Nazi victory, charged British scientists to develop a means to intercept and obstruct these deadly radio signals. The struggle for technical superiority that ensued between British and German scientists Churchill called the Wizard War. During 1940–41, British scientists figured out how to distort the beam by strengthening only half of it, thereby causing German planes to drop their lethal loads in nearby fields instead of on populated towns. In *Their Finest Hour*, the second volume of his history of World War II, Churchill wrote:

> Unless British science had proved superior to German, and unless its strange sinister resources had been effectively brought to bear on the struggle for survival, we might well have been defeated, and, being defeated, destroyed.[1]

This book describes a new Wizard War, the struggle between the U.S. and the Soviet Union to command the world's most advanced technology. The increasing sophistication of high technology, along with the blurring of peaceful and combative uses of high technology, has raised the stakes for maintaining technical superiority. Given the U.S. lead in most technological areas, the Soviets resort to acquiring U.S. technology, from chips to actual computers, through whatever means best serve their purpose, including espionage and export diversion. Once Western high technology reaches Soviet hands, it often appears in Soviet computers, some used to direct rockets into space and some used to produce submarine propellers.

The battlefield for this technological one-upmanship is not clearly defined, reaching outside the United States to Japan and West Germany, countries that serve as conduits for U.S. technology to the Soviet Union. Other participants in the new Wizard War include both allies and neutral countries.

This book investigates the ways in which the United States is safeguarding its most advanced technical secrets. It isolates the issues confronting government policymakers, industry executives, and the academic community. Unfortunately, a way in which to effectively guard this technology is not readily apparent: Each time the United States restricts its technological assets by curbing academic freedom or by prohibiting high-technology exports, it limits scientific progress and economic growth. Ultimately, the freedom inherent in our democracy is at stake.

Current events in the Soviet Union are forcing the United States to rethink its battle plan for the new Wizard War. In 1985, General Secretary Mikhail S. Gorbachev announced to the world his country's vigorous commitment to join the Western economic community. To do so, he said, requires that the Soviet Union launch a massive drive for acquiring Western technology. A campaign of this sort is not entirely new for the Soviet Union, but its intensity and sophistication are.

In only three years, the Soviet Union has attempted to alter its demeanor from an imperialist warmonger, insensitive to human rights, to a peace-loving promoter of democracy enhanced with an expedient sprinkling of capitalism. One motive behind this ideological facelift is the Soviet Union's need to assure Western nations that it no longer poses a threat to world peace and is therefore to be trusted as a recipient of critical and sometimes militarily useful technology through an expansion of U.S.-Soviet trade. The successful transformation of the Soviet economy will depend in part on many separate victories in the new Wizard War, from a loosening of U.S. trade restrictions to the capture of a defense contractor's secret missile specifications.

The push to acquire U.S. high technology appears not only in expanded trade channels and diplomatic initiatives but in covert operations such as spying and illegal exporting. Both activities continued and even increased in the 1980s. From 1985 to 1987, twenty-seven individuals were arrested for spying on behalf of the Soviets in order to obtain U.S. technology. From 1981 to 1987, fifty-eight export-control cases were tried, all involving the illegal diversion of high technology to the Soviet Union.

During the 1970s, the years of détente, the Soviet Union demonstrated that improved superpower relations served to whet its appetite for U.S. high technology: They obtained technology both through increased trade and through a flurry of clandestine activities. And the Soviets have no reason to curtail covert acquisitions while successfully gaining technology through legitimate sales of high-technology products. Stanislav Levchenko, a former KGB officer who defected to the United States in 1979, exhorts naive Americans to expect Soviet espionage to continue alongside a warming of superpower relations. In an interview with the author in May 1988 he said:

> Leaders of the Soviet intelligence organizations consider high-technology espionage as the most profitable business in the Soviet Union. For an investment of $50 to $100,000, representing payment to an American spy recruited by the KGB, the Soviet Union receives half a billion dollars of research and development.[2]

The United States is in a better position than it was in the late 1960s to prepare itself for this new era in U.S.-Soviet relations. Lawmakers and businesses can learn from a détente halted by the invasion of Afghanistan, from the techniques of U.S. spies who delivered secret U.S. technology to the KGB, and from companies that engaged in unprofitable joint ventures with the Soviet Union. These lessons lead to a better understanding of the risks inherent in Soviet joint ventures and the persistence of Soviet agents in locating and obtaining critical technology. To ignore these hard-earned lessons of the past would be to unwisely surrender billions of dollars' worth of U.S. research and development.

On the other hand, some increased U.S. trade with the Soviets or not encouraging exchanges of students and private citizens would be both provincial and shortsighted. Relationships that bring a more informed understanding can only better the chances for mutual survival, but we need not rush headlong into joint ventures and scientific cooperation without assurance that *perestroika* will produce permanent change in the Soviet political and economic system.

With its touted reforms and arms-control initiatives, the Soviet Union appears to be controlling the superpower relationship. The United States needs to assert its own role. Instead of calling the new era of U.S.-Soviet relations a "new détente," the United States should christen this period an era of pragmatism. This period should be distinguished by judiciously written joint venture agreements, a streamlined list of controlled technology exports, and tough penalties for spies and export diverters. U.S. businesses should expect the same financial returns from a Soviet business deal that they would from a European deal. The U.S. strategy of investing in a long-term business relationship makes little sense with a country that has offered only short-term windows of opportunity. The assumption of risk should be compensated for in financial terms, preferably in hard currency. And business agreements should be written with short-term returns on investment in mind.

Critical to the success of a pragmatic position is the role of U.S. citizens. Although government controls and policies form the basis for controlling access to U.S. technology, industry executives, academicians, and individual scientists form the front line of defense of U.S. technological assets. They must become familiar with the issues so that they can negotiate U.S.-Soviet business deals and lobby for trade policy from a position of informed authority.

Another line of defense is a firm commitment by the U.S. government and private industry to research and development. According to the National Science Foundation, U.S. research and development cost as a percentage of U.S. gross national product has been hovering near 2.8 for the past decade. With a cutback in U.S. defense spending, a major source of research and development investment, the United States may even lose a percentage point during the next decade. By maintaining and increasing its technological lead through research and development, the United States can better compensate for technology loss through espionage, diversion, and trade. Projects such as the Strategic Defense Initiative are important from the standpoint of a major commitment of resources to the development of advanced technology. The continuation of the U.S. space program with participation of private industry contributes to technological progress.

Armed with a renewed commitment to research and development, an industry awareness of espionage and export diversion techniques, and a streamlined and rigorously enforced system of export controls, the United States can enter the new superpower dialogue with its technical superiority firmly intact.

The new Wizard War is bound to continue. A cautious balancing of the interests of an open society, international competitiveness, and national security will ensure that the United States emerges from the struggle a victor.

NOTES

1. Winston S. Churchill, *Their Finest Hour*, vol. 2 of *The Second World War* (Boston: Houghton Mifflin, 1949), pp. 381–82.
2. Stanislav Levchenko: Interview, May 2, 1988.

1

THE
BATTLEGROUND

On a warm summer day in 1986, the Bow Street Prison in London held the man most wanted by the United States for illegally diverting sophisticated technology to the Soviet Union. Forty-six years old at the time, Werner Bruchhausen was finally on his way to trial in the United States after several years of eluding American law enforcement officials. Five years earlier, he had been indicted by a U.S. grand jury, but he had successfully—and flamboyantly—lived as a fugitive in Europe from 1981 until 1986. After unsuccessfully appealing his case all the way to the House of Lords in England, Bruchhausen was about to jet across the Atlantic for a courtroom showdown.

Between 1977 and 1980, Bruchhausen smuggled more than $8 million[1] worth of high technology and military equipment through various front companies in California to other front companies in Europe and on to his Soviet customers. Bruchhausen owned and controlled at least twelve corporations in California and two in West Germany. He based his operation primarily in southern California with the help of three accomplices: a Russian-born, naturalized U.S. citizen, Anatoli Maluta (alias Tony Metz), of Redondo Beach, Calif.; a German-born, naturalized U.S. citizen, Sabina Tittel, of Palos Verdes, Calif.; and Dietmar Ulrichshofer, of Austria, whom Bruchhausen helped establish in the illegal business of selling strategic technologies to the Soviets.

Bruchhausen's world began to crumble one day in 1977, when a letter from one of his former employees arrived at the U.S. consulate in Düsseldorf. Although to this day no one knows who the employee was or why the letter was sent, handwriting analysis revealed that it may have been written by a woman. The letter sketchily outlined Bruchhausen's illegal technology-smuggling operations in the United States and Europe. Nothing was done, and another letter arrived at the consulate in 1978; in 1980, the letters finally came to the attention of Robert Rice of the U.S. Commerce Department and Stephen C. Dodge of the U.S. Customs Service. After word reached Commerce, Customs officials were assigned to the case, and they gradually pieced together Bruchhausen's story.

Bruchhausen ran one of the most successful supply routes of U.S. high technology to the Soviet Union during the late 1970s, using his offices in California and Germany to export equipment to both the Soviet Union and other Eastern bloc customers. Although he specialized in finding semiconductor manufacturing equipment for the Soviets, he also assisted them through his front companies in acquiring electronic testing equipment, communications systems, computers, and computer components. By the time Bruchhausen was apprehended, the Soviets had received Data General Eclipse computers, Fairchild test equipment, semiconductor manufacturing equipment, Watkins-Johnson military microwave-communications receiving equipment, antenna equipment, microwave tuners, Memorex disk drives, Intel single-board computers, and Motorola microcircuits. Although the equipment was worth only about $8 million in the United States, eager Soviets had parted with at least $30 million of precious U.S. hard currency to become proud owners of the latest U.S. technology.[2] The Soviet purchases often came in pairs: one for the purpose of "reverse engineering"[3] and another for use in military, general scientific research, or industrial applications.

The requests for technology that were forwarded to Bruchhausen usually came from several Soviet foreign-trade organizations (FTOs), such as Elektronorgteknika (Elorg), which is responsible for international purchases of computers and electronics and reports to the Ministry of Foreign Economic Relations (formerly the Ministry of Foreign Trade) in Moscow. The officer who signed the Request for Quotations (RFQs) for most of the equipment was Viktor Kedrov, a former Soviet military intelligence officer and vice president of Elorg. Bruchhausen used what became a classic route for high-tech smugglers that followed in his footsteps, and his shipments went through the same general sequence of countries each time. Equipment would leave a company in California, California Technology Company (CTC), run by Anatoli Maluta, and go to a front company in Germany, from there on to another front company in either Austria or Switzerland, and then often to Schiphol Airport in Amsterdam, where it was shipped to Moscow on an Aeroflot plane.

Before Commerce and Customs began investigating the case, U.S. electronics firms became suspicious of the CTC orders for equipment. In 1979, Robert Markin, Perkin-Elmer's director of administration, contacted Commerce and told it that his corporation, a manufacturer of precision electric components and analytical instruments, had received an order from CTC for $150,000 worth of equipment from a company that it suspected was a front for the Soviet Union. In 1980, when Fairchild Test System Group questioned CTC's orders, Maluta insisted that he needed the equipment for his security business in Arizona and Alaska. Despite Maluta's insistence, Fairchild delayed a delivery of $740,000 worth of semiconductor memory test systems. When Maluta refused installation and maintenance contracts for the equipment and denied Fairchild the right to on-site inspections after delivery, Fairchild felt it had reason to suspect Maluta's purchase. But because the company could not produce concrete evidence of an illegal sale, it let the shipment proceed. Again in 1980, another company, Watkins-Johnson, notified the Commerce Department that something was not right: It had received orders for equipment from a company that had changed its name six times between Jan. 16, 1975, and Jan. 29, 1980.[4] The company, CTC, belonged to Maluta. At the time, both Customs and Commerce were just beginning to hear about Bruchhausen, and action was not taken immediately. After the Fairchild and Perkin-Elmer incidents, a case was finally opened, and the investigation went into motion in March 1980.

At that time, Gasonics Inc. notified the Commerce Department about a suspicious order from Maluta's company. Customs agents then attempted to track the shipment through Bruchhausen's smuggling route. The shipment consisted of two HiPox High Pressure Oxidation furnaces used in the semiconductor manufacturing process. The agents had a southern California packer fabricate crates identical to the Bruchhausen-bound ones. The false crates were then filled with 10,000 pounds of sand, enough to equal the weight of the equipment. Just after the crates with the equipment reached the Lufthansa plane's loading area in Los Angeles, Customs officials switched the original crates with the sand-filled ones, and the bogus shipment left for Frankfurt, West Germany. Upon arrival in Frankfurt, the crates were trucked to a small town on the Austrian border where Dietmar Ulrichshofer operated a front company. The shipment was then sold to another Ulrichshofer front company in Vienna and left on a different truck for the city. In Vienna, the crates were destined for an Aeroflot flight bound for Moscow via Amsterdam.

While the shipment sat in an Austrian customs' goods-in-transit area of a warehouse in Vienna, officials believe that Ulrichshofer, tipped off about the U.S. Customs effort, entered the warehouse with a crow-bar, opened one of the crates, and discovered the sand. According to Ulrichshofer, he opened the crate to insert an operator's manual. The ruse was at an end, and Customs and Commerce officials had a paper trail proving the intent to ship the equipment from the United States to Moscow.

On Aug. 18, 1981, Bruchhausen and his three accomplices—Maluta, Tittel, and Ulrichshofer—were indicted on sixty counts of violating both the Export Administration Act and the Arms Export Control Act. They had illegally shipped restricted technology to the Soviet Union, falsified export documents, made false statements, and neglected to obtain vali-dated export licenses. Tittel and Maluta were found guilty after a Los

Angeles trial, and both were sent to jail, but Bruchhausen eluded arrest and left the United States. That made him a free man with time on his hands to spend the millions he had netted from his smuggling operations. Ulrichshofer remains a fugitive, and his firm is no longer allowed to export U.S. goods.

Even though Bruchhausen's network was disrupted, he resumed his smuggling operation in 1981. Thomas Albert Gosselin, an American computer systems programmer living in Rhode Island, went into business with Bruchhausen through the diverter's firm in West Germany, Analogue und Digital Technik. That company was a holding company for two other firms, Techma and Elmash, that sold high technology to the Eastern bloc. Gosselin traveled to West Germany to meet with Bruchhausen on several occasions. There, Bruchhausen showed him the Soviet "shopping list" of high-technology items. Bruchhausen confirmed his intent to purchase all items on the list from the United States and to divert them to the Soviet Union. Gosselin returned to the United States and contacted the Federal Bureau of Investigation (FBI). During the next few years, Gosselin continued his work for Bruchhausen while informing the FBI and the Customs Service of the transactions and of Bruchhausen's behavior.[5]

It was not until May 1985 that Detective Inspector Vernon Williams from New Scotland Yard, on behalf of U.S. Customs agents, pounced on Bruchhausen after he entered England. Carrying a Brazilian passport, Bruchhausen was traveling under the alias of Ernesto Hause. While in a London prison, he managed to delay extradition to the United States by appealing his case all the way to the House of Lords. When the final appeal was denied, his time had run out. In the fall of 1986, U.S. Customs authorities announced that Werner Bruchhausen was being extradited for wire fraud in connection with violating U.S. export laws. (Wire fraud is the transfer of illegally obtained funds through the use of telephone or other electronic communications.) Never before had the United States succeeded in extraditing a diverter of its high technology. The authorities hoped that other smugglers were taking note: The United States was getting tough.

Once in California, Bruchhausen was tried on fifteen counts of wire fraud. As the prosecutor, Assistant U.S. Attorney William F. Fahey, put it,

the wire fraud was in connection with a "scheme to defraud U.S. manufacturers and the U.S. government in obtaining high-technology electronic and military equipment for ultimate diversion to Soviet bloc
countries." Bruchhausen used a classic defense: ignorance. He said that
he believed he was operating within the provisions of existing export
laws. His trial revealed, however, that he and his partners consistently
either neglected to obtain export licenses or willfully falsified information submitted to the U.S. Customs Service and the Department of Commerce. In March 1987, he was convicted on all counts, sent to jail for
fifteen years, and fined $15,000, the severest possible fine for wire fraud
but a paltry sum for Bruchhausen. U.S. authorities were unable to touch
the millions sitting in foreign banks that he made through his transactions with the Soviets.

The Werner Bruchhausen case is a paradigm of how the Soviets illegally acquire U.S. high technology. It illustrates that the Soviets are
willing to pay inflated prices for the technology, even 215 percent over
the cost of equipment they disbursed to Bruchhausen. The types of technology that Bruchhausen diverted to the Soviet Union, such as semiconductor manufacturing equipment, reveal the sophisticated buying
behavior of the Soviets, who understand both the role of semiconductors
as the building blocks of most electronics and computer-based electronics
and the need to manufacture semiconductors internally for use in military research and development.

Bruchhausen showed how large quantities of valuable high-tech
products could be stealthily moved out of the United States—shipments
involving a variety of sophisticated electronic equipment—unnoticed except by a few companies that detect and act upon unusual buyer
behavior. The Bruchhausen case also illustrates the classic techniques of
utilizing multiple front companies, falsifying export forms, and lying to
electronics manufacturers. And it points up the critical role that international contacts play, particularly neutral countries that are not members
of the Coordinating Committee for Multilateral Export Controls (Cocom),
an international committee charged with controlling the export of high
technology to the Soviet bloc.

After Bruchhausen's trial, U.S. government intelligence agencies,
the departments of Commerce and Defense, and the Customs Service

heaved a common sigh of relief as their most sought-after technology thief landed in prison. But Bruchhausen's activities represent only a few ripples in the continuing stream of U.S. high technology to the Soviet Union. Various U.S. agencies keep thick files documenting cases of illegal diversion and espionage by the Soviet bloc to obtain U.S. high technology during the past two decades, and many are still open. They demonstrate that the Soviets have an organized strategy for such nefarious acquisitions.

That strategy is not aimed at the wholesale, indiscriminate collection of U.S. technology. As several high-ranking Soviet officials have stated, the Soviet Union is interested primarily in America's latest and most advanced technology. Furthermore, rather than simply coveting the state-of-the-art products themselves, the Soviets want contracts with U.S. firms that deliver the ability to design and manufacture a particular item. Referring to the Soviet interest in U.S. computer technology, the late Boris N. Naumov, director of the Soviet organization responsible for introducing personal computers into the manufacturing sector, stated, "We must buy modern products, not old ones. These must have compatible software with our own, like UNIX or something else we want to use, and have high-level interfaces for instrumentation."[6]

WHAT'S THE FUSS ALL ABOUT?

According to the FBI, between 1985 and 1987, twenty-seven individuals were arrested for assisting the Soviets with the illegal collection of technology such as hardware, software, and documentation. Some spies were employees of the U.S. military, others of U.S. computer companies, Soviet intelligence organizations, or both. In addition, between 1981 and 1987, fifty-eight export-control cases marched through U.S. courts, revealing the details of high-technology smuggling either directly to the Soviet Union or to other countries used as way stations for illegal exports to the Soviets. The number and frequency of these cases have received increasing attention, especially from computer industry executives, who believe that their businesses are being penalized for these technology thefts through complex federal export regulations. U.S. government agencies and politicians say that the growing number of arrests confirms their concerns about the easy accessibility of U.S. technology and justifies stepped-up enforcement efforts.

Most legislators and policymakers—Republicans and Democrats, liberals and conservatives alike—agree that protecting U.S. technology assets is more important than ever before because of the abundance of new U.S. technology available, the speed with which it is being developed, the aggressive methods employed by the Soviets to obtain it, and the potential for high-technology leaks compromising U.S. national security. On Oct. 3, 1983, Senator William V. Roth, Jr. (R-Del.) said, "The KGB [Soviet secret police] has admitted that its goal is to steal American technology."[7] Representative Don Bonker (D-Wash.), opening congressional hearings in 1987 on the sale of naval propeller-milling equipment to the Soviets by Japan's Toshiba Machine Company and Norway's Kongsberg Trade Company, said:

> Let me emphasize at the outset—and I think I can speak on behalf of all members of the committee—the grave concern we have over the illegal diversion of technology. This...case has vividly demonstrated the serious damage such illegal sales can have on Western security interests and the critical need for effective multilateral export controls.[8]

But there the agreement ends. On the subject of Soviet access to U.S. high technology, opinion divides sharply into two camps, both of which argue from premises basic to the American political consensus. On the one hand is the point of view, rooted primarily in deep concern over the Soviet threat to the national security of the United States and to American interests around the globe, that at all costs the United States must stop the flow of its national technological secrets beyond its own and its allies' borders. On the other hand, many free-market economists suggest that stringent controls of American trade, whether with friends or enemies, are destructive of American business and should be levied only in extreme circumstances. Proponents of the former view would likely cite the observation attributed to Lenin that the capitalistic United States, ever eager to expand its markets internationally, will sell the communists the "rope we will use to hang them."[9] Those arguing the latter viewpoint envision U.S.-Soviet rapprochement and fear that strict export controls inhibit U.S. high-technology manufacturers from exporting their equipment, thereby harming American "global competitiveness," a current political battle cry.

Between these two points of view are the technology-export controls and a range of governmental and private security programs, the mechanisms for modulating the flow of U.S. technology to the Soviet bloc. First and foremost among these mechanisms are export-control laws, enacted by Congress, that direct all exporters of controlled products to seek licenses from the Commerce Department or risk severe penalties, including fines and jail. Commerce maintains a list of controlled high-technology products, among them computers, semiconductors and semiconductor manufacturing equipment, software, lasers, telecommunications equipment, and scientific instruments. The list designates the countries to which specific products may or may not be shipped. Before approving applications to export products with military uses, Commerce consults with the Defense Department and often the State Department too. In addition, Commerce may ask for the input of the Energy Department, the intelligence community, and sometimes the international committee, Cocom.

Federal enforcement agencies follow up the license-approval process and investigate cases, such as the Bruchhausen affair, in which it appears that the law has been broken. The Treasury Department's Customs Service and the Commerce Department take the lead in policing high-technology exports under Customs' increasingly successful Operation Exodus, begun in 1981, and Commerce's Office of Export Enforcement. (See Chapter 7 for a thorough review of export controls.) The FBI and the Central Intelligence Agency (CIA) spearhead attempts to interrupt Soviet espionage: They direct counterintelligence activities to thwart the collection of critical U.S. technology.

Those on both sides of the issue admit the necessity of federal regulation of high-technology exports and tighter security but disagree over how stringent policies must be. The trade controls have been debated with increasing fervor since the beginning of the cold war in the late 1940s, and efforts to disrupt Soviet espionage have been thwarted by government strictures on surveillance and an increasing American proclivity to spy for extracurricular income. Since then, public and legislative opinion has moved between pro- and anti-Soviet sentiments, sometimes calling for intensified protection of U.S. interests in the face of Soviet aggression and espionage, at other times seeking new understanding and cooperative ventures between the United States and the Soviet Union.

NATIONAL SECURITY AND THE PENTAGON PERSPECTIVE

All participants in the debate agree that it is critical for the United States to maintain a strong technological lead to safeguard national security and protect American lives. This is in large part because the U.S. military depends so heavily on high technology, especially computers and electronics. The Soviets have long held a quantitative military lead. They have enjoyed an advantage in the number of conventional forces in Europe for several years. For example, during 1986, the North Atlantic Treaty Organization (NATO) had 121 "fully reinforced"[10] divisions in place while the Warsaw Pact had 230.[11] In most cases, the U.S. counters this numeric superiority with superior technology. As Richard N. Perle, then Assistant Secretary of Defense for trade policy, said during a 1985 Senate hearing, the United States should "ensure that the Free World's technological lead is not so eroded that our young people in uniform end up having to face our weapons in the battlefield...."[12]

Nowhere is the reliance on high technology for military pursuits more apparent than in the space-based defense systems both nations are currently devising. What many in the United States had known for some time was finally admitted by General Secretary Mikhail S. Gorbachev in his NBC interview on Nov. 30, 1987, just before the Washington summit conference: that the Soviets have been conducting basic research on their own space-based missile defense system.

The U.S. Strategic Defense Initiative (SDI), unveiled by President Ronald Reagan in 1983, quickly became a high-profile effort involving thousands of scientists and billions of dollars. By mid-1987, the United States had spent more than $6 billion on SDI-related research into technologies such as laser beams and planned to spend an additional $37 billion by 1990.[13] The SDI has become the biggest government-sponsored research project since the Apollo space program set out to put a man on the moon in the 1960s.

Since its inception, the Soviets have loudly and consistently protested the SDI. Not only are they concerned about the U.S. military gaining the edge in space; they are worried that the results of SDI research could propel U.S. cutting-edge technology far ahead of their own in other military and even nonmilitary areas. The SDI has also caused the Central Committee of the Soviet Communist party to place pressure on the KGB to keep the military supplied with the latest Western technology. Furthermore, the Soviets worry that new SDI technology will render their conventional weapons obsolete. Soviet Chief of the General Staff Sergei F. Akhromeyev is concerned that SDI research could lead to significant advances in Western conventional weapons, as was the former Soviet Chief of the General Staff Nikolai V. Ogarkov.[14]

Mark Kuchment, a Soviet emigré and scholar at Harvard University's Russian Research Center, confirms the Soviet Union's angst over the SDI and its concern that it will not be able to sustain technological progress without tapping Western technology both legally and illegally. At Stanford University on Jan. 21, 1987, Kuchment pointed out how "unsettling" the SDI is for the Soviets because "it touches technologies where the Soviets aren't very strong...computer technologies and certain areas of quantum electronics."[15]

To label espionage or diversion efforts as particular to SDI research is difficult because a number of SDI-related technologies, such as laser beams, have multiple uses. Other SDI-related technologies include free-electron lasers, particle-beam weapons, microwave inceptors, heavy-lift space transport vehicles, and kinetic energy weapons. But several diversion cases appear to have been specifically motivated by Soviet interest in acquiring SDI technology.

In the fall of 1986, the Pentagon reported that in 1985 Customs had uncovered a huge cache of illegally exported Western high-tech products with secondary applications to the SDI as well as civilian matters. The equipment included forty advanced Tektronix workstations that could be used for computer-aided design of semiconductors. The cache also contained an unknown number of Control Data disk drives that could be used to store complex data bases needed for designing weapons. By tracing the shipment to its manufacturers, Customs agents determined that it had been purchased by a German businessman, Wolfgang Lachmann, who purported to represent an important client that wanted anonymity. Lachmann purchased $11 million worth of equipment from the two vendors; he had planned to ship it to a company called Electro Import-Export in Belgium, then to Vienna, and on to the Soviet bloc.[16] U.S. Customs officials snagged most of the goods, but Lachmann slipped through their hands and remains at large.

Later, in the fall of 1987, a small computer company in Silicon Valley moved into the limelight as the victim of technological espionage allegedly related to the SDI but more than likely related to general military applications. The company, Saxpy Computer Corporation, founded in 1985 with the help of $15 million in venture capital, manufactures a supercomputer called Matrix I. The machine, of potential use in antisubmarine warfare, can enhance a strategic defense system by calculating potential missile trajectories. The software and documentation for the design of this high-speed, parallel processing device was almost acquired by the Soviets after one of Saxpy's software engineers, Ivan Pierre Batinic, stole it in mid-1987 and transferred it to a middleman, Kevin Eric Anderson.[17] Anderson, a Silicon Valley software programmer born in 1951, contacted Charles McVey in Canada. McVey, an infamous illegal exporter of high technology to the Soviets, was arrested in Canada on August 18, 1987. When McVey was arrested in Teslin, in the Yukon Territory, law enforcement officials found Saxpy materials in his briefcase. (See Chapter 4 for more information on McVey's technology diversions.) The two Batinics and Anderson were detained at the airport in Vancouver, B.C., on August 9, 1987, as they were attempting to reenter the United States with $16,200 in large denominations. Customs officials, their suspicions aroused by cash the men carried, also found items belonging to Saxpy. The men confessed that the cash was given to them in a taxicab in Canada by Carlos Julio Williams, an alias used by McVey.

Between August and October, when the three men were arrested in Santa Clara, Calif., U.S. Customs agents monitored Anderson's activities. Anderson traveled to McVey's home in Malta and to the Soviet Union in

September. He hoped to sell the Saxpy software to the Soviets for $4 million. Court documents filed in San Jose, Calif., allege that Anderson had discussions with the KGB during the course of negotiating the sale and had planned to transport software to the Soviets through Mexico. Stevan Batinic, Ivan's brother and an auto mechanic, assisted by copying and transporting some software for Anderson. In early October 1987, Customs and FBI agents searched Anderson's rented storage locker and found an assortment of computer tapes, diskettes, and manuals. The agents substituted dummy materials and arrested the three men. Anderson was convicted on May 27, 1988, the first conviction in the United States for illegally exporting printed technical data.

Although the SDI has received a great deal of publicity during the last few years, high technology has, since World War II, also become increasingly important to the operation of both the U.S. and Soviet conventional military systems. For example, computers and electronics form the backbone of military communications, particularly command, control, communications, and intelligence systems (C[3]I). Computers enable missiles to find their targets. The navy's Theater Mission Planning Center uses sophisticated computer software to manage missions for the Tomahawk Land Attack Missile.[18]

This increasing importance of computers and electronics to military systems is underlined by the acquisitions of electronics companies by military contractors: General Motors (GM) acquired Hughes, Lockheed acquired Sanders Associates, and Boeing acquired ARGOSystems. Almost 20 percent of U.S. military expenditures in 1986 was for electronics, and 70 percent of the cost of a 1986 LHX scout/attack helicopter was for electronics.[19]

Much of the technology developed for military use in the United States had its beginnings in the private commercial sector and originally may have been designed with civilian applications in mind. It is just this kind of equipment that has received the most attention from technology-export regulators. So-called dual-use technology constitutes the largest part of the Soviet "wish list" for American technology and the list of items subject to control by U.S. officials.[20]

An example of such a product is the Intel 80386 microprocessor, which is currently used in scientific supercomputers and Army tank-command systems. Also, a data encryption scheme for a communications system is similar to those used in a credit card data communications link and a military intelligence computer network. Many other such examples of technology with dual civilian and military use are on the Commerce Department's "control list" of items that can be exported only after specific licenses are approved by trade officials. Increasingly, however, items of advanced technology that may not have dual use are also being placed on the control list in case their acquisition by the Soviets might one day jeopardize U.S. national security.

A WELL-ORGANIZED CAMPAIGN

A white paper published by the CIA in 1985, entitled *Soviet Acquisition of Militarily Significant Western Technology*, discusses the structure of the Soviet campaign to acquire U.S. technology. The prologue to this 34-page document captures the military perspective on the subject and justifies the Pentagon's insistence that the United States continue to strengthen export laws that protect critical U.S. technology:

> In recent years, the United States Government has learned of a massive,
> well-organized campaign by the Soviet Union to acquire Western
> technology illegally and legally for its weapons and military equipment
> projects. Each year Moscow receives thousands of pieces of Western
> equipment and many tens of thousands of unclassified, classified, and
> proprietary documents as part of this campaign. Virtually every Soviet
> military research project—well over 4,000 each year in the late 1970s
> and over 5,000 in the early 1980s—benefits from these technical
> documents and hardware. The assimilation of Western technology is
> so broad that the United States and other Western nations are thus
> subsidizing the Soviet military buildup.[21]

The report goes on to say that the upper reaches of the Soviet government ask that its military, intelligence, and research organizations gather more than 3,500 specific requests for Western high-technology equipment and information each year and that one-third of the desired technology is collected, with the remaining requests carried over to the next year's list. The technology requests are organized into twelve categories: aviation, projectiles and explosives, armor and electro-optics, missiles and space, communications, radars and computers, nuclear and high-energy lasers, shipbuilding, electronics and microelectronics, chemicals, electrical equipment, and petroleum and petrochemicals.[22] Of all the technology requested in the early 1980s, about 60 percent was of U.S. origin, while 70 percent was critical and under some form of restriction or secret classification. The report estimates that the Soviets spend as much as $1.4 billion on technology espionage annually and gather as many as 10,000 pieces of equipment and 100,000 documents a year from Western sources.[23] The Soviets have also begun a drive for new technology to develop new military systems: A commitment to more spending on military hardware was made by the Twenty-Seventh Party Congress in February–March 1986.

The Department of Defense has also carefully researched Soviet efforts to gather U.S. high technology and has assembled a list of military developments that the Soviets have directly copied from American models. According to the Defense study, at least 150 American weapons systems have been subject to Soviet reverse engineering. Included in this list are laser range finders similar to those on U.S. tanks; look-down shoot-down radar systems resembling those on the U.S. F-15; cruise missiles that employ many components identical to those of U.S. cruise missiles; and the Atoll air-to-air missile, which duplicates the U.S. Sidewinder right down to its only left-hand-threaded screw.[24] Western technology also helped accelerate construction of the MiG-29 and SU-25 ground attack fighter and interceptor aircraft, improve weapons-aiming systems aboard jet fighters, and analyze the airfoil and wind resistance for the SU-25.[25] Soviet sonobuoys and microprocessors used in the sonobuoys were copied from U.S. expendable, air-dropped sonobuoys. The Soviets found a U.S. one and reverse-engineered it, even copying the Intel logo on the chip.

THE IMPACT

Soviet collecting of U.S. high technology erodes the qualitative edge of the American military, but it harms U.S. national interests in another way as well. Every time the Soviets obtain high-technology equipment and put it to military use, the United States must spend more research and development (R&D) money to counter the new Soviet capability. That money has to be taken from somewhere else in the budget, or the deficit will be enlarged; in either case, inflationary pressures are increased. For example, a VAX computer manufactured by Digital Equipment Corporation and acquired by the Soviets through a diversion scheme headed by a German, Richard Müller, between 1978 and 1983, is probably being used by the Soviet military to design high-speed semiconductors for missile guidance systems with computer-aided design software. As a result, the U.S. military had to surpass the new Soviet capability with more advanced chip technology. Conversely, every time the Soviets steal equipment, they save the amount of money Americans spent developing it, less

More Than 5000 Soviet Military Research Projects Benefiting from Western Technology

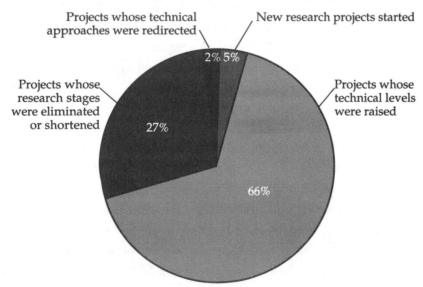

Courtesy of the Defense Department, from "Soviet Acquisition of Militarily Significant Western Technology: An Update," 1985.

their acquisition expenses and the cost of reverse engineering. Intel, for instance, spent $100 million and four years to develop its 80386 chip. If the Soviets obtained the design and manufacturing facilities for this powerful chip, they would save at least the equivalent amount of R&D resources.

The French, who study the impact of Soviet acquisitions of Western technology almost as rigorously as Americans, have come up with some revealing statistics. According to French research, the Soviet Ministry of Aviation Industry saved almost $256 million in R&D by acquiring Western technology for high-performance aircraft between 1976 and 1980. They also found that the Soviets saved $60 million in research in 1979, three times the 1978 savings of $20 million.[26] In 1983, the French intelligence service obtained a letter allegedly written by a Soviet aviation minister. Printed in 1985 in *Le Monde*, the document expressed the impact in another way. The minister wrote:

> The use of the positive experience of foreign countries has made it possible for our country to make favorable developments of a higher technical standard in shorter periods of time. The use of this experience has also made it possible to industrialize some progressive technological processes.[27]

Although the acquisition of U.S. technology has both cost the United States and saved the Soviet Union money, many believe that were it not for U.S. efforts to stand in the way of such acquisitions those sums would be even greater. In a February 1985 Defense Department report, then U.S. Secretary of Defense Caspar W. Weinberger stated that long-term restraints on technology trade to the Soviets could save U.S. taxpayers $20 billion to $50 billion a year in defense expenditures. The report went on to say that the effectiveness of U.S. export controls to thwart Soviet high-technology acquisition would save Moscow $6.6 billion to $13.3 billion in defense costs between 1985 and 1997 through "direct military weapon production efficiencies" gained from Western technology acquired in 1983 and 1984.[28]

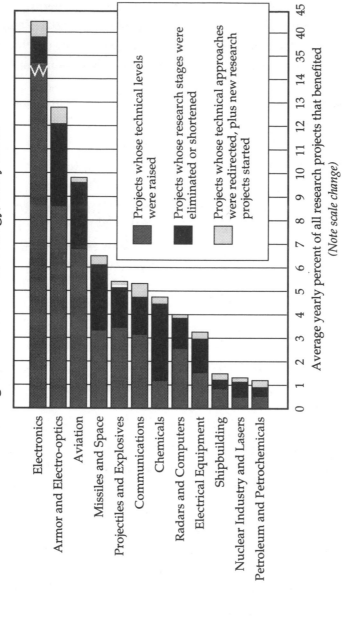

Rank Ordering of Industries by Soviet Military Research Projects Benefiting from Western Technology, Early 1980s

Legend:
- Projects whose technical levels were raised
- Projects whose research stages were eliminated or shortened
- Projects whose technical approaches were redirected, plus new research projects started

Industries (top to bottom):
Electronics
Armor and Electro-optics
Aviation
Missiles and Space
Projectiles and Explosives
Communications
Chemicals
Radars and Computers
Electrical Equipment
Shipbuilding
Nuclear Industry and Lasers
Petroleum and Petrochemicals

Average yearly percent of all research projects that benefited
(Note scale change)

0 1 2 3 4 5 6 7 8 9 10 11 12 13 14 35 40 45

Courtesy of the Defense Department, from "Soviet Acquisition of Militarily Significant Western Technology: An Update," 1985.

THE COST OF CONTROLS

Despite the ominous Soviet successes in capturing U.S. high technology, many U.S. high-tech companies chafe at what they depict as the restraint of trade imposed by current export laws. And security restrictions limiting academic freedom, individual rights, and physical access cause some Americans to question the costs of cracking down on Soviet bloc spying. But the overall economic impact of U.S. efforts to limit Soviet access to high technology is complex and difficult to measure, in part because unrestricted trade between the United States and the rest of the world has not been practiced for at least forty years.

During the past ten years, export controls have clearly dampened trade, particularly in high technology, between the United States and the Soviet Union. Of all the manufactured products sold to the Soviet Union by the United States in 1975, 32.7 percent were high-technology[29] products. By 1982, after export controls became more stringent, that figure declined to 5.4 percent. In 1975, the United States sold $219 million worth of high-technology items to the Soviets. By 1983, sales of high-technology products had fallen to $39.1 million. The Department of Commerce points out that during that year the United States ranked eleventh out of sixteen Western countries in exports of high technology to the Soviet Union. West Germany supplied the Soviet bloc with the largest quantity of high-technology items, $711 million worth in 1983, followed by France with $363 million and Japan with $227 million.[30]

But while export controls have reduced trade to the Soviets, the controls appear to have also impaired U.S. high-technology exports to European allies, a potentially harmful side effect. (Other depressants to U.S. trade to the Soviets between 1980 and 1986 were the strengthening dollar and the increasing sophistication of European high technology. According to a 1987 National Academy of Sciences study, *Balancing the National Interest*, export controls may have cost the United States $5.9 billion in lost revenue. But the subject of economic loss to the West is controversial, and sufficient trade data to substantiate the claim are unavailable.[31] Many industry observers believe that if export controls were loosened the United States could significantly increase sales to Europe while becoming an international competitor for Soviet business, but precisely what effect such a loosening would have, even on U.S.-U.S.S.R. trade, is unknown.

Deeply concerned about the U.S. export controls, however, is the U.S. high-technology industry, which is keenly aware of the electronics-trade deficit. According to the American Electronics Association, the 1986 electronics-trade deficit was $13.1 billion, 49 percent higher than in 1985, most of it coming from an imbalance in trade with the Japanese. Many Silicon Valley executives, including former U.S. Representative Ed Zschau (R-Calif.), feel that the high-technology industry could become more competitive if the costs of complying with export controls were lowered—costs incurred because of bureaucratic inefficiencies.[32] He also feels that the United States should focus restrictions on militarily critical technology but try to open trade for other technologies. Many industry executives agree. They typically support their companies' efforts to expand their business opportunities, even if those opportunities are in the Soviet Union, but they also oppose selling the Soviets critical high technology.

A 1985 survey by the commercial section of the U.S. consulate in Frankfurt, West Germany, found that because of the restrictions some European companies were looking for alternate supply sources for technology, including electronic components and computers.[33] Some European countries have come to prefer non-U.S. suppliers to avoid confronting U.S. export-control laws. The study found that if some of the more exercised European critics of U.S. export policy were to have their way they would build a self-sufficient European technology market not subject to a superpower's possibly overcautious export policy. Europeans appear to be annoyed with the administrative hurdles that U.S. export laws require them to overcome and are also suspicious that Cocom may be stifling competition by enabling such non-Cocom members as Hong Kong and South Korea to sell computers and other products to the Soviet Union while the West loses the business. They have not forgotten how the United States used Cocom to manipulate international trade during the shift in U.S.-Chinese relations. Before the United States became friendly with China, the United States used Cocom to restrict technology trade with the country. After 1979, when the United States established normal diplomatic ties with China, both the United States and Europe began to pressure Cocom to open up trade with the Asian giant so that their firms could benefit.

The most significant question remains unanswered: Can export controls stop people such as Bruchhausen? It can be argued that export controls make the lives of diverters more dangerous and necessitate the use of expensive, complex networks of front companies and aliases. But the export laws do not stop spies, although the trend toward stiffer espionage laws and the increasing public awareness of spying activities have made high-technology espionage more difficult, as have stricter corporate security and the high-tech industry's awareness of the Soviet spy's modus operandi.

THE SOVIET PERSPECTIVE

Whether today's export and espionage laws actually protect U.S. high-technology assets, the Soviet commitment to acquiring US high technology is as strong as it has ever been, if not stronger. Work for the state and dedication to the communist ideology form the basis for Soviet values that the state expresses in terms of industrial quotas and growth statistics. Technology forms an important part of the Soviet strategy for realizing true communism, because the benefits of new technology are necessary to achieve the perennial goals of increasing economic productivity and military strength, the dual backbones of the Soviet political system. And although the application of technology plays a central role in Soviet thinking, internal deficiencies require the Soviets to turn to the outside world for much of their high-technology equipment instead of developing it themselves. Because the Soviet bureaucracy has been highly inflexible and the economy and all scientific development have been subject to rigid centralized control, the Soviet Union has never developed broad-based policies that give incentives for technological advances and investment. As a consequence, the Soviet Union has achieved superpower status although it has an economy more in line with those of Third World countries.

Gorbachev wants to change this. As he wrote in his book *Perestroika*, published in the United States in 1987:

> The path in our country from a scientific discovery to its introduction in production is too long. This enables enterprising foreign industrialists to make money out of our ideas. Of course, such a situation does not suit us.[34]

The vehicle for change is his program *perestroika* ("restructuring"), of which *glasnost* ("openness") is a prime component. It is too soon to tell if recent initiatives promoted by him will result in significant structural changes that produce tangible economic results.

The Soviet government is hopeful that the new *glasnost* will invite a loosening of U.S. export controls and new business ties, both of which would result in greater access to U.S. high technology. Evidence of *glasnost*, such as the willingness to make token concessions regarding dissidents, the apparent relaxation of cultural and artistic rules of the past, and the careful easing of media controls, has made the Soviets appear less hostile and more approachable.

But the Soviets are shrewd negotiators, as the United States witnessed during the frenzied few days before the signing of the INF treaty in December 1987. They are now willing to give up a few degrees of centralized economic and political control for access to valued Western know-how and investment. Without these two catalysts, the Soviet Union would remain manacled by a stagnant economy and threatened by an increasingly prosperous middle class intent on demanding greater rewards from the revered political system.

GORBACHEV'S U.S.S.R.: HIS AGENDA, U.S. TECHNOLOGY

Lessons from history often influence world leaders as they create policies to take them into the future. Gorbachev is no exception as he and his economic advisers look back to the 1920s and Lenin's New Economic Policy, that temporarily successful experiment with private enterprise and capitalism, elements of which Gorbachev appears to be bringing back in the late 1980s. Gorbachev realizes that revitalizing the Soviet economy is the key to his country's survival. Before Gorbachev assumed control of the Soviet state in March 1985, Soviet economic growth had slowed every year from the rule of Joseph Stalin to that of Gorbachev's predecessor, Konstantin U. Chernenko. Although growth statistics during Gorbachev's tenure may improve, the full impact of his initiatives has not yet been felt in the economy. Steep price hikes, not yet implemented, will surely elicit an immediate response from the Soviet people. Even with some of the more innovative changes going into effect, the Soviet government is not likely to meet the aggressive and optimistic economic targets of the Five-Year Plan ending in 1990.[35] The Soviets again announced a poor grain harvest for 1987 and began buying U.S. grain and soybeans once more. Furthermore, the Soviet labor force has continued to shrink.[36] Therefore, about 60 percent of the economic growth projected for Eastern bloc countries between now and the year 2000 must be achieved through increased efficiency and productivity.[37]

To increase productivity from a shrinking, little-motivated labor force, Soviet industrial equipment, much of it older-generation machines, desperately needs the improvements offered through new technology. Technology takes a front seat in the statewide program to improve the Soviet economy that was announced by the Politburo in 1985. Later, during the Twenty-Seventh Party Congress in February–March 1986, M. S. Shkabardnya, minister of instrument making, automation, and control systems, stated that "it is quite obvious that in this matter, it is impossible to take a somewhat appreciable step ahead without the broad introduction of automation, without modern computer technology and programmable equipment."[38]

Recent comments by Gorbachev indicate that he is looking to the Eastern bloc nations for help. As the *Christian Science Monitor* pointed out in February 1987, Gorbachev "needs higher-quality goods from his allies to invigorate his economy, and he hopes that greater alliance cooperation will help close the technology gap with the West."[39] To attain these goals, Comecon[40] started a program in December 1985 called the "Comprehensive Program for Scientific and Technological Development." The program promoted Soviet leadership of a drive to develop computer-related products. Also, Eastern bloc countries are committed to upgrading the technology-based products they export.

But some of the countries are not happy with the new Gorbachev initiatives. Until recently, they had built their economies around ongoing trade with the West. Hungary relies on Western technology trade to invigorate its economy. One of its computer companies, Novotrade, sells software to Western companies, including the International Business Machines Corporation (IBM). Novotrade and other firms would find it necessary to cut new trade relationships to comply with the mandate to increase trade with the Soviets. They view this as a technological and economic step backward.

The Soviets are also attempting nontechnological solutions to their economic problems. For one, the government wants workers not only to work harder but to work more intelligently, a goal reinforced by Gorbachev's move to require enterprises to base wages on quality in addition to the traditional measure of productivity. Also, in early 1986, Gorbachev gave trade rights to twenty-one ministries and sixty-eight enterprises and increased the number of FTOs.[41] This initiative is aimed at expanding international trade and thereby giving the Soviet Union access to hard currency. Some enterprises, ministries, and collective farms are also beginning to operate on the basis of profit-and-loss accounting, what the Soviets call "full-cost accounting," a concept that will be extended to all enterprises.

Since Gorbachev announced the new initiatives giving enterprises more autonomy and responsibility for profitable operation, Soviet bureaucrats have realized that their enterprise managers are ill-equipped to function in a decentralized environment. To address this problem, the State Committee for Science and Technology (GKNT), an organization responsible for setting technology-acquisition priorities, has been given the assignment of sending Soviet enterprise managers into Western corporations to learn Western business-management techniques. Although Western business has little to gain from this arrangement and may risk exposing business practices and production techniques to the Soviets (as it did to the Japanese during the 1960s and 1970s), some Western countries, including the United States and West Germany, are considering ways they can assist in training the Soviet managers.

Along with these unusual moves, the Soviet government appears to be courting the country's intelligentsia. Gorbachev realizes that the changes he must make to revitalize the Soviet economy will need the input and support of this highly influential and vocal group. It includes Soviet scientists and engineers, who are perhaps the most essential to the implementation of needed changes.

Despite his energy and optimism, Gorbachev has a difficult job ahead of him. The thinking that dominated the Central Committee during the past ten years continues to be a force with which Gorbachev must reckon. Some economic indicators, possibly fixed by Gorbachev's detractors in the Soviet government, show that the Soviet economy may have slowly begun to awaken from its deep sleep without Gorbachev's additional stimuli. Official Soviet net material product (NMP) statistics indicate a 3.1 percent growth in 1985 and a 3.6 percent growth in 1986.[42] Even more glowing reports emerged from the Joint Economic Committee of Congress, saying that Soviet gross national product (GNP) grew by more than 4 percent in 1986. Official Soviet statistics indicate, however, that the growth may have been closer to 8 percent for both years.[43] Among other experts, Ed A. Hewitt, a senior fellow at the Brookings Institution who followed the statistics as they were released from the former Soviet Central Statistical Committee, suspects that the Soviet old guard wants to present an optimistic picture of the economy to their people so that Gorbachev's new initiatives will appear unnecessary. But in 1988, the Central Intelligence Agency estimated that the Soviet economy grew at a rate of only one-half of one percent in 1987, a sharp drop from the 1986 rate. It also stated that industrial production for 1987 increased 1.5 percent. The Soviets claimed that for the first quarter of 1988 industrial production increased 5 percent. Soviet statistics appear inflated by propaganda aimed at demonstrating the effectiveness of the new reforms.

Although Gorbachev has removed some shackles that bound past Politburo thinking, he has even had problems with some new thinkers. In the fall of 1987, Boris N. Yeltsin was removed from the Politburo for being too outspoken and impatient with the speed of reform. U.S. observers are watching conservative members of the Politburo as they apparently press for a more cautious approach to reform. Yegor K. Ligachev, a prominent member of the Politburo and secretary of the Central Committee, is a supporter of *glasnost* but also a conservative and an archdisciplinarian. He will not endorse a hasty transformation of Soviet society.

The new economic initiatives may also only create new problems because of several differences between the Soviet economy of the 1980s and that of the 1920s. One potential obstacle facing the economic initiatives is the current predominance of collective farms; any moves toward individual ownership would require revolutionary changes, even a fatal erosion of the socialist system. When the economy was liberalized in the 1920s, agriculture was not massively collectivized as it is today. The population was less literate and educated than now; today's middle-class Soviet citizen may be reluctant to accept major job and compensation restructuring and certainly will not accept serious price hikes passively.

Although the new *perestroika* aims to build new technology to revitalize the economy, the Soviets intend to maintain control over the flow of information and the economy. Economic pluralism, which tolerates both free-market economics and socialism, will be pursued cautiously, because it may pose a threat to the firmly established Soviet government. Western Sovietologists and economists argue that the free flow of information is a prerequisite to efficient use of technology. It is a contradiction for the Soviets both to advance technically and to continue an authoritarian system. A radical interpretation would lead to support for a U.S. policy that encourages a massive infusion of Western technology, particularly computer-related technology, creating a serious threat to the Soviet political system by providing the tools for the uncontrolled dissemination of information.

WOOING THE WEST, OR *PERESTROIKA* FOR PROFITS

As the Saxpy case suggests, and despite the *glasnost* initiatives, the Soviets are continuing to take full advantage of opportunities to acquire technology illegally. Under Gorbachev, however, entirely legitimate, open means of purchasing U.S. cutting-edge technology may become fruitful for the Soviets in a way unheard of since the policy of détente relaxed U.S.-Soviet relations in the 1970s. The Joint U.S.-Soviet Summit Statement, issued during the December 1987 summit in Washington, outlined a specific but still cautious commitment to increasing trade between the two superpowers. It said the two countries "agreed that commercially viable joint ventures complying with the laws and regulations of both countries could play a role in the further development of commercial relations."[44] More telling, however, was the secret meeting of U.S. company representatives, Commerce Department representatives, and Soviet officials during the summit. Details of the meeting are unavailable to the public but would likely reveal the program now in place to expand U.S.-Soviet trade while linking the two superpower economies. Commerce Department head C. William Verity, Jr., and Soviet economist Abel G. Aganbegyan joined U.S. company representatives from such companies as Archer Daniels Midland in making effusive comments to the press after the meeting about a potential $10 billion in U.S.-Soviet trade.

In addition to directly affecting the Soviet economy, Gorbachev's recent moves appear designed to enhance his nation's image in Western countries, which may indirectly improve the Soviet economy. When the Chinese began to open their doors, the United States offered them trade, technology, and investment; the Soviets are eliciting the same reaction with what amounts to a public relations campaign. Although political optimists resist thinking of glasnost as a public relations campaign (one translation of glasnost is, in fact, "publicity"), historically, the Soviets have never made concessions on such matters as human rights without specific objectives in mind.

Considering this, the apparent Soviet reforms must be viewed with pragmatism and caution. Gorbachev's "intellectual mentor" and adviser on new initiatives is Aleksander N. Yakovlev, an accomplished economist, member of the Communist party Central Committee and Politburo, and author of the book *On the Edge of an Abyss: From Truman to Reagan—The Doctrines and Realities of the Nuclear Age,* published in 1984. Known to be a behind-the-scenes architect of glasnost and the new economic initiatives, he is also known to have a strong distrust of anything American and to be a hard-line Soviet ideologue and Marxist-Leninist thinker. He has been careful to distance glasnost from Western-style democracy. He says, "We [the Soviets] are moving away from [democracy]. We think, and even hope, that in certain aspects you [Americans] will follow our

example and catch up with us."[45] He is, moreover, the secretary for propaganda of the Communist party and knows how to make effective use of
the media. As an exchange student in 1959–60 at Columbia University
and later as the Soviet ambassador to Canada, he gained a useful understanding of the West.

Another key player in developing the *glasnost* strategy is Anatoly F.
Dobrynin, the former Soviet ambassador to the United States. During his
twenty-four-year tenure at the Soviet embassy, he became particularly
familiar with American ways and the U.S. media. He was recalled to the
Soviet Union to apply his well-honed understanding of the American
psyche to Gorbachev's agenda. His skills have been helpful in developing
a restructuring process that is attuned to American values; he has also
promoted Gorbachev's reforms in ways that appeal to Americans. With
such men as Yakovlev and Dobrynin at Gorbachev's right hand, Americans may want to think carefully about the intention of the reforms and
the role the United States should take in assisting Soviet economic
progress. Clearly, Gorbachev hopes that role will be as active as possible.

One step Gorbachev has taken to modernize the Soviet economy by
acquiring Western technology is to launch a campaign for Western-Soviet
joint ventures. During the Twenty-Seventh Party Congress in Moscow,
held in February–March 1986, Nikolai Ryzhkov, chairman of the Soviet
Council of Ministers, stated that the Soviet government "envisages a con-
siderable expansion in foreign economic ties. They will be concentrated
on the priorities, focused on scientific and technological goals, and used
extensively for attaining social goals."[46] On the eve of the December 1987
summit, U.S. Commerce Secretary Verity expressed interest in the new
and large Soviet market available to U.S. businesses. In August 1987, *The
Wall Street Journal* ran a twelve-page advertisement, paid for by the
Soviets, heralding Soviet trade opportunities for American companies.
Ads for Soviet products touted everything from jewelry to a software
package written in Fortran IV, a programming language developed in the
United States by IBM. A six-page color advertisement in the December 14,
1987, *Business Week*, prepared by the Soviet Foreign Trade Advertising
Agency, extolled the benefits of doing business with Moscow while re-
minding readers that the new trade initiatives "do not mean that the state

is abandoning its monopoly on foreign trade." In January 1987, *The New York Times* wrote that "the Soviet Union has begun a whirlwind courtship of Western partners aimed at creating the first genuine joint ventures on Soviet soil."[47] James H. Giffen, president of the privately run U.S.-U.S.S.R. Trade and Economic Council[48] since 1974, has acknowledged that U.S. businesses are taking steps to explore potential ventures while the Soviets are attempting to sweeten the terms available to American business.

Requests for proposals have found their way into the sales departments of U.S., Japanese, and European companies. But during the past decade, U.S. businesses have developed a skeptical, and sometimes even cynical, attitude toward Soviet overtures to Western companies, especially because, in the past, the Soviets have appeared to want U.S. technology more than they want to share profits. Many in industry recall the Soviet Union's confiscating U.S. assets in the 1920s after American business tried to tap Soviet markets. Concerns about the reliability of the Soviets as trade partners, and more patriotic concerns as well, may keep U.S. industry from exporting more high technology to the Soviet Union, even without trade controls. Also, because the Soviets need hard currency, most contracts in the past have stipulated that profits must stay within Soviet borders. Furthermore, the conflict of political ideologies has made negotiations seem fraught with uncertainties, and many tenets of Soviet society and government have precluded Western management styles and financial structures.

The Soviets, eager to strengthen ties with Western companies that can bring both high-quality, technology-based products and know-how to their economy, issued new joint-venture rules in early 1987. These allow foreign investment partners to own as much as 49 percent of a joint venture. The Soviets assert that Western countries can now take out their profits in hard currency but only if a joint venture produces earnings in foreign trade. Previously, Western countries had to work out complicated barter arrangements to gain access to profits earned through joint ventures with the Soviets. Many U.S. companies remain skeptical about how profits will be calculated and question whether the Soviets will indeed part with their limited supply of hard currency. If the Soviets follow through with the hard-currency promise, and if today's exchange rates persist, they will lose money because the exchange rate favors the West. The Soviet government has also eliminated the need for some Western companies to work through FTOs; now they may work directly with enterprises and some ministries. Furthermore, profit taxes can be paid on a deferred plan called a "tax holiday" by the Soviets. More reforms favorable to joint ventures may still be in the offing.

Even after learning of the Soviet interest in gaining access to Western technology through these joint ventures and realizing the ambiguities in some Soviet terms, some U.S. companies are eager to do business with the Soviets. Amtorg, the Soviet trading company in New York City, indicated in mid-1987 that at least fifteen U.S. companies were negotiating with them on possible venture deals.[49] In June 1988, the Soviets announced that the number of joint ventures with Western countries rose from twenty-three to fifty-two during the previous six months. Seven involved U.S. companies. The Soviets held a news conference in the spring of 1986 to encourage Western inquiries and to answer objections raised by prospective clients. At that time, they said, they had received 200 proposals, were interested in 121, and 13 were "practically implemented."[50] In October 1987, for example, a Spanish company, Telefónica Nacional de España, signed an agreement with the Soviets to produce telecommunications equipment. In the same month, an Italian subsidiary, FATA European Group S.p.A., of Babcock International, signed an agreement for a venture, to be 73 percent Soviet-owned, for the production of refrigeration equipment.

Monsanto Archer Daniels Midland (a chicken-raising and grain-storage firm), Honeywell Bull, Ford Motor Company, RJR Nabisco, Kodak, Johnson & Johnson, Dresser Industries (equipment and technical services to the energy and natural-resources industries), SSMC (formerly Singer Sewing Machine Company, a manufacturer of computer equipment in addition to sewing machines), and Chevron Corp. are currently negotiating contracts with the Soviets for joint ventures.[51] Archer Daniels Midland would like a joint venture in oilseed processing, Ford Motor Company would like the Soviets to purchase its European-manufactured cars, Kodak would like to make floppy disks in the Soviet Union, Johnson

& Johnson would like to market its pharmaceutical products to the Soviets, and Nabisco is anxious to see Muscovites munching on Oreos. PepsiCo Inc. bottles its soft drinks on Soviet soil, and McDonald's Restaurants of Canada, Ltd. signed an agreement in April 1988 (after twelve years of talks) to provide Muscovites with Big Macs. Earlier, in September 1987, Pepsi signed an agreement to open two Pizza Hut restaurants in Moscow.

A contract signed in November 1987 by Combustion Engineering of Stamford, Conn., with the Soviets involves high technology, calling on the U.S. firm to assist in improving productivity in the oil-refining business. The contract could lead to a classic joint venture, eventually enabling the Soviets to manufacture their own instruments and control gear. Combustion Engineering has agreed to provide process-control equipment and engineering technology to the Soviet Ministry of Oil-Refining and Petrochemical Industries. The know-how includes U.S. management skills and technical engineering expertise; in other words, the agreement calls for the U.S. firm to train Soviet personnel. Combustion Engineering will also provide computer software and $8 million, half of the funding for the venture. The Soviets own 51 percent of the joint venture, which will enable them to manufacture control valves, electronic transmitters, gas chromatographs, infrared and ultraviolet analyzers, microprocessor-based controllers, and integrated control systems.

Combustion Engineering was careful in securing the proper export-license clearances because the venture does include computer-based control systems and optimization software. The U.S. government will only allow the company to assemble the systems in the Soviet Union, not to manufacture them. Both the U.S. government and Cocom have to approve the company's licenses. In January 1988, William Zolner, vice president for marketing of the company's Engineered Systems and Controls, was hoping that the Commerce Department would eventually grant a special license for manufacturing the equipment. Consistent with the new rules allowing more hard currency to leave the Soviet Union, Combustion Engineering will receive a onetime fee in U.S. dollars for technology transfer plus later payments based on a percentage of the joint-venture sales. (Combustion Engineering already had one $12 million contract with the Soviets to upgrade the process-control system at a large ethylene plant, and in June 1988 it announced that it plans to build two petrochemical plants in Western Siberia, a deal worth more than $20 billion.[52])

In June 1988, Occidental Petroleum, long a promoter of U.S.-Soviet trade, signed an agreement to build and operate a $6 billion petrochemical complex in the Soviet Union with the help of companies in Japan and Italy.[53] Later, in April 1988, Occidental Petroleum continued to cash in on its long-term relationship with the Soviets. It signed another agreement, this time for the construction of two plastics factories in the Ukraine, a contract worth at least $300 million.[54] Even high-technology companies are pursuing ventures with the Soviets. In May 1988, Advanced Transducer Devices, a division of Televideo Systems Inc. in Sunnyvale, Calif., announced a joint venture agreement that would enable the Soviets to assemble U.S. personal computers in Moscow. The deal, brokered by another Silicon Valley firm, California Microelectronic Systems Inc., provides for Advanced Transducer to export 4,000 IBM AT-compatible computers and kits to Moscow the first year. The plan is for the Soviets eventually to take over the assembly facility after the U.S. firm sets up the operation and provides training. The U.S. government had not approved the deal as of June 1988.[55] More ventures of this sort are in the works, all resulting from the Soviets' intensifying campaign to win over U.S. businesses, from the Soviets' need for hard currency, and from Western corporate needs for international expansion.

The Reagan administration responded to the Soviet trading overtures by encouraging U.S. companies to embark on "nonstrategic" trade ventures with the Soviets as a gesture of goodwill at a time when the arms agreement signed during the December 1987 Washington summit was being negotiated. U.S. officials also hoped that an increase in trade might further encourage the decentralizing forces that seemed to be at work in Moscow.

Two efforts to increase trade were made in April 1988. First, the U.S. Cabinet signed an initiative in support of U.S.-U.S.S.R. trade, and second, a group of U.S. businesses combined to form a consortium whose purpose is to negotiate trade deals with the Soviets. Called the American Trade Consortium, the private group consists of such companies as Johnson & Johnson, RJR Nabisco, and the Ford Motor Company.[56] The consortium's president is James H. Giffen. The group may also act as its own banker, providing loans as necessary.

High-technology firms looking to expand their markets into the Soviet Union and realize short-term gains were warned by the Defense and Commerce departments of the Soviet desire to acquire products that are controlled by U.S. export laws and Cocom. The Soviets apparently hope the joint ventures will eventually bring them Western automation and manufacturing facilities, including sophisticated computers, lasers, and robots, all items on the Commerce Department's list of items that may not be exported to the Soviet Union.

In the past, such initiatives have resulted in the transfer of U.S. technology to the Soviets that, at the time, seemed harmless but later came to have military use. In 1973, for example, the United States allowed the Soviets to purchase millions of dollars' worth of equipment, including an IBM 370 computer system, for the Kama River truck factory in the city of Naberezhnye Chelny. In 1979, the Commerce Department discovered to its chagrin that trucks from the factory were rumbling toward Afghanistan during the Soviet invasion of the country.

To turn the current Soviet trade initiatives into reality, Western banks are willing and eager to lend money not only to Soviet-Western ventures but also directly to the Soviet government. A German bank loan made possible the petrochemical joint venture of a Soviet enterprise and a West German company.

The Soviets continue to receive financial aid from Western banks despite their weak hard-currency position. In early 1988, the Soviets entered the Eurobond market with bonds backed by $78 million worth of Swiss francs. The bonds, issued by a Soviet bank, are not especially attractive to Western banks looking at the 5 percent coupon; only in 1986, England settled its dispute with the Soviets over repayment of Tsarist Russian bonds.[57] In May 1988, Germany announced a second bond sale, this time a bold $294 million worth. Deutsche Bank AG plans to establish a consortium for the purpose of providing the Soviets 3.5 billion marks' worth of credits.[58] And closer to home, Los Angeles-based Security Pacific Corporation has also provided financing for Western exports to the Soviet Union. A British unit of Security Pacific agreed in December 1987 to provide $146.2 million in financing for Western exports to the Soviet Union.[59]

Many loans sought by the Soviet Union are "untied," that is, not lent for a specific purpose. Such loans enable the Soviet Union to use money for development of trade but also for military R&D. In November 1987, U.S. Representative Jack Kemp (R-N.Y.) introduced a bill that would require U.S. banks to disclose untied loans given to the Soviet Union. The bill would also give the president the right to stop lending by U.S. banks if the lending activity threatened U.S. national security.

These Western banks, including Morgan Grenfell and Co. Ltd. in England and Deutsche Bank in West Germany, have obviously been willing to lend money to the Soviets, although they are sometimes discouraged by their governments from doing so. The Soviets can also raise money through Eurocurrency consortium loans in Western Europe. Or, they can raise money through government guarantees collateralized by capital goods exported from countries other than the United States.

By the end of 1986, the estimated Soviet net hard-currency debt was about $26 billion, up from $19 billion in 1985, most of the debt provided by Western banks and governments.[60] By the end of 1987, it had risen to $38.2 billion.[61] This "debtor's leverage" may later place the United States in an untenable position during foreign-policy and security negotiations. Some Western bankers also worry that the threat of default on these loans could give the Soviets the leverage to force the West into providing additional economic assistance. This has been done from time to time by other nations with massive Western debt that they are unable to repay on schedule. In addition to its voracious appetite for these new loans, the Soviet Union wants to align itself with Western economic interests by becoming a member of the General Agreement on Tariffs and Trade (GATT) and the International Monetary Fund (IMF). In June 1988, the European Community (EC) announced an agreement on cooperation between its members and Comecon, a gesture representing the first time the Soviet bloc recognized the EC.[62] The agreement lays the groundwork for other agreements representing technology and financial assistance.

THE SOVIETS AS COMPETITORS?

Besides using Western high technology to boost its economy, the Soviet Union may eventually use the equipment it acquires to produce goods and services that will one day compete with those of the United States. In *Perestroika*, Gorbachev wrote that his country had "started the necessary research and development and the production of what we once proposed to purchase, so Western firms will ultimately be the losers."[63] His stated objectives indicate an interest only in gaining technical know-how from the West that will enable the Soviet Union to free itself from purchasing products in the long run. According to his book, he wants the forthcoming commercial ventures as a technical "shot in the arm," not as the beginnings of a long-term commercial partnership.

This longer-range goal of Soviet economic independence and even competitiveness should suggest caution to many in U.S. industry about selling too much know-how to the Soviets. That the Soviet Union wants to become a force in the international high-technology markets is evidenced by its campaign to attract customers for commercial satellite launchings using its Proton and Vertikal rockets. On Jan. 7, 1987, the Soviets announced that foreign companies could ship their satellites in sealed containers to the Soviet Union for launching, meaning that the equipment did not have to be inspected by Soviet customs officials. Western companies had previously been hesitant to send their treasured satellites to the Soviet Union for launching because of the assumption that they would be scrutinized, copied, and perhaps tampered with en route to the heavens.

The Soviet pitch also allows Western companies to send their technicians with the satellite all the way to the Baikonur Kosmodrome launch site in Central Asia. Giving the impression that they possess the ingenuity of capitalist sales reps, the Soviets have offered flight insurance for their new customers, a necessity that would otherwise have to be acquired on the open market. The cost of the launching service to Western customers is low compared with most Western alternatives and half the cost of a U.S. launch; a Soviet launch costs as little as $18 million to $20 million, compared with $40 million for a French Ariane rocket launch.[64]

The sales campaign has borne fruit: The Soviets launched an Indian satellite in March 1988, and the West German company Kayser-Threde signed an agreement in December 1987 to conduct scientific experiments on board a Soviet space probe between 1989 and 1992.[65] General Motors and General Electric have complained to the U.S. government that its restrictions have prevented them from benefiting from the Soviets' inexpensive launching services. But in February 1988, Payload Systems Inc. of Wellesley, Mass., signed a contract with the Soviets to launch a commercial payload. The contract enables the U.S. firm to send a device for growing protein crystals aboard the *Mir*, a manned Soviet space station currently in orbit. Approved by both the Commerce and Defense departments, the venture provides for Soviet cosmonauts in *Mir* to tend the experiments and to make necessary observations.[66]

The Soviets are seeking other ways of becoming internationally competitive in space technology. They have offered their *Mir* space station for Western-Soviet scientific cooperative ventures; earlier, in November 1987, they announced that they would enter the business of selling Soviet satellite photos to Western customers. And in August 1988 the Soviets planned to launch their space shuttle. Asked by U.S. journalists before the launch about the appearance of the Soviet shuttle, Gen. German Titov, a former cosmonaut, answered, "It looks just like yours."[67]

THE DILEMMA

Whether U.S. technology finds its way to the Soviet Union through a commercial venture or through an illegal exporting scheme, the same issues challenge America's continued high-technology superiority and national security. These issues range from the role of government in restricting the export of high technology to the Soviets to the enforcement problems facing U.S. authorities as more Americans succumb to the perceived financial rewards of spying for the Soviets. The issues are complex, and the solutions are not simple or readily apparent. But the stakes are high: U.S. competitiveness and national security are at risk each time the government or industry negotiates for more or less access to U.S. high technology by the Soviet Union.

The Soviets' new direction adds up to a dilemma for the United States and for its high-technology industry. On the one hand, the United States may look at *glasnost* and the accompanying Soviet initiatives as providing opportunities to expand internationally and help put American competitiveness back on course. Yet American businesses must assess the possibility that an investment today in a Soviet joint venture may be lost tomorrow if, with a change in leadership, the initiatives are reversed. Also, the United States must beware of seeking profits at the possible expense of America's technological edge and national security. And as much of an opportunity as there might be, American firms can only go so far in exporting high technology to the Soviets before they collide with U.S. export regulations.

On the other hand, U.S. trade regulators and Cocom may take too cautious an approach. This could signal to the Soviets that they should more actively seek business relations in other nations, especially those that are competitive with the United States but take a less restrictive approach to controlling exports, including Brazil and Singapore. Not only could this threaten the effectiveness of U.S. export controls, but it could also drive a wedge between the United States and its current economic and political allies by causing them to rethink their allegiance to U.S. export policy. The Soviets could gain increased involvement in markets now dominated by American business.

U.S. government and industry, thus, must together walk a fine line in determining policy on access to high technology by the Soviets. In choosing their path, an understanding of past Soviet technology acquisition practices is important, as is coming to grips with the current technical capabilities of the Soviet Union and the areas in which they seek to harvest, whether openly or clandestinely, the fruits of America's research and development. Also important to consider are the methods the Soviets use to obtain high technology, in the United States and around the world, as well as the roles other nations play in diverting U.S. equipment and know-how to the Soviet bloc. Finally, it is crucial to assess the measures taken in the United States, both by the government and private industry, and those taken by other nations to keep vital technology out of Soviet hands. The ultimate course the United States chooses in selling technology to the Soviets will affect not only the vitality of America's high-technology industry and its ability to compete internationally but also America's continued national security.

NOTES

1. In all, Customs and Commerce officials identified more than 300 illegal shipments. One hundred and three were used in the indictments, and 13 of them were used in the trial. These 13 shipments yielded the $8 million figure. But company records indicated that the 13 shipments included $10.5 million worth of equipment. Federal investigators found that Bruchhausen had sent Anatoli Maluta $100,000 per week between 1975 and 1980; those transactions would indicate that the total worth of the equipment was almost $21 million.

2. Stephen C. Dodge, U.S. Customs Service, Los Angeles, Calif.: Interview, Nov. 15, 1987; "$30 Million to the Soviets," *Customs Today*, No. 3, 1987, pp. 1–7.

3. Reverse engineering is the activity of taking apart a product and studying its assembly and technology for the purposes of designing and manufacturing a similar product.

4. Testimony by Fred Asselin, investigator for the U.S. Senate, in U.S., Senate, Committee on Government Affairs, permanent subcommittee on investigations, *Transfer of United States High Technology to the Soviet Union and Soviet Bloc Nations*, 97th Cong., 2d sess., 1982, pp. 397–99.

5. Affidavit of Thomas Albert Gosselin, No. 85-652, taken by Francis J. Boyle, chief judge, U.S. District Court, Providence, R.I., July 25, 1985.

6. Paul Tate and David Hebditch, "Opening Moves," *Datamation*, Mar. 15, 1987, p. 43.

7. Senator William V. Roth, Jr., "Soviet Theft of American Technology," *Congressional Record*, Oct. 3, 1983, H7856.

8. Representative Don Bonker, chairman, House Subcommittee on International Economic Policy and Trade of the Committee on Foreign Affairs, at Hearings on Enforcement of Multilateral Export Controls, Nov. 3, 1987, as dictated by telephone to the author in November 1987 by Rep. Bonker's office.

9. A column by William Safire in the *New York Times Magazine*, Apr. 12, 1987, p. 8, discusses in detail the frustrations of finding the source of the quotation, which, after intensive sleuthing on Safire's part, cannot be directly verified. Safire comes closest to verification through his discovery of a man named Annenkov who claims to have copied portions of Lenin's personal papers in Moscow. Annenkov came up with the following close approximation of the same sentiment: "The whole world's capitalists and their governments, as they pant to win the Soviet market, *will close their eyes* to the above-mentioned reality and will thus transform themselves into men who are *deaf, dumb, and blind*. They will give us credits...they will toil to prepare their own suicide." Whether precisely stated by Lenin or not, the United States has evidence that the intent to acquire Western technology is well established in Soviet thought.

10. "Fully reinforced" includes North American reinforcements and all Warsaw Pact forces west of the Urals.

11. *Soviet Military Power, 1987*, 6th ed. (Washington, D.C.: Government Printing Office, 1987), p. 93.

12. Testimony by Richard N. Perle, assistant secretary for international security policy, U.S. Department of Defense, in U.S. Senate, Committee on Government Affairs, permanent subcommittee on investigations affairs, *Foreign Missions Act and Espionage Activities in the United States*, 99th Cong., 1st sess., 1985, pp. 75–76.

13. Lt. Col. Terry Monrad, SDI Office, U.S. Department of Defense, Washington, D.C.: Interview, Mar. 16, 1987.

14. Alex Gliksman, "The Soviets' 'Star Wars' Dread," *Christian Science Monitor*, Nov. 25, 1986, p. 17.

15. Kathleen O'Toole, "Soviets May Be Reorganizing Science for Star Wars," *Stanford Daily*, Jan. 28, 1987, p. 6.

16. "Stealing Star Wars," *Time*, Oct. 20, 1986, p. 71.

17. Patrick J. Kiger, "Techno-bandit Case: The Stuff of a Spy Yarn," *Orange County Register*, Nov. 9, 1987, p. 1.

18. John Mann, Delphin Systems, Sunnyvale, Calif.: Interview, Apr. 14, 1988.

19. "Military Electronics: The Heat Is On," *Electronic Business*, Jan. 15, 1986, p. 84.

20. The term "dual use technologies," embedded in almost every discussion about export controls, first appeared in a 1976 report titled "Defense Science Board Task Force on Export of U.S. Technology: A DOD Perspective," according to J. Fred Bucy, former president of Texas Instruments, who worked on the panel that produced the report.

21. Central Intelligence Agency, *Soviet Acquisition of Militarily Significant Western Technology: An Update* (Washington, D.C.: 1985), Prologue.

22. Ibid. pp. 31–34.

23. Tom Morganthau, "Moscow's Prying Eyes," *Newsweek*, Sept. 30, 1985, p. 30.

24. Robert S. Dudney, "How Soviets Steal U.S. High-Tech Secrets," *U.S. News & World Report*, Aug. 12, 1985, p. 33.

25. Jack Vorona, "Technology Transfer and Military R&D," in C. M. Perry and R. L. Pfaltzgraff, Jr., eds., *Selling the Rope to Hang Capitalism? The Debate on East-West Trade and Technology Transfer* (Elmsford, N.Y.: Pergamon Press, 1987), p. 18.

26. Ted Agres, "Documents Unveil Soviet Methods of Obtaining Western Technology," *Research and Development*, June 1985, p. 48.

27. "The Price of Technology Leaks," *Wall Street Journal* (editorial), May 10, 1985, p. 24.

28. "Assessing the Effect of Technology Transfer on U.S./Western Security: A Defense Perspective," U.S. Department of Defense, (Washington, D.C.: 1985), office of the under secretary of defense for policy, Department of Defense, pp. E5, E6.

29. The Department of Commerce included twenty-eight technologies in its definition of high technology: jet and gas turbines for aircraft; nuclear reactors; calculating machines (including electronic computers); statistical machines (punch card or tape); parts of office machinery (including computer parts); machine tools for metal; glassworking machinery; pumps and centrifuges; parts and accessories for machine tools; ball, roller, or needle-roller bearings; cocks, valves; telecommunications equipment; X-ray apparatus; primary batteries and cells; tubes, transistors, photocells; electrical measuring and control instruments; electron and proton accelerators; electrical machinery (including electromagnets), traffic control equipment, signaling apparatus; aircraft, heavier than air; aircraft parts; warships; special-purpose vessels (including submersible vessels); optical elements; optical instruments; image projectors (might include holograph projectors); measuring and control instruments; photographic film; and gramophones, tape recorders, and video recorders.

30. U.S. Department of Commerce, International Trade Administration, *Quantification of Western Exports of High-Technology Products to Communist Countries Through 1983* (Washington, D.C.: 1985), pp. 12, 28, and 29.

31. Mitchell B. Wallerstein, project director, National Academy of Sciences: Interview, Jan. 12, 1988; National Academy of Sciences staff et. al., *Balancing the National Interest, U.S. National Security Export Controls and Global Economic Competition* (Washington, D.C.: National Academy Press, 1987), pp. 266–67.

32. Ed Zschau, "Export Controls and America's Competitive Challenge," *High Technology Law Journal*, No. 1, 1986, p. 4.

33. "Overkill in Export Control," *Financial Times* (editorial), Oct. 20, 1986, p. 16.

34. Mikhail S. Gorbachev, *Perestroika: New Thinking for Our Country and the World* (New York: Harper and Row, 1987), p. 94.

35. The Soviets have never met the original goals of their five-year plans, but they have often revised the goals downward so they can appear to be living within them.

36. The absolute number of people employed continues to rise, but the rate of growth of the labor force is decreasing. The working-age population (ages 20–59) increased by 30 million between 1970 and 1985 but is expected to increase by only 6 million between 1986 and 2000. (Source: Dr. Murray Feshbach, Georgetown University, Washington, D.C.)

37. William Echikson, "Energy Crunch Hits East Bloc," *Christian Science Monitor*, Feb. 2, 1987, p. 9.

38. Speech by M. S. Shkabardnya, minister of instrument making, automation, and control systems, during the Twenty-Seventh Party Congress, February–March 1986, *Pravda: Organ of the Central Committee of the CPSU* (St. Paul, Minn.), Feb. 27, 1986, p. 5.

39. William Echikson, "Gorbachev Proves a Hard-Nosed Trader," *Christian Science Monitor*, Feb. 18, 1987, p. 1.

40. Comecon is the Council for Mutual Economic Aid, founded in 1949 and consisting of the U.S.S.R., Bulgaria, Czechoslovakia, Hungary, Romania, East Germany, Mongolia, Cuba, Vietnam, and Poland.

41. "Prospects for Profits," *Business International*, Mar. 16, 1987, p. 84.

42. "Reversing Russia's Slide," *Economist*, Oct. 3, 1987, p. 101.

43. Michael R. Gordon, "CIA's Report Revives Soviet-Growth Debates," *New York Times*, Mar. 29, 1987, p. A14.

44. U.S. White House Office of the Press Secretary, "The Joint U.S.-Soviet Summit Statement," Dec. 10, 1987, p. 8.

45. Foreign Broadcast Information Service, Daily Report–Soviet Union, Mar. 16, 1987, p. G14.

46. Report by N. I. Ryzhkov on the Twenty-Seventh Party Congress, *Pravda: Organ of the Central Committee of the CPSU* (St. Paul, Minn.), Mar. 4, 1986, p. 4.

47. Bill Keller, "Does Moscow Mean It This Time?" *New York Times*, Jan. 18, 1987, p. III, 4.

48. The U.S.-U.S.S.R. Trade and Economic Council was created in 1973 under the Nixon-Brezhnev trade agreement. The group of more than 300 American companies and 150 Soviet trade organizations and representatives has offices in New York and Washington, D.C.

49. Sergei Frolov, senior economist, Amtorg Trading Company, New York: Interview, Apr. 12, 1987.

50. Mark D'Anastasio, "Capitalists Wary of Moscow's Hard Sell to Invest Joint-Venture Enterprises," *Wall Street Journal*, Apr. 6, 1987, p. 20.

51. Ibid.

52. Bob Willis, manager of media relations, Combustion Engineering, Stamford, Conn.: Interview, Apr. 23, 1987; Timothy Hentage, "Biggest U.S.-Soviet Ventures Announced," *San Francisco Examiner*, June 2, 1988, p. C3.

53. Roman Rollnick, "U.S. Firm in Deal for Plant in Russia," *San Francisco Examiner*, Nov. 19, 1987, p. C10.

54. "U.S. Company to Build Plants in Russia," *San Francisco Examiner*, Apr. 13, 1988, p. C3.

55. Kathleen Sullivan, "Computer Deal with Soviets Not Yet Final," *San Jose Mercury News*, May 26, 1988, pp. D1, D4.

56. Peter Gumbel, "American Companies Form a Consortium to Cope with Soviet Trade Bureaucracy," *Wall Street Journal*, Apr. 14, 1988, p. 25.

57. "Soviet Bank Taps Eurobond Market for $78 Million," *Wall Street Journal*, Jan. 6, 1988, p. 22.

58. Peter Gumbel, "German Banks Increase Loans to Soviets and Introduce Moscow to Bond Markets," *Wall Street Journal*, May 16, 1988, p. 12.

59. "Security Pacific U.K. Unit, Soviets Sign a Trade Pact," *Wall Street Journal*, Dec. 16, 1987, p. 22.

60. Phillip Hanson, University of Birmingham, England: Interview, May 7, 1987.

61. "Going Into the Red," *Wall Street Journal* (editorial), Dec. 7, 1987, p. 20.

62. Paul L. Montgomery, "Soviets' European Trade Bill," *New York Times*, June 11, 1988, p. Z21.

63. Mikhail S. Gorbachev, *Perestroika: New Thinking for Our Country and the World* (New York: Harper and Row, 1987), p. 94.

64. Mark D'Anastasio, "Soviets Step Up Efforts to Win Share in Launching of Commercial Satellites," *Wall Street Journal*, Jan. 6, 1987, p. 33, and Melinda Gipson, "What is Glavkosmos?" *World & I*, March 1987, p. 99. The prices depend on the size and weight of the item launched. A commercial Titan launch costs about $110 million; U.S. costs are much higher because U.S. booster manufacturers do not have to compete on costs, and quantities are much lower in the Soviet Union. The Soviet Proton rocket has six engines, while U.S. rockets have two. Considering the increasing frequency of Soviet launches, it appears that Soviet costs are driven downward by larger equipment production runs. (Source: Letter to author, Jan. 5, 1988, from Arthur H. Dula, Dula Shields & Egbert, Houston, Tex.)

65. "West German Firm to Do Tests in Soviet Space Run," *Christian Science Monitor*, Jan. 13, 1988, p. 2.

66. William Broad, "American Company and Soviets Agree on Space Venture," *New York Times*, Feb. 21, 1988, p. A1.

67. Felicity Barringer, "U.S. Reporters Get First-Hand View of Soviet Space Launching," *New York Times*, May 19, 1988, p. A7.

2

FROM IRON TO
SILICON

Soviet high-technology espionage and the illegal export of high technology to the Soviet Union have become a fact of life. In 1978, members of Congress and the American people were shocked to learn that Christopher Boyce, a young man working at TRW, had sold highly sensitive satellite specifications to the Soviets through their embassy in Mexico City. During congressional hearings in the late 1970s, leading up to the Export Administration Act of 1979, Senate and House members heard from Boyce, who came to be known as the Falcon, how easy it had been to acquire and sell top secret information critical to U.S. national security. But long before Boyce's actions, the Soviets had made a regular habit of reaching out to the West for technology. At least since the time of Tsar Peter the Great, Russia had an appetite for Western scientific know-how. And since the Bolshevik Revolution in 1917, the Soviet economy has moved through cycles of insularity and open relations with the West; four times since 1917 (not counting the most recent opening), the Soviets have made overtures to the United States and initiated internal reforms to obtain Western high technology.

Because the Soviets' rigid system does not allow for innovation, historically they have developed an unhealthy reliance on Western technology for industrial and economic progress. However, acquiring technology from external sources instead of developing it internally is less a communist characteristic than a Russian one, although the Soviets have advanced it to an art form. Russians, however, are not singular in the art of technology filching. It is virtually a truism of history that developing nations will go to great lengths to acquire the technology of their advanced rivals.

TECHNOLOGY THIEVES: FROM PETER THE GREAT TO THE GREAT COMMUNICATOR

The pre-twentieth century Russian economy was based to varying degrees on serf labor. Because serfs earned little or nothing for better harvests, they had no incentive to improve their farming methods. This lack of incentive carried over into Russian industry. Even before the reign (1682–1725) of Peter the Great, Russians began to seek outside know-how rather than develop it internally. Peter's father, Alexis (reigned 1645–76), looked to the West for ideas, skills, and know-how. Much of the know-how was brought to Moscow by Germans who settled in their own suburb, a favorite visiting place of Alexis' son, Peter. The foreigners brought with them a variety of sought-after crafts. For example, the German settlement included architects, engineers, and doctors who offered their skills to Moscow residents.[1] And as early as the mid-1500s, Western European laborers brought industrial skills to Russia; for example, Swedish and English workers brought modern ironworking know-how. In 1632 a Dutchman was the director of the first Russian ironworks to use water power.[2] But it was Peter the Great who first sprinkled Western innovations over the Russian economic system to extract increases in productivity from a systemically unmotivated work force.

Tsar Peter concentrated his forays in Europe on his search for ways to bring industrial know-how to Russia. He brought home weapons, and with them came skilled technicians who could teach the Russians how to manufacture and repair the weapons. Peter appeared to have had a similar goal of, and approach to, modernizing the military as his Soviet counterparts have today.

Peter sometimes brought Western ways into Russian society with a fervor akin to religious fanaticism. At one point, his travels convinced him that his male compatriots should shed their beards, a symbol, in his opinion, of Russian uncouth appearance in contrast to that of forward-thinking, unbearded Westerners. Motivated by both his Western observations and his obsession with taxation, he demanded that Russian men shave off their beards, personally and abruptly removed some of them himself, and issued small medallions to be carried by those paying a tax that enabled them to keep their beard.[3] When Peter set his sights on making Russia a preeminent naval power, he began spying in other countries. The original catalyst for his campaign was his desire to keep up with Dutch and particularly English naval developments. He ordered the clandestine observance of foreign naval vessels and shipyards and the recruitment of foreign expertise to accomplish his goal. Dutch naval expertise came in the person of Cornelius Cruys. Major General Patrick Gordon from England brought English naval know-how to Russia. Various pilots, engineers, and doctors followed him after a trip Peter made to Europe in 1698.[4]

THE CONTINUOUS THREAD: FROM THE REVOLUTION

Just as in today's Soviet Union, the motivation for modernization in Russia during the 1800s under the Romanov emperors depended on the state, and the result was an inability to keep pace with the Industrial Revolution that was taking place in the West. During that period, particularly under Nicholas II (reigned 1894–1917), many European and American firms contributed significantly to Russia's technological base. The French assisted with the building of the Trans-Siberian railway in the late 1800s, the English, French, and Belgians with the establishment of mining operations in the Donets Basin, and the Swedish and British with the development of the oil fields near the Caspian Sea. John Hughes, the Englishman mostly responsible for assisting the Russians with their metallurgical technology, was heralded as the "iron king" and honored when the Donets Basin factories were named after him. American companies came to Russia offering two industrial innovations—the sewing machine and agricultural equipment. Both Singer Sewing Machine and International Harvester had large, vigorous operations in Russia until the October Revolution. By 1914 Singer had a sales force of 27,000 in Russia, selling and servicing sewing machines.[5]

In 1916, the American-Russian Chamber of Commerce was incorporated "to foster trade, encourage and generally promote the economic, commercial, and industrial relations between the United States of America and Russia." In 1950, when it was dissolved, E. A. Emerson of Armco International Co., T. H. Mitchell of RCA Communications Inc., Reeve Schley of Chase National Bank, Arthur Walsh of Thomas A. Edison Co., and Thomas J. Watson of IBM, among others, were members of the chamber's board of directors. Earlier, representatives of such companies as Westinghouse and Ingersoll Rand also sat on the board.[6] In 1917, the swell of events in Moscow nullified the chamber's plans for the near future.

ONE STEP FORWARD

The Russian Revolution in 1917 indelibly marked every aspect of Russia's political, economic, and social institutions. V. I. Lenin, the first Soviet leader (1917–24), condemned Western capitalism as an exploitation of the workers by the owners of industry and expropriated all Western assets, including threshing and sewing machines. Early revolutionary attitudes toward scientists further curtailed economic and technological progress. Revolutionaries viewed science as an effort to question the central importance of the individual to the new political order and feared that it offered the potential for replacing the human work force with machines. The new Soviet government also felt threatened by individualistic scientists and made the nationalization of science and technology an important part of its agenda. More independent-minded scientists were branded enemies of the proletariat and often tormented or even killed. Many fled the country.

Russia's economy during its first communist year was dismal. In 1918, Lenin said:

> Now comes the most critical moment, when hunger and unemployment are knocking at the doors of an ever greater number of workers, when hundreds and thousands of men are suffering the pangs of hunger, when the situation is aggravated by the fact that there is no bread.[7]

Money was losing its value faster than it was being issued. Between November 1917 and June 1918, the gross yield of grain crops dropped from 641,000 tons to 2,000 tons.[8]

During the period of "war communism" immediately following the Bolshevik victory, the government officially discouraged any efforts to seek Western assistance and ideas, including technology, particularly because Britain, France, and the United States intervened on Soviet soil during World War I. Lenin's forces attempted to eliminate the vestiges of opposition to their new order. A wave of anti-Semitism brought with it pogroms that swept away some of Russia's most gifted scientists. (Such purges continued to escalate, especially under Stalin, until the early 1950s.) But the Bolshevik party soon realized its need for Western expertise. In the spring of 1919, the party congress recommended that "ideological purity be overlooked in drawing on the expertise of scientists."[9]

In 1921, Lenin attempted to improve the economic situation by instituting the New Economic Policy (NEP). The NEP permitted concessions to Western entrepreneurs, allowed for technology-assistance contracts with foreign engineers, and approved Soviet experts' exchanges with their Western counterparts. Far from being an innovative experiment in economic management, the NEP was an emergency plan for rescuing the economy to the point that it might feed the population. The peasantry had grown hostile as a result of dismal agricultural conditions. To make things worse, the peasants were threatened because of the new regime's forced requisitioning of agricultural surpluses. The NEP attempted to improve the situation by changing agricultural and industrial policy. Instead of forced requisitioning, the NEP provided for a tax on production and a means for placing some produce on the free market.

Similar to Gorbachev's new initiatives, the NEP enabled farmers to lease land, hire some labor, and exercise a degree of local autonomy. Small businessmen were allowed to manage some enterprises and, to a limited extent, practice free trade. They were pressured to institute more rigorous management principles and to show increased profits. As early as 1922, the economy began to improve, and Lenin's new policy laid the groundwork for the Soviet Union's first Five-Year Plan.[10] Thus, the Soviets compromised communist principles to maintain the regime. Times continued to be unsettled as Lenin tried to lead a starving, embattled people who had known no peace since the beginning of World War I. Lenin referred to his program as taking "one step backward in order to take two steps forward," surprising his fellow revolutionaries by stating that "communists must learn to trade."[11] His plan carried with it the hope that the influx of Western skills and assets would develop the store of natural resources that blessed the Soviet Union. He also hoped that the NEP would bring with it the momentum of industrialization that had transformed the West. Several European countries signed trade agreements with the Soviets, including Great Britain in March 1921. The Soviet foreign-trade company, Amtorg, was also created under the NEP, as was another trading company in London called Arcos. Germany extended credits to the Soviet Union for the purchase of German machinery.[12]

As a result of this risky reach for the benefits of capitalism, the Soviets granted almost 200 concessions to foreign firms, giving each one the right to engage in a specific commercial activity for a specific period.[13] The concessions were aimed at acquiring Western, mostly U.S., production processes, training engineers, and creating institutes for applied and basic research. U.S. banking interests also played a role. When concessions continued during the first years of Stalin's rule, the Chase Manhattan Bank, then known as the Chase National Bank, held all of Amtorg's accounts.

The contracts ushered in a period of unprecedented Westernization of Russian technology, both in equipment and know-how. International Barnsdall Corporation, for instance, introduced U.S. rotary drilling and pumping technology; by the end of the 1920s, 80 percent of all Soviet drilling operations used the rotary technique.[14]

Although the concessions had the immediate effect of bringing new life to Soviet industry, they had a longer-term negative impact. The infusion of Western technology began to take away what little incentive there was for internal innovation and development. The consequences were felt in the Soviet economy until 1941, when World War II intervened and the demands of creating and maintaining a huge war machine led to the revival of internal R&D.

Lenin died in 1924, to be succeeded ultimately by Joseph Stalin. For the rest of the decade, those agreements already reached with foreign firms remained in effect, but the number of new concessions dwindled. Instead, state planners concentrated on technical-assistance contracts with individual foreign firms. Western ways had come to be the dominant force in the Soviet economy. In his 1979 *Commentary Magazine* article, Carl Gershman wrote that by 1928

> there was not a single important industrial process—from mining, oil, production, metallurgy, chemicals, transportation, communications, textiles, and forestry to the production of industrial and agricultural equipment and the generation of electrical power—which did not derive from transferred Western technology.[15]

Anthony C. Sutton, a historian specializing in Soviet history, concludes that U.S. technical assistance to the Soviets between 1917 and 1930 was "the most important factor in the survival of the Soviet regime."[16]

American industrialists greeted Soviet markets with enthusiasm. Thomas Watson, founder of the new calculating machine company, IBM, warned Americans to "refrain from making any criticism of the present form of government adopted by Russia," in an effort to keep the doors wide open for business opportunities.[17] Between 1918 and 1933, U.S. companies active in this transfer of technology included Curtiss-Wright Corporation (aviation), Sperry Gyroscope Company (marine instruments), International General Electric Company, and the Radio Corporation of America (electronics).[18] For their part, Soviet engineers had absorbed U.S. technology in large measure via the concessions, and manufacturing centers were becoming self-sufficient enough to do without the massive infusion of U.S. expertise and technicians. When imports from the United

States began to taper off, the Soviet Union prepared to internalize its newly renovated industrial society.

But American technical input had not come to an end. Between 1930 and 1945, technology-assistance agreements continued to replace the concessions of the 1920s. During that time, an industrial design firm in Detroit, Mich., Albert Kahn Inc., designed and built plants called for by the first Five-Year Plan (1928–33) using non-Soviet equipment. This effort was central to providing American technology so desperately needed by the Soviets to implement their first Five-Year Plan. Other American firms went to the Soviet Union to work under individual contracts with the government. Arthur G. McKee Company managed the construction of the world's largest steel plant, Du Pont constructed two nitric acid plants, and General Electric designed and built electric generators and turbines. Even automobile plants rose in Moscow and Yaroslavl with assistance from A. J. Brandt and the Hercules Motor Company.[19]

TWO STEPS BACK

Under Stalin's direction, the government continued to monitor Western technical literature and to duplicate some prototypes obtained during the concessions period. Stalin's economic policy initially continued to move the country toward industrialization. Some companies were denationalized in an attempt to stimulate the growth of a competitive marketplace and to compensate for the decrease of Western investment in the Soviet economy. But Stalin quickly moved away from NEP policies, in part because of Lenin's ambiguity concerning whether he intended the NEP to be a temporary program or a permanent fixture of the Soviet economy.

During the infamous show trials of the late 1920s and early 1930s, Stalin charged Western technicians with sabotage and "wrecking." Much to their chagrin, U.S. firms saw their assets expropriated by the Soviet government. Only those Americans with significant economic and political clout, most notably Armand Hammer and W. Averell Harriman, emerged from the concessions experiment unscathed,[20] receiving reasonable compensation for their business interests. Hammer, whose father was instrumental in founding the U.S. Communist party in 1919, represented thirty-eight U.S. firms during the concessions period. Harriman was a director of the U.S. bank Kuhn, Loeb & Co., one of four U.S. financial institutions active in lending money to the Soviet government.

In 1936, operating under his new constitution and with the second Five-Year Plan in full swing, Stalin officially condemned Lenin's NEP in favor of his own economic policy. (In fact, the NEP lasted only until 1924.) In a speech before the Extraordinary Eighth Congress of Soviets, he described the NEP as "based on old, obsolete, poor technique and agriculture." He went on to say that it "resembled an immense ocean of petty individual peasant economies with their obsolete medieval technique." The economy under his policies would grow "to giant strength...based on a new, rich, modern technique with a strongly developed heavy industry...."[21]

If reliance on foreign technology under the NEP had slowed internal Soviet R&D, the totalitarian measures carried out by Stalin in support of his new policies virtually stultified it. Free thinking and individualism, personality traits of many great scientists, hardly fit the Stalinist vision of the U.S.S.R. Concerned that scientists could pose an intellectual if not a political threat to his rule, Stalin sent many of the country's leading men of science to the gulags.

Although Stalin's reforms, especially the collectivization of agriculture in the 1930s, had been intended to put the Soviet economy on an equal footing with the economies of the Western powers, by late in the decade, the economic situation was starting to decline. Collectivization took with it the lives of millions of peasants and drastically destabilized the economy. Stalin starved the peasants by selling requisitioned grain for hard currency that he used to purchase foreign technology for the military. In large part the victim of Stalin's extremism, economic progress had also suffered the inability of the technicians remaining at their posts to apply and improve on the expertise gathered under the NEP. Stalin thus began, in the 1940s, to bring scientists back from the labor camps in the hope that they could advance Soviet technology and pump new life into the economy and the military. Scientists were given a privileged position in society, so much so that Stalin once told his staff, "Don't bother our physicists with political seminars. Let them use all their time for their professional work."[22]

WORLD WAR II: A TECHNOLOGY WINDFALL

World War II again opened the door to U.S. technology. Once the Soviet Union and the United States were allied against Germany, technical assistance began to flow between the two countries. The Lend-Lease Act, passed in 1941, provided for the United States to sell, lend, or lease materials, including machinery incorporating important technology, to its allies in return for in-kind repayment or other vaguely defined assets. Anatoly P. Aleksandrov, the outgoing president of the Soviet Academy of Sciences, claimed in 1986 that assistance from the West during this period "served as the material foundation for our great victory in the struggle with fascism."[23]

William Corson and Robert Crowley, in their book *The New KGB*, argue that, under Lend-Lease, Soviet agents in the United States, posing as trade representatives, made off with any equipment they could put their hands on. Although proving this assertion is difficult, under the act about $167 million worth of electrical-plant shipments—a priority for the Soviets—also reached the Soviet Union via legitimate channels. As provided by the Lend-Lease Act, everything from tanks, trucks, locomotives, and motor vehicles to army boots, telephones, and radio components reached the Soviets under protocol agreements signed between 1941 and 1945, when the war ended. In addition, from 1940 to 1942 alone, at least 1,300 industrial plants opened up with some assistance from the United States in the Soviet Union. By 1944, this U.S. assistance increased Soviet wartime capacity by 20 percent.[24] In all, the Soviets received more than $11 billion in technical aid. (The U.S.S.R. was one of the last recipients to finish its repayment, which it did in 1972, more than 30 years after the act was signed.)

Stalin, U.S. President Franklin Delano Roosevelt, and Winston Churchill recognized that their nations would emerge from the war as the world's preeminent powers. Accordingly, each attempted to maneuver into a position that would leave his country with the advantage when fighting ceased. Their common cause of defeating Hitler, however, kept relations superficially cordial even as they competed with each other. This was to change in the war's waning days.

When, in early 1945, Nazi defeat appeared inevitable, the Allies turned their attention to dividing the spoils of victory, which, considering Germany's advanced industrial and scientific community, were substantial. Thus began what Winston Churchill called the Wizard War, the Soviet and American effort to commandeer the Third Reich's technicians and technology.

As war reparations, the Soviets dismantled entire German factories and moved them lock, stock, and barrel to their own country. Similarly, they moved complete laboratories to the Soviet Union, along with a great many German technicians. Sometimes the facilities proved difficult to reassemble, and the absence of know-how or accomplished scientists who did not go to the Soviet Union with their labs made it difficult to run them.

In the end, the most visible technological battle was won by the Americans. They and the Soviets had realized that the awesome V-rocket, the "vengeance weapon" used by Hitler to terrorize London during the war's final months, bore the promises of space travel and military superiority for whatever nation first mastered its power. In 1945, Wernher von Braun, the inventor of the V-rocket, sought refuge with the Americans in anticipation of a German defeat. To protect his invaluable technical papers, von Braun buried them in an abandoned mine shaft in southern Germany. After surrendering to an American soldier in Germany, he and other key rocket experts were whisked to America. Arriving later at their New Mexico testing grounds were the critical technical papers, retrieved by the Americans after von Braun had told them where the stash could be found, and all the rocket equipment U.S. forces could salvage from the underground Nazi rocket factory at Peenemünde, in what was to become the Soviet-controlled Eastern zone. The Soviets, meanwhile, had all along eyed the German rocket facilities and personnel as a top priority for their own use. When the war ended, the Soviets raced to Peenemünde only to find deserted buildings.[25]

FROM THE COLD WAR TO DÉTENTE

After World War II, Soviet-American relations plummeted to a low point, ominously called the cold war. On the one hand, the Americans became suspicious and even paranoid as they recognized the Soviets' position of strength bolstered by their domination of a portion of German land and eventually, by 1948, of Poland, Hungary, Bulgaria, Romania, and Czechoslovakia. The United States saw the Soviet Union as the second most powerful country, a superpower with confirmed expansionist behavior. Furthermore, Americans quickly became aware of strong anti-American propaganda emanating from the Soviet government.

On the other hand, Stalin continued to consolidate his power by aggressively and often brutally eliminating anything and anyone who threatened his dictatorship. The U.S. was portrayed as the country's most feared enemy, and Soviet-sponsored international peace movements conveyed the image of a warmongering America. The struggle against capitalism was reignited in the Soviet Union, and by 1948, both the United States and the U.S.S.R. were consumed with mutual distrust and fear. And by the war's end, industrialization under Stalin was threatened because thousands of skilled workers had perished.

The cold war was also fueled by covert attempts to steal U.S. technology. Lavrenti P. Beria was a slightly balding, bespectacled man who headed the Soviet security agencies for the second half of the Stalin era (the NKVD from 1938 to 1946 and the MGB from 1946 to 1953)[26] but was executed in 1953 during the internal power struggle after Stalin's death. Stalin and Beria are thought to have regarded each other with mutual contempt, yet each was too powerful for the other to destroy. Lavrenti Beria was the godfather of Soviet military research and development. In the early 1940s, he championed the development of the Soviet atomic bomb, assembling first the best and brightest of Soviet scientists and, later, captured German scientists. Under pressure from Stalin, Beria sent agents to the United States (as well as to Britain and Canada, which were also doing atomic research) in an effort to gather information about the Manhattan Project. In 1949, the Soviets had their atomic bomb.

Although controversy still surrounds the case, one of the most successful Soviet espionage plots appears to have led to the Rosenberg trial. Harry Gold, David Greenglass, and Ethel and Julius Rosenberg were apparently recruited and subsequently ordered, in the early 1940s, to steal and then pass on to the Soviets both materials and information relating to U.S. nuclear research developments. Julius Rosenberg had worked as an electrical engineer and was also in the U.S. Army Signal Corps. David Greenglass, Ethel Rosenberg's brother, managed to enter the Los Alamos, N. Mex., facility and steal highly sensitive material. He appears to have passed it to the Rosenbergs, who then passed it to the Soviets. Another member of the spy ring, Harry Gold, also passed information from Greenglass to a Soviet contact in New York City, Anatoly A. Yakovlev. The Rosenberg trial in 1951 was highly controversial, particularly its procedures and the motivation of the prosecution, which some thought were tainted by anti-Semitism.

But the Rosenberg case was the most publicized espionage trial involving the loss of critical U.S. technology until the 1970s. All codefendants were found guilty: The Rosenbergs received the death penalty for espionage and were executed in 1953. Harry Gold received a 30-year prison sentence as did another codefendant, Morton Sobell, and David Greenglass served a 15-year prison term.

Nikita S. Khrushchev, Soviet leader from 1953 to 1964, led the country when it broke two different records. In 1961, Yuri A. Gagarin made an unprecedented orbit around the earth in *Vostok I* while agricultural failures brought food production to record lows. Soviet science, particularly aeronautics and rocketry, was making impressive progress, and scientists were being accorded prestigious positions in Soviet society. Khrushchev announced the usual ambitions for his country in the speech detailing the sixth Five-Year Plan, 1956–60.

In an attempt to improve relations and to seek Western economic and technical assistance, Khrushchev visited the United States in 1959, the first time a Soviet premier had stepped on American soil. There he took a close look at U.S. technical advances. During the visit, President Dwight D. Eisenhower and Khrushchev confirmed their mutual interest in a 1960s version of détente and talked of increasing trade relations between the two countries. In the spirit of closer economic ties, the Economic Club of New York gave Khrushchev and his delegation a dinner hosted by W. Averell Harriman, former governor of New York. While visiting San Jose, Calif., Khrushchev toured an IBM factory manufacturing calculators.[27] Although he may have been disheartened by the technological gap between his country and the United States, he returned to the Soviet Union enthusiastic about its ability to reach similar heights.

The building of the Berlin Wall and the Bay of Pigs incident, both in 1961, and the Cuban missile crisis in 1962 as well as generally mounting American anticommunism brought U.S.-Soviet relations to an icy impasse. When Khrushchev came to power, he had realized that he could not count on the cooperation of the United States, but he nevertheless set about trying to obtain U.S. support for improving Soviet technology. Khrushchev realized that the only way to close the technology gap between his country and the United States would be to arrange for another period of open technical acquisition from the United States, particularly in computers and electronics. The early 1960s thus foreshadowed the era of détente that was to follow a decade later.

Although U.S. export controls restricted sophisticated technology sales, the increasing Soviet chemical production, a goal of the sixth Five-Year Plan (1956–60), opened the doors to the U.S. chemical industry: The Soviets purchased fifty chemical factories from the West between 1959 and 1961.[28] Agricultural production had begun to improve in 1958, and the Soviet Union wished to open trade channels once again, hoping that the trade would be technical in nature. Even though a crop failure in 1963 temporarily set back Soviet expectations for further commercial dealings with the United States, the harvests gradually improved, and trade maintained its upward momentum.

Recently declassified documents reveal that President John F. Kennedy was ambivalent about these transactions. In a letter to Commerce Secretary Luther H. Hodges on May 16, 1963, Kennedy wrote:

> It is not my judgment that the gains to our national security which can be achieved by denying the Soviets access to American machines and factories of the kind we are discussing, many of which they can get in Europe at any event, balance the cost to our national security of making it more difficult to deal with the Soviets on vital military and political issues.

Later that same day, in a memo from the White House, Kennedy posed a question: "Are we being adequately compensated in these sales [to the U.S.S.R.]?" And he added: "We know the Soviets are using American machinery to copy our technology."

In the mid-1960s, the Soviets signed more than 160 contracts with Western firms and 105 scientific and technical cooperation agreements.[29] But they were not planning to open the doors for long; the agreements were designed to expire in ten years. On a commercial level, the government began to arrange purchases of computer technology from American electronics firms. In 1965, the Soviets purchased $5,000 worth of computers. A mere two years later, they spent $1,079,000 on U.S. computer equipment.[30]

Many U.S. companies approached the Soviet Union to build trade relationships. Among those seeking new Soviet business were IBM and Control Data Corporation (CDC). Encouraged by the U.S. government, CDC sold its by then outdated 1604 computers to the Soviets. The 1604 had been CDC's first computer and the first ever to be completely transistorized. The computer was about 10 feet long; punched paper tape was used to input data. Sales such as this paved the way for trading protocols between the Soviet State Committee for Science and Technology (GKNT) and U.S. companies.

Following in Khrushchev's footsteps, Premier Aleksei N. Kosygin (1964–80) told the Twenty-Third Party Congress in 1966 that the Soviet Union would import more technology from Western countries as a means of improving its economy. He stated that importing technology from abroad would limit Soviet investment in internal research and improve productivity in factories and in agriculture. Furthermore, General Secretary Leonid I. Brezhnev (1964–82) followed up the Twenty-Third Party Congress with economic reforms that sound similar to those being promoted by Gorbachev in the 1980s. Enterprises were given more freedom to plan, and profit was emphasized as the basis for performance evaluation.[31]

Also in 1966, new automobile technology came to the Soviet Union through a deal with Fiat, which by 1972 would give the Soviets the equivalent of their own Fiat factory. The Soviet space program continued to build momentum during the early 1960s, sending more than 320 artificial earth satellites into the heavens.[32] And in 1975, Americans and Soviets rendezvoused in orbit to conduct scientific experiments. Kosygin's commitment to building a strong defense industry also supported large scientific projects aimed at developing new military technology.

AN ERA OF GENEROSITY?

Although the United States began moving toward détente, Soviet economic growth was still declining despite efforts during the 1960s to improve its technical assets. The continuation of the technical-exchange agreements signed during the mid-1960s kept U.S. companies optimistic about the prospects for larger contracts with the Soviets. A few sizable deals were made, but as CDC would later realize, the larger contracts gave the Soviets the expertise to carry on the technology without the U.S. company as soon as the contract expired.

As the 1970s began, U.S. President Richard M. Nixon and Brezhnev initiated an era of détente that was to last nearly the entire decade. The Nixon administration allowed the export of some U.S. technology to the Soviet Union as part of its efforts to promote friendship with the Soviets. Americans who believed in détente championed the expansion of both national and personal contact with the Soviets as a means of attaining harmonious relations. The new American approach also supported the concept that increased transfers of technology could increase chances of rapprochement with the Soviet Union. At the time, the United States, cautious in its international involvements after the tragic conclusion of its Vietnam experience, struck a diplomatic posture of conciliation and cooperation rather than confrontation and intervention.

Efforts on both sides were directed toward encouraging business, especially technology-related business, between the two superpowers. The U.S.-U.S.S.R. Trade and Economic Council was formed in 1973 by companies in the United States and representatives from the Soviet government with the sole purpose of developing business.[33] The Soviets, particularly the KGB, found the relaxed American attitude supportive of their continuing drive to acquire U.S. technology. Activity within the Soviet intelligence agencies responsible for illegally acquiring U.S. technology began to increase. As a result of its far more cautious foreign policy and the cutback of counterintelligence and counterespionage activities after the Watergate scandal, the U.S. had dropped its guard. The KGB and the GRU (Soviet military intelligence directorate) stepped up espionage activities directed at penetrating key U.S. centers of technology development. Along with the increases in legal access to U.S. high technology, gained through technical and scholarly exchanges, these clandestine forays brought a great deal of classified and unclassified technology to the Soviet Union.

In the 1970s the Soviet Ministry of Aviation requested the Council of Ministers to obtain electronics used in American cruise missiles. Their request was granted, and the KGB soon obtained the technology with the help of 170,000 rubles from the Soviet government. Also during this period, the Ministry of Electronics Industry illegally obtained chip memory testing equipment from the United States. Four and one-half million rubles were allocated to the ministry, most likely for the purpose of paying for that particular acquisition.[34] In 1972, Bryant Grinder Company (of Springfield, Vt.) sold 164 precision grinding machines to the Soviets. (The sale had been turned down by Commerce a number of times before.) Then, as might have been (but was not) expected, the machines were used to produce precision ball bearings highly useful for military purposes such as milling missiles. In 1980, the U.S. Defense Intelligence Agency announced that the grinding machines had given the Soviets the ability to produce more accurate missile guidance systems. This particular tech nology leak provided the defensive impetus for U.S. efforts to develop the MX missile.[35]

When Nixon and Brezhnev held their summit meeting in May 1972, the number of Soviet trade missions and representatives began to proliferate as never before. Americans were as hopeful as the Soviets that they would benefit from the agreements. Nevertheless, while the Soviets sent numerous trade representatives to the United States to develop business, the United States sent only one Commerce Department officer to staff a U.S. trade office in Moscow.[36] Armand Hammer, an avid and longtime promoter of trade with the Soviets, took advantage of this improvement in U.S.-U.S.S.R. relations in 1972 to transact billions of dollars' worth of business for his company, Occidental Petroleum. The arrangement, for a five-year scientific and technical cooperation agreement between the Soviet Union and Occidental Petroleum, was considered at the time the largest business deal in the history of the Soviet Union, worth about $20 billion dollars.[37] (The Soviets were so pleased with Hammer's successful efforts to bring U.S. businesses to the Soviet Union that they awarded him the Order of Friendship Between Peoples in 1978.)

In October 1972, Nixon and Brezhnev signed several trade agreements as an expression of détente. One agreement provided for reciprocal, nondiscriminatory trading, extolling a "new era of commercial friendship," and cited industrial cooperation as a desirable objective. But these agreements needed congressional authorization before they could be implemented.

The 1974 Trade Act incorporated these agreements, including one that arranged for the Export-Import Bank to finance Soviet purchases of technology using long-term loans. It also extended most favored nation tariff treatment to the Soviet Union. At the same time, however, Richard N. Perle, then a staff member of the Senate Committee on Government Operations and Committee on Armed Services and the Arms Control Subcommittee and a key member of Senator Henry Jackson's (D-Wash.) staff, spearheaded an initiative linking the act to Soviet restrictions on granting its Jewish citizens exit visas. His initiative resulted in the Jackson-Vanik Amendment to the 1974 Trade Act, which called on the Soviets to allow more open emigration before trade agreements could proceed. The so-called (Adlai) Stevenson amendment limited Export-Import credits to the Soviet Union to $300 million. The amendments, in effect, canceled the trade and banking agreements. Further limits to high-technology trade, halting all U.S. sales of oil and gas equipment, were invoked by President Jimmy Carter in January 1980 as a protest against the Soviet invasion of Afghanistan. Carter's action dramatized the U.S. government's new connection between its foreign and trade policies.

Although America was thus reminded that export controls could be a valuable tool, the U.S. government continued a laissez-faire posture toward further high-technology trade restrictions during the 1970s. The U.S. role in Cocom (see Chapter 7) during this period illustrated this ambivalence. The U.S. asked for and received from the committee more exceptions than any other member country to allow its firms to sell goods that were on the international control list. The list, developed by the Cocom member countries, describes the technologies that may not be exported to Communist bloc countries without special permission of the committee.

THE BARN DOOR CLOSES

By the early 1980s, U.S. public opinion had taken a discernible turn to the right. Détente lost its appeal as anxieties about Soviet aggression and military strength, combined with continuing human rights abuses, caused the U.S. again to cool its relations with the rival superpower. The invasion of Afghanistan in 1979 and growing Soviet presence in Central America fueled the perception in the United States that it needed to guard its home front, including its critical technology, with more diligence. (See Chapter 7 for a discussion of U.S. export-control policy and laws.)

In 1981, when Ronald Reagan became president, the U.S. government considerably tightened its policy regarding the export of high technology. Richard Perle, who was assistant secretary of defense during most of Reagan's two terms in office, became one of the most vocal critics of exporting technology to the Soviets. Largely as the result of his sharp rhetoric, the Department of Defense increased its say in export-control policy.

The succession of Yuri V. Andropov as Soviet leader in 1982 signaled a new sophistication in methods of technology acquisition. He had demonstrated his affinity for high-technology theft as head of the KGB from 1967 to 1982. His sense of discipline and organization permeated the organization. Through Directorate T, the KGB agency responsible for scientific and technical intelligence gathering, Andropov directed an efficient campaign for acquiring classified U.S. military technology. The acquisition of classified information concerning U.S. reconnaissance satellites provided by Christopher Boyce was just one of his successful espionage coups. Andropov left his mark on the Soviet Union by appointing Viktor M. Chebrikov to head the KGB in December 1982 and by grooming his eventual successor as general secretary of the party, Mikhail Sergeyevich Gorbachev.

When Andropov died in 1984 and Konstantin V. Chernenko took the reins, the Reagan administration was building steam as its policies resulted in an economic recovery. The two agencies responsible for administering and enforcing U.S. high-technology export-control laws, the Commerce Department and the Customs Service, were in the process of renewing cooperation after a long period of rivalry. Also, the Defense Department was becoming a strong force in determining trade policy for restricted technology. Together, these agencies launched new efforts to keep U.S. technology out of Soviet hands and to discover and punish those breaking U.S. export laws. Between 1979 and 1984, industry also began to recognize that past U.S. high-technology export policy had seemingly allowed the Soviets to obtain sophisticated, even secret, U.S. equipment. Media attention to newly discovered spies, such as John Walker and Jerry Whitworth, put additional pressure on both houses of Congress to require more rigorous enforcement of export controls. America's technical generosity had come to at least a temporary end.

On Mar. 10, 1985, an ailing Chernenko died, and Gorbachev came to power as general secretary of the Communist party. Apprenticed by the best of the party leaders, a protégé of Andropov, this new leader came upon the scene with the realization that only drastic measures would resurrect the Soviet economy. At the Twenty-Seventh Party Congress in 1986, Gorbachev announced that he was not afraid to talk about the country's problems, including alcoholism, corruption, and the weaknesses of the state's economic system. Heads rolled, and new initiatives passed the party's approval, but it did not become immediately clear whether Gorbachev would be able to maintain the support of party leaders or whether the new moves would revitalize the economy. It also remained unclear whether the efforts at loosening some of the Soviet government's controls would bring with them political and social unrest and have the potential for causing the new leader to retrace his steps. However, it appeared that efforts by the Soviets to gain access to Western high-technology reserves were not about to abate. Gorbachev's strong viewpoint that the acquisition of technology would be necessary to improve the economy was seen in almost every speech made during the 1986 congress.

It thus appears that Gorbachev is not about to turn his back on an age-old Russian habit of seeking new technology from beyond his borders. He voices strong hopes that he can rebuild the economy and introduce new incentives to innovate. Nonetheless, the Soviet Union, while technically sophisticated in some specific areas, continues to need foreign technology to modernize its large industrial base, to replace tired methods in its scientific community, and to energize its economy. A thorough examination of high technology, especially computer science and electronics, in the U.S.S.R. today shows how strong the need is for outside technical assistance.

NOTES

1. Henri Troyat, *Peter the Great* (New York: E. P. Dutton, 1987), p. 45.
2. Jesse D. Clarkson, A History of Russia (New York: Random House, 1961), pp. 168–69 and 207–9.
3. Troyat, p. 119.
4. Ibid., p. 107.
5. Carl Gershman, "Selling Them the Rope: Business and the Soviets," *Commentary Magazine*, Apr. 1979, p. 2.
6. J. M. Tatcher Feinstein, *Fifty Years of U.S.-Soviet Trade* (New York: Symposium Press, 1974), pp. 63–64.
7. Clarkson, p. 506.
8. Ibid., p. 511.
9. Vera Tolz, "Aleksandrov's Speech to the Twenty-Seventh Party Congress: The Role of the U.S.S.R. Academy of Sciences," *Radio Liberty Research Bulletin*, RL 108/86, Mar. 5, 1986, p. 1.
10. Donald W. Treadgold, *Twentieth-Century Russia*, 6th ed. (Boulder, Colo.: Westview Press, 1987), pp. 180–82.
11. "A 1921 Lesson for Russia," *Economist*, Jan. 24, 1987, p. 45.
12. Clarkson, p. 558.
13. Gershman, p. 3.
14. Anthony C. Sutton, *Western Technology and Soviet Economic Development 1945–1965* (Stanford, Calif.: Hoover Institution Press, 1973), p. 411.
15. Gershman, p. 3.
16. Sutton, p. 412.
17. Ibid.
18. William Rogers, *Think* (New York: Stein & Day, 1969), p. 109.
19. Feinstein, p. 63.
20. Gershman, p. 3.
21. Clarkson, p. 627.
22. Gary Taubes and Glenn Garelik, "Soviet Science: How Good Is It?" *Discover*, August 1986, p. 43.
23. Speech by A. P. Aleksandrov, *Pravda: Organ of the Central Committee of the CPSU* (St. Paul, Minn.), Feb. 27, 1986, p. 5.
24. Sutton, p. 394.
25. Walter A. McDougall, *The Heavens and the Earth: A Political History of the Space Age* (New York: Basic Books, 1985), pp. 42–46.
26. The NKVD, or Narodnyi komissariat vnutrennikh del (People's Commissariat of Internal Affairs), was founded in 1934, nominally to secure Russia's borders, ensure internal peace and order, and protect state property. It was the Soviet Union's largest employer during the 1930s. In fact, it was among the organs used by Stalin to control, discredit, and destroy any threat to his totalitarian order. (Source: Treadgold, p. 269.) The NKVD was succeeded in 1946 by the MGB,

or Ministerstvo gosudarstvennoi bezopasnosti (Ministry of State Security). The present security agency, the KGB, was established in 1954.

27. Roy Medvedev, *Khrushchev,* tr. Brian Pearce (Garden City, N.Y.: Anchor Press, Doubleday, 1983), p. 148.

28. "What It's Like Building Plants in the U.S.S.R.," *Chemical Week,* Mar. 11, 1961, p. 53.

29. George D. Holliday, *Technology Transfer to the U.S.S.R., 1928–1937 and 1966–1975, The Role of Western Technology in Soviet Economic Development* (Boulder, Colo.: Westview Press, 1979), p. 50.

30. Sutton, p. 321.

31. Treadgold, p. 466.

32. Basil Dmytryshyn, *U.S.S.R., A Concise History* (New York: Charles Scribner's Sons, 1971), p. 333.

33. As of 1987, 275 U.S. companies, including high-technology firms, belonged to the council, along with 130 Soviet trade organizations. Incorporated in the State of New York and with offices in New York and Moscow, the council has never revealed its American membership. Today, member companies on the council's board of directors include FMC, Dresser Industries, Chase Manhattan, Seagram's, Occidental Petroleum, PepsiCo Inc., Litton Industries, and Corning Glass Works.

34. Tom Morganthau, "Moscow's Prying Eyes," *Newsweek,* Sept. 30, 1985, p. 30.

35. "Kremlin Spies Target U.S. Electronics Knowhow," *Business Week,* Sept. 20, 1982, p. 77.

36. William R. Corson and Robert T. Crowley, *The New KGB, Engine of Soviet Power* (New York: William Morrow & Co., 1985), p. 366.

37. Armand Hammer, with Neil Lyndon, *Hammer* (New York: G. P. Putnam's Sons, 1987), pp. 401–2.

3

FROM WHERE THEY SIT: SOVIET HIGH TECHNOLOGY

A close look at computer science and industry in the Soviet Union, both past and present, reveals that the Soviets are virtually addicted to importing Western technology. Such an inspection will also help Western interests to anticipate the priority areas for future technology acquisitions by the Soviets.

THE TECHNOLOGY GAP

Each day, as millions of New Yorkers squeeze onto the subway to commute to work, they are unwittingly reaping the benefits of Soviet technology. In 1982 the New York City Transit Authority purchased a portable welding plant, using flash butt welding[1] developed by the Soviets in the early 1970s. In late 1987 it was still used for repairing subway tracks. This same unique Soviet welding process is also used by some twenty other cities in the United States and Mexico. An American firm, the Holland Company of Chicago Heights, Ill., licensed and sold the portable welding plants.[2] Although most Americans assume that the United States is far ahead of the Soviet Union in high technology, flash butt welding is one area in which the Soviets have surpassed Americans.

As it is measured in the United States, the perception of the size of the so-called technology gap between the two nations fluctuates from year to year and in unison with U.S. foreign-policy changes. The gap's size is also measured and expressed in as many ways as there are people who measure it. American Sovietologists and scientists agree, however, that the United States is ahead in most areas of technology.

The most publicized opinions about the size of the U.S. technology lead come from government experts who study the relationship of Soviet computer science to Soviet military systems. The dependence of advanced military systems on computers requires that the U.S. Department of Defense and the intelligence community carefully monitor developments in Soviet electronics. Although much of the information gathered by the U.S. government about Soviet military systems is classified, both the Defense Department and the CIA periodically publish reports that analyze their perception of the technology gap as it relates to military systems.

In 1986, the Defense Department studied twenty technologies that affect military capabilities and concluded that the Soviets were equal to the United States in six and behind in fourteen. According to the report, they are equal in aerodynamics/fluid dynamics, directed energy (lasers), conventional warheads (including all chemical explosives), nuclear warheads, optics, and mobile power sources (including energy storage).[3] The report pointed out that in several areas, such as propulsion and submarine detection, Soviet technical abilities were approaching the U.S. level of sophistication, a conclusion agreed to by the CIA in its 1985 report, *Soviet Acquisition of Militarily Significant Western Technology*. The Pentagon concluded that the Soviets used Western technology to decrease the qualitative military lead that the United States had enjoyed in the past.

Another study, prepared by the Office of Science and Technology Policy in December 1985, states that the United States leads in computer science, molecular biology, experimental astrophysics, condensed matter physics, oceanology, and atmospheric physics.[4] In the area of computers and electronics, the Defense Department rates U.S.-Soviet capabilities according to the number of years the United States leads the Soviets. In 1987, the United States led by eight to nine years in microprocessors, eight to ten years in minicomputers, eight to twelve years in mainframes, ten to twelve years in supercomputers, and seven to eleven years in software.[5]

As illustrated by these reports, comparisons of U.S.-Soviet scientific capabilities are made with a variety of yardsticks and perspectives. A theme in each report is that the Soviets seem ingeniously able to apply their outdated equipment effectively; in addition, they enjoy parity in the theoretical dimensions of most technologies.

Soviet claims to scientific leads are often questioned by the United States and by the international scientific community. Nuclear fusion, which was advanced by military research, was once thought to be a Soviet stronghold of innovation and scientific leadership. But Dr. Bernard Cotti, a physicist at the Massachusetts Institute of Technology (MIT), takes issue with that assertion. According to him, a single Soviet nuclear physicist, Lev Artsimovich, in the 1960s and early 1970s temporarily placed the Soviet Union in the forefront of nuclear fusion research. But after his death in 1971, the Soviet Union lost its edge in this area despite R&D budget cuts and project mismanagement in the United States.

Both superpowers chauvinistically bandy about claims that appear to put each ahead of the other in scientific areas. Physics and mathematics are areas in which Soviets have earned an international reputation. The Soviets purport to have discovered a superior way for confining plasmas (charged particles), and since 1976, they also have the world's largest single-mirror telescope (albeit with serious problems), the 6-meter Zelenchukskaya, high in the Caucasus Mountains. But Soviet scientists often make claims about Soviet technical prowess that are unsupported. They say that the Soviet Union built the first proton synchrotron in the late 1950s (a device for giving extremely high speeds to protons through the use of a high-frequency electric field and a low-frequency magnetic field used to study matter). But Dr. Lee Teng, associate director of the Fermi National Accelerator Laboratory in Batavia, Ill., confirmed that the British built the first one in the late 1940s in Birmingham, England. The Swiss and then the Americans each built proton synchrotrons before the Soviets, in 1959 and 1961, with energy ratings of 30 GeV (gigaelectron volts). The Soviet synchrotron was actually completed in 1967 at the Institute for Nuclear Physics in Serpukhov (near Moscow), and was at the time the most powerful in the world, with an energy rating of 12 GeV.[6]

With the U.S. space program handicapped by the Challenger disaster, budget constraints, and the need to develop new designs, safety standards, and testing procedures, the Soviets have vaulted into the lead in the space race. The Soviets clearly surpass the United States in long-duration space flight and heavy-lift rocketing.[7] In 1986, the Soviets launched ninety-one missions; the United States launched six.[8] As of 1987, Soviet cosmonauts had spent a combined total of nearly twelve years in space, more than twice as long as their American counterparts. Although not immune to disasters—in 1967, the first *Soyuz* spacecraft tumbled to earth, killing cosmonaut Vladimir M. Komarov—the Soviet space program continues to amass enormous resources. Furthermore, the Soviets plan to launch their first shuttle mission in August 1988, before the United States has a chance to restart its space shuttle program.

The Soviets, however, are not ahead of the United States in advanced space technology, but they apply their comparatively less sophisticated space technology with impressive results. The United States also has technically superior space electronics. Both the United States and the Soviet Union are compiling similar data about space, although the United States obtains the data through technically superior means.[9]

A well-known analyst of the Soviet space program, Nicholas L. Johnson, at Teledyne Brown Engineering in Colorado Springs, Colo., confirms that the Soviets do not lay claim to any superior space technology other than the ability to use their advanced welding know-how to build structures in space. Before *Sputnik* circled an incredulous world in 1957, the United States had developed a comprehensive space technology infrastructure with plans in the works for launching communications and weather satellites vastly superior to the Soviets' headline-grabbing one, which was little more than a sphere equipped with a radio transmitter.

Although the Soviets have made enormous strides in space pioneering, the products of their space labs have been much less reliable than those of their American counterparts. For example, their spacecraft do not last as long; only 5 percent of the Soviet satellites launched by 1982 still functioned by the mid-1980s; 18 percent of the U.S. satellites launched during the same period were still operating.[10]

SOVIET SDI

An area in which both superpowers are scrutinizing each other's technical ability is space defense technology. That the Soviets have their own "strategic defense initiative" program has not been widely publicized. In the mid-1960s (and perhaps earlier), the Soviet military undertook research in space-based antimissile defense weapons systems. Their program absorbed almost $80 billion during the 1970s.[11] Andrei D. Sakharov, the well-known physicist who was involved in the Soviet hydrogen bomb development, apparently wrote an article as early as 1965 on technologies similar to those used in U.S. space-based missile systems, although the article never left the Soviet Union. Anatoly Fedoseyev, formerly a designer of Soviet missile radars and now a resident of the United States, suggests even earlier Soviet efforts, saying in 1987 that "since the beginning of Soviet SDI about 35 years ago, this project has never been interrupted or delayed. And I'm sure it never will be."[12]

The program has continued in the 1980s and includes research into laser, microwave particle-beam, and kinetic-energy weapons as well as optical, early warning, and tracking systems. Because the Soviet military is free from the types of restraints placed on the U.S. Defense Department (such as public accountability), it is allowed to move forward with its own "star wars" program impeded only by the limits of the political system and scientists' abilities. According to the CIA, between 1976 and 1986 the Soviets spent $150 billion, fifteen times more than the United States, on their strategic defense program.[13]

That this momentum exists is backed by U.S. government claims that more than 10,000 Soviet scientists and engineers are working on laser research, mostly at the Sary-Shagan Missile Test Center in eastern Kazakhstan. The Soviets are world leaders in X-ray lasers, which use a short wavelength to increase penetration.[14] The Soviets have also developed ground-based lasers capable of attacking U.S. satellites. Hard at work on particle-beam technology since the 1960s, the Soviets could advance it enough to be capable of disrupting U.S. satellite operations by the 1990s.[15] Soviet developments in kinetic-energy technology also began during the 1960s, when scientists experimented with a gun, potentially based in space, that would project streams of small metal particles capable of hitting ballistic missiles. A story in the *Los Angeles Times* on Jan. 2, 1987, asserted that "the Soviets match or lead the United States in the basic technology of lasers and particle beams—and perhaps even in converting the exotic technology into weapons." The same article notes, however, that the Soviets still lag in those computer-based technologies that are critical for operating and managing space-based missile systems. CIA Deputy Director Robert M. Gates confirmed this observation while also acknowledging the great strides the Soviets have made with lasers.

R&D Activities

The Soviets' strategic defense system is a classic effort of their research and development community. To be a research scientist in the Soviet Union is to be blessed with a generous budget and government support. Almost half the world's scientists reside in the Soviet Union.[16] In 1983, the large Soviet technical community included approximately 1.5 million scientists and engineers, compared with 750,000 in the United States. And in 1983, the Soviets spent about 3.9 percent of their gross national product on research, while the United States spent 2.6 percent.[17] These figures indicate that Soviets meet scientific challenges with brute force, large deployments of personnel, complex research projects, and infusions of government investment. Despite the huge size of the Soviet research community, the quality of its work tends to lag well behind that of the United States. For example, as of 1986 the Soviets and Russians had received only 10 Nobel Prizes; U.S. scientists had received 132 prizes.[18]

Soviet scientists are currently treated well by both the Soviet government and the general population. Science is a revered profession because its practitioners are depended on not only to provide military technology but also equipment and processes that will lift the sagging economy and, perhaps, provide prosperity to Soviet citizens. Soviet scientists often receive salaries that are 10 to 15 percent higher than those of most people who have industrial jobs, even though scientists' salaries are low by Western standards.[19] Many get perks such as the use of a dacha or a prime apartment in Moscow. But attractive as it may seem, the scientists' status may have its down side. The profession sometimes attracts those who seek the perks rather than those who are driven by innovation or creativity. Furthermore, Communist party membership and its correlative politics often stifle originality and creativity.

The best arrangement for a Soviet scientist is to be involved in military research. The military has top priority for access to the best scientists, equipment, and funding, and if Soviet scientists can demonstrate a military application for technology they are developing, they are more likely to receive adequate funding and even access to Western equipment. Because the military does most of the illegal and legal acquiring of Western technology through its intelligence organ, the GRU, a Soviet scientist involved in military research is likely to receive coveted Western technology. It is estimated that at least half of all Soviet scientists are involved in military research. According to Leonard L. Lederman, head of the Special Analytical Studies Section of the National Science Foundation, only about 35 percent of U.S. scientists work on military-related research.

Only 10 percent of Soviet scientists work in the Soviet Academy of Sciences, originally conceived by Peter the Great in 1724 and founded by his widow and successor, Catherine I, in 1725 to promote scholarship and research.[20] The remaining 90 percent are employed either by secondary ministerial research organizations in which research flourishes or in higher education, which is only minimally involved in actual R&D.[21] But the scientific community is being revitalized and restructured. The expansive trend of the 1970s that led to excessively large research projects began to reverse itself during the 1980s. About 150 research institutions were closed, and others merged into leaner organizations. There is no moratorium on the creation of new research facilities, but new ones may require careful justification.

In many cases, research projects are chosen either by the Council of Ministers or by the heads of the government-run research institutes. Although the Academy of Sciences traditionally performs basic theoretical research, recent activities indicate that it has shifted emphasis to developing new technologies for priority industries such as the military. The academy has also created committees and divisions, including those for informatics, computing, and automation. Most Soviet researchers are concentrated in research institutes and research centers affiliated with the Academy of Sciences, the majority of which are in Moscow. Ministry institutes, which perform more than 90 percent of Soviet engineering, have no relationship with the academy. Research and implementation activities are thus isolated from each other.

Despite generous funding and an immense number of scientists, Soviet science suffers from the lack of a free flow of ideas. Freedom of thought, expression, and communication has long been a hallmark of successful science. Government secrecy and censorship, the emphasis on military technology, and the state's authoritarian style all inhibit the development of a scientific community built on the exchange of concepts, theories, and basic and applied research. Scientific disciplines appear to be isolated from one another as are the research institutes. Restrictions placed on access to information and bureaucratic control of scholarly publishing often delay the publication of research results. Also, most Soviet scientists do not have the opportunity to attend international technical conferences as freely as Westerners. For the most part, they cannot work outside their small circles and are thereby unable to exchange ideas broadly and at will. An exception to this general rule are Soviet space-exploration teams, which have been allowed to reach out internationally for joint research and commercial ventures.

Many leaders of the research institutes have to play an active role in Soviet politics to ensure the success of their research programs. The party mandates research priorities. This situation may worsen, because the Politburo appears to be increasing its role as the arbiter of technological priorities and demanding that positions in scientific institutions be approved by the party. A strong party relationship also enables scientists and researchers to travel abroad and to obtain access to much needed resources. This pressure to maintain close party ties is felt not only by heads of research institutes but also by individual scientists who depend on government support for career advancement.

Soviets struggle to bring the findings of research out of the lab and apply them to commercial or practical tasks. One option a scientist has is to pass a discovery up to the GKNT in the hope that it will pass it back down to an industrial research institute. Each Soviet ministry[22] operates a group of such institutes that attempt to apply advanced scientific concepts to practical tasks. The development of the first Soviet computer, the vacuum-tube-filled MESM (Small Electronic Calculating Machine), conceived at the Institute of Precise Mechanics and Computer Technology in Moscow, followed this route.

The application of research is a goal shared by most Soviet bureaucrats and is mirrored in the official rhetoric. But actions speak louder than words, and the tendency to rely on Western innovations still dominates Soviet R&D. During the Twenty-Seventh Party Congress, Anatoly P. Aleksandrov, the then 83-year-old president of the Academy of Sciences, denounced with great embellishment the Soviet dependence on Western technology, citing it as a key reason for the stagnation of Soviet technological progress. He said, "...there is nothing wrong with making foreign purchases of better samples for comparison with our products and being up on state-of-the-art scientific or technical solutions. But it is absolutely necessary to develop quickly those branches of our science and technology in which a lag has been observed." He also pointed out that the Academy of Sciences had completed more than 300 research and development projects that had yet to find their way into the national economy. Aleksandrov reminded the party of the formation of new industrial complexes for the purpose of linking the research organizations with industry. The prototype of these engineering centers is in the Ukraine. He also discussed the creation of "interbranch scientific-technical complexes," the first of which is reportedly a laser center near Moscow. At least sixteen other such complexes have been documented by Radio Liberty Research, a group associated with the U.S.-funded radio network that broadcasts programs into communist countries.[23] These announcements reflect the stated Soviet goal of using research to produce economic growth.

But the practical application of research is often hampered. Although funding for most research projects can be abundant, the Soviets have not been under the same pressure as U.S. scientists to justify costs with benefits. They undertake large research projects regardless of whether the results can be effectively put to use. Because research projects and bodies originate at the top of the organizational structure and move down, an individual has little opportunity or incentive to initiate a project in anticipation of its adoption by the research institute.

The habit of copying international research efforts also keeps Soviet scientists from taking the technological lead. Some research projects begin as a response to similar U.S. efforts, and Soviet scientists may have to wait years for approval of a project until the United States initiates research in that area.

During periods when technology flows more freely, the Soviets tend to lose sight of their commitment to innovate. For example, during the 1970s, the U.S.-Soviet détente permitted an increase in the flow of high technology to the Soviet Union. As a result, the Soviets relied on acquired technology instead of internal research and development.[24] In addition, they used U.S. or Western equipment directly, which meant that they did not have to reverse-engineer U.S. high-tech products. Later, under Andropov, the Soviets say their scientists began to innovate in their own labs. That happened because the United States had tightened the flow of its technology through stricter laws (the Export Administration Act of 1979) and better enforcement (under Operation Exodus, which began in 1981), and so had Cocom. Now the Soviets say that their previous reliance on Western technology was detrimental to their research and development progress, and they are working to avoid such dependence in the future. Despite these statements, current Soviet efforts to engage U.S. companies in joint ventures to gain access to U.S. technology point to continued reliance on Western know-how.

Conditions remain uninspiring for Soviet scientists. Their compensation is usually based on political or bureaucratic standards rather than scientific achievement. In 1986, the Soviet press mentioned a proposal for shifting compensation within the Academy of Sciences toward a merit system, one Gorbachev hopes will be based on "concrete contributions to scientific-technological progress."[25] Resistance to this proposal is coming from older academy members.

Soviet scientific research is inhibited by an aversion to risk. Because the political system emphasizes consistency, loyalty, and job security, Soviet scientists tend not to veer far from accepted and approved theories. Promotions result from toeing the line, not from creativity. The general unwillingness to risk manifests itself in a primarily evolutionary approach to scientific and computing development as opposed to the U.S. approach, which is revolutionary.

The copying of the IBM 360 hardware and software for their own Unified System (ES), or Ryad, mainframes is a classic example of the Soviets' lack of imagination in the early 1970s. The ES series computers use the same assembly language, error codes, and software as the 360, as well as identical technical documentation; for a time, the documentation was left in the original English. It was eventually translated into Russian; as late as 1979, however, error messages appeared on the screen in English. Control Data Corporation (CDC) once purchased a Soviet ES computer to test its compatibility with IBM software. Its engineers found a very high level of compatibility between the ES and IBM machines.[26] The Soviets' dogged allegiance to IBM 360 and 370 architecture in every mainframe of the ES series also testifies to their evolutionary rather than revolutionary method of scientific achievement.

Harley D. Balzer, director of the Russian Area Studies Program at Georgetown University, points to the "blackboard rule" as one reason the Soviets fail to achieve ongoing and significant scientific breakthroughs. The rule refers to their attraction to theoretical rather than applied science. Many Soviet scientists have to manage with inadequate equipment or no equipment at all for experimenting and proving research. This discourages them from applying practical solutions to industrial and economic problems.[27] As a result, scientists turn to their blackboards on which theory can be pursued indefinitely. Although Soviet technical advances have led to licensing arrangements with U.S. companies, converting theoretical research to practical industrial solutions is the exception rather than the rule in the Soviet Union. Ironically, these stumbling blocks may prod some Soviet scientists into changing the methods with which they accomplish their research. Some fabricate their own equipment, barter for much needed supplies, or find other ways to circumvent problems that existing limitations place on them.

GETTING IT, USING IT: TECHNOLOGY TRANSFER AND IMPLEMENTATION

Although the plethora of espionage and diversion cases involving dual-use technology demonstrates that U.S. high technology has arrived in the Soviet Union, many U.S. computer scientists believe that their Soviet colleagues are unable to utilize the acquired equipment and know-how in any efficient manner. When hardware arrives from the United States, Soviet scientists must figure out how to operate it, either with or without documentation. And if the equipment has been illegally obtained, they certainly have to forgo the luxury of calling the manufacturer's service representative for assistance. Even if the equipment comes with documentation, chances are good that it is not in Russian.

Seymour E. Goodman, a professor of management information systems in the College of Business and Public Administration at the University of Arizona, classifies the means of technology transfer to the Soviet Union according to combinations of active and passive, overt and covert methods. The most efficient way for a Soviet scientist to acquire U.S. technology is through active means, which include legal purchases of American goods. The buyer can arrange for service contracts, spare parts, and hardware and software upgrades. Passive acquisition includes the use of copying machines to duplicate technical publications and equipment documentation that have already found their way into the Soviet research community. That forces the Soviet scientist or bureaucrat to learn about technology secondhand without actually seeing a device.

Active and passive acquisition may be overt or covert. An active overt acquisition would be the legal purchase of, for example, IBM personal computers for use in schools in the Soviet Union. An active covert acquisition would be, for example, the illegal purchase of technology on the U.S. and Cocom control list via European middlemen. An example of passive overt acquisition would be a subscription by a Soviet scientist to a foreign scientific or technical journal. The copying by a Soviet intelligence agent of the plans for an American supercomputer on the U.S. export-control list would be an example of passive covert acquisition. Most Soviet acquisitions are passive covert, which Professor Goodman says puts the Soviets in "the worst conceivable part of the technology transfer circuit." But even though it may take them a long time to obtain a particular technology by passive covert means, the acquisition may be sophisticated enough to have a great impact on Soviet computing progress.

The Soviet Union appears unable to manufacture large quantities of products based on acquired Western high technology. When the Soviets become aware of a particular technology through technical literature or even acquire a product through illegal diversion, moving the technology from their own R&D into manufacturing is difficult. Prototypes and small quantities tend to be easily produced, but manufacturing significant quantities has not been feasible. One reason for this is that U.S. computer scientists or engineers rarely accompany the transferred technology. Without those who have experience working with and testing the technology, the Soviets are handicapped in their efforts to adapt it to meet their specific needs. These circumstances may change if U.S. high-technology companies establish joint ventures with the Soviets that transfer know-how and engineers in addition to products.

SOVIET COMPUTERS: U.S. CLONES?

Soviet computers, like American ones, are derived from a collection of technologies, including software, semiconductors, magnetic storage, and telecommunications, any of which may be compared with its U.S. counterpart. For example, mainframe computers are derived from such a diverse collection of technologies, some more advanced, some less, that it is difficult to determine the technical gap between the Soviet Union and the United States even within that single area.

That complexity aside, most observers believe that measurements are possible for the aggregate of technologies applied in the computer industry. In the mid-1980s, the Foreign Applied Sciences Assessment Center (FASAC), a consulting organization that provides government agencies with information about Soviet basic and applied science research, studied Soviet science and technology. Released in April 1985, their report, which is entitled *Selected Aspects of Soviet Applied Science*, declared that the Soviet Union was ten years behind the United States in significant areas of computing technology and in the base requisite to produce significant innovations.

SOVIET COMPUTING: A SHORT HISTORY

Because the Soviet Union carefully restricts information about its scientific, governmental, and military activities, factual knowledge of past and present computer developments comes only through U.S. observations made in the Soviet Union under somewhat controlled circumstances, in addition to U.S. government-provided publications and Soviet media. U.S. intelligence agencies are, of course, hard at work by clandestine means to understand Soviet technical capabilities. Defectors and emigrés also provide insight into the environment and background for Soviet computer science.

Computer science in the U.S.S.R. came into being roughly in parallel with U.S. developments. In its incipient stage, it struggled against ideological barriers unfamiliar to early U.S. computer scientists. One such barrier was the initial resistance to cybernetics, the mathematical theory of control processes involving the comparative study of information-handling machines, such as computers, and the nervous systems of animals and humans. Ministerial infighting and centralized resource allocation also stood in the way of early Soviet computer science, as did trade embargoes, lack of incentives for R&D, and even the huge expanses of land and cultural differences that separated centers of research, development, and manufacturing.

In the 1930s and 1940s, the U.S. Army sponsored many of the first developments in the then primitive field of computers. By that time, American computer science had gathered momentum and pushed far ahead. Government needs for ballistics analysis and census data initiated several computer-research efforts. Universities and private industry also played a role. One of the first milestones was reached in 1930, when Dr. Vannevar Bush built the differential analyzer at MIT, an analog calculator that could compute with 98 percent accuracy. And IBM jointly sponsored the development of the Mark I with Harvard University. In January 1943, the Mark I digital computer was demonstrated at IBM's Endicott, N.Y., plant. Fifty-one feet long and eight feet high, the Mark I employed dial switches that crunched out three additions a second. In 1946, J. Presper Eckert and John W. Mauchly placed the United States firmly in the lead in computer science by completing the ENIAC (electronic numerical integrator and computer), the first electronic digital computer. Used in the development of the Manhattan Project at the Los Alamos Laboratory, the ENIAC could perform 4,500 additions a second. (By comparison, the Apple Macintosh II can process 2 million instructions a second.)

Early Soviet efforts focused on basic, theoretical concepts rather than on practical applications. Andrei N. Kolmogorov, a brilliant Soviet applied mathematician, and his researchers were absorbed in theoretical work on algorithms. Soviet computer developments continued to lag behind those in the United States because of the country's isolation created by its own ideology and Western foreign policies.

During the Stalin era (1924–53), Marxist political ideology combined with Stalin's suspicions of intellectuals and free thinking impeded the development of Soviet computer science. Even though Marx and Friedrich Engels (a German political theorist and contributor to Communist philosophy) saw science as giving workers the means to achieve greater productivity and defeat capitalism, their theories objected to applying principles of hard science to human behavior. Cybernetics, which provides much of the philosophical basis for computer science, relies on a mechanistic interpretation of the individual and society, a belief that the laws of chemistry and physics can explain life. Marx's philosophy of dialectical materialism holds, however, that life is constantly changing and evolving. Stalinist thinkers interpreted Marxism to imply that cybernetics threatened the integrity of workers, because automation promised to lessen the dependency on human labor for certain tasks.

At the same time, Stalin's totalitarian vision did not leave much room for the development of new sciences; indeed, it viewed as potential threats any intellectual breakthroughs without readily apparent application to state-directed policy. As a result, cybernetics was declared a pseudoscience in several influential articles that appeared during the Stalin regime. Although Western historians have exaggerated the early Soviet condemnation of cybernetics, the fact that it was considered

"bourgeois" by some in high circles was enough to deter rapid developments in computer science.

Despite the lowly position of cybernetics, Soviet computer science
moved ahead, albeit at a snail's pace compared with American developments. In 1952, A. A. Lyapunov taught the first course in programming at
Moscow M. V. Lomonosov State University.[28] (The first computer programming course in the United States was taught at Harvard University
in 1944.[29]) Clearly, though, computing was not to catch fire in the Soviet
scientific community as it did in the United States because of U.S. commercial interest and support.

In 1953, an article attacking cybernetics with renewed enthusiasm
appeared in a Soviet philosophical journal, *Problems of Philosophy*. The article marked a turning point because scientists debated it until previous
objections to the science fell away. The formation of the Scientific Council
of Cybernetics in 1958[30] confirmed the acceptance of the discipline in
Soviet science. Soviet computer scientists were finally able to study cybernetics and apply it without fear of punishment, and they embraced it with
the fervor of the newly converted. An anthology edited by A. Berg in
1961, called *Cybernetics in the Service of Communism*, expounded the ways
in which the new science could be utilized in the Soviet economy.[31] By the
early 1960s, Soviet exchange students in the United States anxiously
sought anything they could get their hands on about cybernetics.[32]

Even before they embraced cybernetics, Soviet scientists had introduced their own computers. The MESM (Malaya Elektronnaya Schetnaya Mashina, "small electronic calculating machine"), their first digital
computer, was completed in 1951 after three years of development. Two
years later, the Strela appeared, but it had no storage capacity and operated with a 10-minute mean-time-between-failure (MTBF) rate. U.S. computers of the time operated with an 8-hour MTBF.

Among the early pioneers who labored without the direct blessing
of the state were S. A. Lebedev, a brilliant designer responsible for the
MESM, and Mikhail A. Lavrentev, a professor of mathematics and
physics at the Ukrainian Academy of Sciences in Kiev, who arranged for
Lebedev to work at a laboratory in nearby Feofaniya.

Once cybernetics became universally acceptable, computer scientists found their work was met by a far more receptive audience. Lebedev

went to Moscow from Feofaniya where he designed the BESM (Bol'shaya Elektronnaya Schetnaya Mashina, "large electronic calculating machine") line. New models of the MESM and BESM were used in rockets. The Soviet supercomputer of its time, the BESM-6, developed between 1964 and 1965, became one of the standard computers for scientific research and engineering; between 150 and 300 were built, and some were still in use as late as the 1980s.

The laboratory in Feofaniya continued to work on computers and became the Kiev Institute of Cybernetics. It has remained an active center of electronics research, concentrating on software development, but its work has been complemented by other centers of computer R&D. For example, the industrial city of Zelenograd was built, beginning in 1959, for the purpose of computerizing the Soviet Union. Its factories, design bureaus, and housing for workers helped it become a leading center for electronics research. The town has a group of design bureaus, all managed by one director. The group, called the Center for Microelectronics, concentrates on computer applications for the Soviet military. Another center for electronics work is Novosibirsk; work there is mostly on civilian computer applications.

HIGH-TECH DEFECTORS

Ironically, two American defectors—Alfred Sarant and Joel Barr—appear to have made significant contributions to the development of both Zelenograd and microelectronics in the Soviet Union. Mark Kuchment of Harvard University's Russian Research Center, a physicist born in Odessa and educated in the Soviet Union, has carefully studied these two men, becoming the U.S. authority on their role in the development of Soviet computer science. Alfred Sarant studied at Cooper Union in New York City and received a Bachelor of Science degree in electrical engineering in 1941. He went on to work on the synchrotron at Cornell University's nuclear physics laboratory as an electrical engineer. Joel Barr was graduated from City College of New York in 1938 and eventually worked for Western Electric and Sperry Gyroscope in 1946 and 1947. During this period he also worked for a short time at Bell Labs. He and Sarant worked together for a time at Fort Monmouth, N.J., the site of a highly sensitive U.S. government communications intelligence research facility. Barr and Sarant had more in common, however; they were both affiliated with the U.S. Communist party. Evidence indicates that they knew each other through mutual friends, Julius and Ethel Rosenberg, and Kuchment suspects that both Barr and Sarant may have been recruited as Soviet agents.

Motivations for their defection to the Soviet Union are unclear. They may have felt an ideological attraction nurtured by their Communist party membership, or they may have been peripherally involved in the Rosenberg case and felt they were on the brink of detection by the FBI. Sarant had strong reasons for feeling he was under suspicion, because the FBI questioned him shortly before he defected.[33] He also had recently started an affair with a friend's wife; he may have wanted to escape his own wife in upstate New York and establish a new life in the Soviet Union with his lover, who fled with him.

Both Sarant and Barr left hurriedly at the same time during the summer of 1950, Sarant from the United States via Mexico and Barr from Paris. Barr had left the United States in late 1947 for Europe, where he traveled and studied music. Both went first to Czechoslovakia, where they worked together on a military-related research project until 1955. In Czechoslovakia, Sarant changed his name to Filip Georgievich Staros, and Barr became Yosef Venyaminovich Berg. In 1956, both moved to the Soviet Union. Soviet computing was about to receive a much needed infusion of microelectronics know-how and Western management skills.

Staros moved up rapidly in the Soviet scientific community, even befriending Nikita Khrushchev and receiving a top Soviet security clearance. Drawing upon his education in electronics and his work experience in the United States, he preached the benefits of microelectronics and Western technology, a message appreciated by Khrushchev, who visited the United States in 1959 to see those benefits himself. Staros is sometimes called the "father of Soviet microelectronics," possibly because he presented a seminal scientific paper in 1958 extolling microelectronics as the key to Soviet military leadership.[34] The Soviet newspaper *Izvestia* hailed Staros's contributions to Soviet science as significant to the "development of national microelectronics."[35]

The Military Industrial Commission (VPK), the organization responsible for determining Soviet high-technology acquisition priorities (see Chapter 4), also benefited from Staros's know-how by using him as a consultant. Staros became chief designer of the Leningrad Design Bureau and continued to have the ear of Soviet scientists and the research community. At the bureau, he built a computer designed for process control called the Elektronika K-200.

Staros's charmed life as a microelectronics visionary began to wane in 1965, one year after Khrushchev was deposed. Those in positions of power in the scientific hierarchy apparently resented his special treatment and individual identification as the progenitor of Soviet microelectronics. They pounced on him as soon as his "sponsor" disappeared. Staros still managed to receive the State Prize in 1969 for designing a transistor based computer called the UM 1 Nld I, the predecessor to the Elektronika K-200. By 1973, Staros had also completed the design for the Elektronika 24-71 at the Leningrad bureau. This device was originally intended to be an inexpensive calculator that would compete for sales with the new Japanese ones. The Soviets hoped that international sales of the calculator would bring hard currency to their economy. Instead, the design firm ultimately took apart a Japanese calculator, stamped the firm's insignia on the parts, and displayed them at a Moscow electronics exhibition to achieve Brezhnev's goal of a good showing of Soviet computing prowess. (The Elektronika 24-71 experience illustrates the early and continuing Soviet frustration with fabricating and manufacturing electronic components. Eventually, the Soviets did mass-produce the calculators but at a cost of about $83 each, hardly competitive with the Japanese counterparts, which might have sold for as little as $10.[36]) After being demoted at the Leningrad bureau, Staros was relegated, in 1973, to the Soviet Academy in Vladivostok. He died in Moscow in 1979 after a heart attack. Berg, Staros's assistant at the Leningrad Design Bureau, was last seen in Leningrad during the early 1980s and may still be living there.

Both Staros and Berg contributed to Soviet computer science through their ability to read U.S. technical literature and to transfer U.S. developments to the Soviet scientific community. Their story illustrates the power and efficiency of human know-how over that of the simple transfer of hardware and software, but their greatest contribution may have been their Western management skills.

Throughout the Staros/Berg era, the Soviets continued to develop computers. By the end of the 1950s, though, the United States still held its lead. Despite Staros and Berg's efforts, the United States had 5,000 installed computers, the Soviet Union only 120.[37]

ENTERING THE COMPUTER ERA: 1960 TO 1980

The State Committee on the Electronics Industry was created in 1961 to coordinate the Soviet development of microelectronics and semiconductors. This committee performed the early development of Soviet microelectronics. The Committee achieved ministry status in 1965 and by 1963 was producing integrated circuits. Not until 1971–72, however, did the circuits go into mass-produced computers.

During the late 1960s, the Soviets introduced their functional copy of the IBM 360 series, called the Ryad-I series. By the time IBM formally announced the 360 series on Apr. 7, 1964, it had invested almost $5 billion during five years of development. The Soviets avoided that massive investment, although they did incur costs in the process of copying the computer. They also began their continuing practice of buying or copying IBM software, which produced significant cost savings in R&D.

The development of the Ryad-I began in 1968–69 as a joint venture involving the U.S.S.R., Bulgaria, Hungary, East Germany, and Poland, which were starting a concerted effort to develop two coordinated groups of computer systems. During the next two decades, the Soviets, along with other Comecon countries, developed hardware and software in two categories: the Unified System (Edinaya Sistema, or ES) for mainframe computers, and the Small System (Sistema Malaya, or SM) for minicomputers and microcomputers. The Ryad computers fall within the ES classification.

In 1965, before work started on the ES, the Ministry of the Radio Industry began the development of another series of mainframes, the Minsk series, incompatible with the Ryad except for the ES-1035. These computers were general-purpose computers, widely used throughout Eastern Europe. Not benefiting from IBM engineering, the Minsk computers never came close to having the Ryad's capabilities. They were slow and had no disk storage, and memory was limited.[38] Yet they served, and still serve, their purpose. Big workhorses of the Soviet computing community,

Minsk series machines continue to provide the Soviet Union with computing power. In 1987, a computer networking engineer working in Silicon Valley visited his native country, India. Out of curiosity, he went to the engineering institute that he had attended almost fifteen years earlier. There he saw the same computer in the lab where he learned to program in assembly language. It was a 37-bit Minsk. The engineer later recounted his story to a Soviet exchange professor in the United States only to elicit a red-faced admission that many of these trusty but outdated machines were still in their original owner's hands more than twenty years after their first use.

Seymour Goodman believes that by the end of the 1960s, the Soviet Union had approximately 8,000 computers compared with America's 40,000. By this time, the U.S.-Soviet computer gap was widening in the areas of new, faster chip technology, storage, and software. With no growing and varied user community and a limited computer equipment manufacturing industry to go along with their state-run development labs, the Soviets were unable to introduce hardware and software as rapidly as those countries that had these resources. The gap was even wider by 1977, when the Soviet Union had an installed base of 20,000 computers while the United States had 325,000.[39]

When IBM followed the 360 with the 370 series in the early 1970s, the Soviets predictably developed an equivalent, the Ryad-II, in the late 1970s and early 1980s. The Soviets announced an improvement on this tried and true architecture, the Ryad-III, in 1976, but had still not shipped the first unit by 1986. Western observers following the introduction of computer models subsequent to the Ryad series believe the newest Soviet computer to be the ES-1066, installed in October 1986 in the Computing Center of the Siberian Department of the Academy of Sciences. The advanced ES mainframes, some of which can store 200 to 400 MB on disk, are hard to come by.[40]

To develop these and other models and to expedite R&D, the Soviets have augmented ongoing technology-espionage activities with legitimate purchases. In 1959, General Electric was selling a range of computers to the Soviets. It was joined by RCA and some British computer manufacturers in the early 1960s. Between 1965 and 1979, after which the United States enacted stricter export controls, the Soviets steadily increased their spending for Western computer equipment. It rose from $5,000 in 1965 to $40 million by the end of the 1960s.[41] And at the height of détente, between 1972 and 1977, the United States sold the Soviets $120 million worth of computers.[42]

SOVIET COMPUTING IN THE 1980s

In 1985, the Soviets produced 4.2 billion rubles' worth (approximately $2.6 billion) of computer equipment. That compares with production worth $40.5 billion in the United States in 1983.[43] And in 1986, the 2,000 BK-0010 personal computers that went on sale in the Soviet Union contrast with the 5 million personal computers that sold in the United States in 1984.[44] Even with the perennial proclamations of the state's commitment to increased production of computers, the Soviet computer industry continues to grow at a slower pace than the U.S. industry and from a much smaller base. Approximately 100,000 mainframes and minicomputers were in use in the Soviet Union in 1987;[45] the number of mainframes and minicomputers in the United States that year was 1.1 million.[46] The Soviet computer industry has been growing at an annual production rate of 11 to 14 percent since 1980, compared with about 18 percent—and on a much larger base—for the U.S. industry. If the Soviets were to double their current growth rate and the U.S. rate were to slow to 10 percent by the year 2000, the Soviets would still trail the United States.[47]

One reason the United States is the acknowledged leader in computers is its existing support system of suppliers, investment channels, manufacturers, and skilled labor. The lack of this infrastructure is a major deterrent to Soviet progress with computers. Individual Soviet computer scientists have difficulty obtaining the parts, lab equipment, sources for materials, labor to build prototypes, organizations that support innovation, and venture capital that are necessary to create an environment for ongoing developments.

Government research organizations, state committees, the military, industrial enterprises, cooperatives, and ministries together design, manufacture, and distribute computer hardware and software. These components of the Soviet computer industry research, invent, test, make prototypes, and manufacture equipment through a network of institutions, all of which are funded by the state. Specific research institutes take concepts from research to testing and leave the manufacture of computer products to industrial enterprises. Government ministries manage the production of computer-related equipment. Seymour Goodman cites at least eight ministries, all charged with various aspects of the computer industry. The Academy of Sciences also weighs in with its heavy research commitment.

The Ministry of the Radio Industry manages the mainframe systems and the more advanced scientific and engineering microcomputers. The Ministry of Instrument Making, Automation, and Control Systems is responsible for the minicomputer and some personal computer systems. A third one, the Ministry of the Electronics Industry, manages and directs electronics research and development in addition to the production of electronic components. Other players in the Soviet computer industry include research institutes, design bureaus, and technical colleges and other ministries which oversee industries that have specialized uses for computers (for example the petrochemical industry's use of process-control computers).

Problems with quality control and the innovation process also plague the computer industry. Because of this, the design and manufacture of semiconductors have presented problems for Soviet scientists. They seem unable to develop sophisticated chips and then mass-produce them. During the 1970s and 1980s, the Soviets sought U.S. chip manufacturing equipment as a top priority in their illegal technology-acquisition activities. They were successful in obtaining this equipment through several infamous diversion schemes but still have difficulties maintaining quality and designing new chips. Both Czechoslovakia and East Germany produce chips for the Soviet market in addition to supplying their own needs.

Software has proved to be a greater problem for the Soviets than hardware. To begin with, the reticent Soviet acceptance of computer science and an emphasis on theory rather than application in the early 1950s delayed research. Today, the lack of both tools and equipment continues to impede software development. Also, programmers cannot benefit from feedback from the kind of varied and plentiful user community that exists in the United States. To hamper their efforts even more, programmers must sometimes input entire programs in English.

Soviet computer scientists are familiar with IBM programming languages and operating systems, such as IBM's MVS and Digital's RSX-11. MS-DOS and Unix are also gaining followers.

The development of management information systems (MIS) software is typical of Soviet programming in most areas. Although American businesses saw their first MIS programs in the 1950s, not until the mid-1960s was a Soviet MIS, called *automatizirovannaya sistema upravlenya predpriatem*, or ASUP, introduced. Part of this delay was due to the lack of demand by Soviet enterprises; they had neither the incentive nor the funds to acquire an MIS computer.

PROLETARIAN PCs?

The existence of computer hackers[48] signals a society moving toward computerization. The exact number of hackers (*fanatiky*) hunched over personal computers in the Soviet Union is not known. But the emergence of this small but significant group reveals a crack in the typically centralized development of computers. Access to personal computers is mainly restricted by limited supply and high prices. Even if the machines were plentiful, the Soviet government envisions an official pool of personal computers to which access is controlled rather than broad, individual, unsupervised ownership of personal computers.

The few hackers that exist—observers in the United States estimate fewer than 5,000[49]—have performed relative miracles to enable their machines to exceed the capacity for which they were designed. Soviet hackers may well have to be more creative than their U.S. counterparts to overcome the inadequate designs of Soviet personal computers. The lucky acquisition of an early-model, Western personal computer by someone belonging to one of the newly formed hacker clubs does not always make life easier. In some cases, printers have to be altered at the chip level to enable them to produce Cyrillic (Russian) characters.

Particularly in metropolitan areas, where research institutes and industrial enterprises spawn computer-literate employees, *fanatiky* pool their incomes to buy simple computers on the black market or from electronics stores. William McHenry, assistant professor at the School of Business Administration of Georgetown University, notes that the only personal computer for sale to the Soviet public is the BK-0010, which is offered without a monitor, printer, modem, or floppy-disk storage; even the Soviet press ridiculed the sale of such a useless device. It became available in 1985 at a price between 800 and 980 rubles, or roughly $500–$600. Soon after, Soviet computer enthusiasts could have a BK-0010 for 550–600 rubles ($345–$375).[50] In 1986, about 2,000 BK-0010s were sold. At home, the hackers add keyboards, displays, memory, cabling—whatever they can get their hands on or make themselves. Although supplies are extremely limited, very primitive (in Hungary, hackers often rely on long outdated Commodore 64s with only 64 KB of internal memory, while their Western counterparts generally use today's ubiquitous personal computers with at least 256 KB of memory), and expensive, the *fanatiky* exercise their ability to innovate and may eventually provide the Soviet economy with a new brand of creative and imaginative computer scientist.

The introduction of personal computers in the Soviet Union in 1983 raised hopes for the widespread use of computers throughout Soviet society. At the same time, it raised a question about their impact on the authoritarian Soviet government. Because the centralized government bureaucracy values large, powerful computing resources for such organizations as Gosplan, the Soviet committee for long-term economic planning, it has struggled to understand the value and implications of distributed and decentralized computing made practical by personal computers. Even though dissidents could broaden their sphere of influence via personal computers, the Soviet government appears committed to developing a broad base of users. But because the Soviet government is promoting the use of personal computers for academic and scientific purposes, the current emphasis is on collective rather than individual applications such as the dissemination of information to a particular user. Their observations of the personal computer revolution in the West have led Soviet bureaucrats to commit themselves to developing personal computers, although they are wary of the decentralizing effects this may have and of the unknown ways in which the computers will be used in Soviet society, industry, and the military.

One estimate places the installed base of personal computers in the Soviet Union at fewer than 20,000.[51] Most personal computers are owned by research institutes and enterprises, and the twelfth Five-Year Plan, which was announced in the spring of 1986, called for the production of 1.1 million personal computers. By contrast, more than 32 million such machines were in use in the United States in 1987.[52]

Thus far, the Soviet authorities have not restricted personal computers. But the ease with which Soviet citizens circumvent their government's restriction on the use of photocopying equipment suggests another reason the Communist party has not yet limited individual use of computers. According to Soviet law, individuals cannot photocopy anything without authorization from their supervisors. Copy-machine operators, however, can easily be paid off by those who want access to copiers. Also, the penalty for unauthorized use is mild, usually no more than a reprimand. Loyal party members can sometimes circumvent any requirements for authorization. Most research institutes and enterprises have more serious problems than the security of their photocopiers, and copying infractions often go unnoticed. Controls on individual use of personal computers would likely be equally ineffective. Although no laws or policy concerning Soviet citizens' use of personal computers existed as of late 1987, some computer experts recommended that they be used only by officially recognized groups. Time will tell whether the Soviet government will back up the rhetoric of Gorbachev's *glasnost* by allowing widespread use of personal computers.

The development of personal computers is the one area of computing most plagued by ministerial infighting. Several ministries, institutes, and state committees claim leadership. Four ministries actually manage personal computer developments, and many more take responsibility for manufacturing personal computer components.[53] This lack of a clearly defined leader diffuses resources and causes a series of fits and starts in the initiation of programs to promote the use of personal computers.

Although the Politburo's computer-literacy program calls for 500,000 computers in secondary schools by 1990, today's classrooms are lucky to have even an Agat, the Soviet "red apple." Much like an Apple II, the Agat first appeared at a Soviet exhibition in 1983, one year after Apple Computer appeared on the Fortune 500 list. It was never manufactured in any quantity, and only about 1,200 Agats still existed by 1987. The Agat thus never had a meaningful installed base. It cost $5,000, or 3,100 rubles, some 17 to 23 months' salary for the average Soviet industrial worker.[54]

Although designed to be portable—its keyboard folds over the screen—it cannot be carried comfortably for more than a few feet. The designer wrote a Cyrillic menu over the BASIC operating system, and each key has three functions. An American eye surgeon who saw the Agat in Moscow described it as "exotic" and felt that demand for it outside the Soviet Union would be nonexistent, "even if they gave it away."[55] The Soviets appear to have discontinued the Agat at the beginning of 1987.

The BK-0010, mentioned earlier, is sometimes used in school programs. It has a 16-bit processor, a cassette tape recorder for storage, and a monitor. A printer, when available, is extra. The BK-0010 is sold through a chain called Elektronika stores.[56] In 1987, the Soviets planned to produce 40,000 units. Most were to go to schools, while 7,000 were slated for sale to the public.[57]

Another Soviet microcomputer is the Elektronika 60. In 1985, Alex Beam, Boston bureau manager for *Business Week*, visited a Soviet secondary school in Siberia and saw twelve computers that had been installed recently. Beam reported that the computers were crudely assembled (imprints of hammers used to seal the metal keyboard casings were visible) and used black-and-white TV sets as displays. The school had to purchase wiring, keyboards, and cables separately because Elektronika manufactures only the computer.

The problem is not that the Soviets cannot manufacture personal computers. They have demonstrated that they can produce mainframes—the Ryad ES series—and minicomputers—copies of Digital's PDP-11 and VAX lines and Hewlett-Packard's 2100 series. But government inertia to date has caused confusion among policymakers. A research center near Novosibirsk released design specifications for a new personal computer based on a 16-bit chip to replace the Agat. The Soviet government adopted the new personal computer design, called the Korvet, in 1987. Although it had not been mass-produced as of late 1987, the Korvet represents the Soviet government's hope that its ambitious computerization project will yet succeed. Production of the Korvet has also been hampered by the lack of peripherals.[58]

As of May 1988, three U.S. firms have plans to assist the Soviets in manufacturing personal computers. One Soviet-U.S. venture, called Dialogue, is a consortium of six Soviet partners and a Chicago-based consulting firm, Management Partnerships International (MPI). Their objective is to manufacture 5,000 IBM PC/XT clones during 1989. The second venture is a partnership between Elorg and three U.S. firms—New Software International (Attleboro, Mass.), Innovation Computer (Cleveland, Ohio), and California Microelectronic Systems Inc. (Campbell, Calif.). The Soviets will assemble IBM PC–compatible computers in the Soviet Union using kits provided by the U.S. partners.[59] The third venture, involving a Silicon Valley firm—Advanced Transducer Devices—is described in Chapter 1.

Until the Soviets can manufacture computers in sufficient quantity, they may attempt to import personal computers for their schools. For example, in 1986 they purchased 10,000 Yamaha personal computers.[60] Not at all state of the art, the Yamaha uses an 8-bit processor and has 6 KB of memory, a music-synthesizing chip, and a color display. The Soviets hoped to use the Yamahas to increase schoolchildren's exposure to computers. They soon discovered, however, that the Yamaha computers were best suited for computer games, not for meaningful instruction.

The Soviet government hopes that Western know-how will rescue the country's personal computer manufacturing efforts. It anticipates that the joint ventures between Soviet enterprises and U.S. computer manufacturers will bootstrap the mass production of high-quality personal computers. Efforts to improve the still unacceptable quality and performance of Soviet personal computers are still superficial. In July 1987, an All-Union Standard was introduced as a quality control requirement for the manufacturing of personal computers. The government now requires each new machine to carry a card stating that it meets or exceeds the quality of engineering found in foreign models.[61]

Purchasing Western computers can never be more than a short-term solution to the Soviet supply problem, because the lack of hard currency limits all purchases of foreign equipment. If purchases could be arranged through credit or barter agreements, the Soviets could use Western suppliers to fulfill their demands quickly. Despite the currency problems (somewhat ameliorated by recent borrowing from Western banks), U.S. personal computer manufacturers continually receive invitations from the Soviets to bid on proposals to purchase large quantities of personal computers for Soviet schools. So far, few sales have resulted from such invitations, either because the Soviets are content to collect technical data from U.S. companies making sales presentations or because of the U.S. export-control laws, which restrict international trade of many personal computer components. But in early 1988, the United States decontrolled the export of 16-bit computers, such as the IBM PC, to the Soviet Union.

NETWORKS AND SUPERCOMPUTERS

It remains to be seen whether the Communist party is willing to open communications between individuals across international borders. Technical limitations on the Soviet side make such links unlikely.

Practical applications of local and long-distance computer networks first appeared in the Soviet Union in the 1980s. Since 1985, the Academy of Sciences, for example, has used Akademset, a packet-switched network that uses networking equipment strikingly similar to Digital's. Eventually, all organizations of the Academy of Sciences, including research institutes, will be linked. The Soviets still struggle with low transmission speeds. In 1985, the Akademset link between Riga, Moscow, and Leningrad ran at 300 bits per second.[62] By comparison, a telephone network that links remote Apple Macintosh computers runs at up to 9.6 megabits per second. A few enterprises and some research institutes have primitive local area networks.[63] Ministries (such as that for the automobile industry), railroads, Tass (the Soviet news agency), and a few enterprises also use wide area networks.

The telephone system remains a major hurdle in the way of network development. In 1985, only 7 percent of rural families and 23 percent of urban families had telephones.[64] Furthermore, because of the scarcity of telephone lines and, perhaps, security considerations, the Soviet government restricts the use of a regular telephone line to 9 minutes an hour for data transmission (and 18 minutes an hour on the All-Union Data Transmission System[65]), which obviously limits transfer of large files. The slow development of computer networks may also reflect the government's realization of the risks in providing access to additional data that could either expose an enterprise manager's low production statistics or reveal military research files held in a research institute's computer.

Supercomputers—those capable of executing more than 100 million operations a second—are also high on the Soviet wish list and are ideally suited to scientific and military applications. The United States and other Cocom nations, however, are galvanized in their efforts to limit Soviet access to U.S. and Japanese supercomputers and have banned them from export to the Soviet Union and Eastern bloc countries. Moving up the ladder of computer sophistication presents greater problems for the Soviets than enhancing past designs.

The Soviets are trying to build their own supercomputer, but so far, U.S. observers do not believe they have—with one possible exception, the Elbrus. As of 1987, Soviet "supercomputers" were only boxes containing complicated collections of outdated technology.[66] Jack Worlton, a laboratory fellow at Los Alamos National Laboratory and author of the book *High Performance Computers in the Eastern Bloc,* thinks that the Soviets are at least five years behind the United States in the development of supercomputers. He points out that because the Soviets are accomplished mathematicians they can reduce the complexity of a problem so that it can be processed faster by their computers, even though they may not yet work at supercomputer speed.

One Soviet computer (fast by Soviet standards but by no means a supercomputer) is the Elbrus I, named after the highest peak in the Caucasus. Soviets claim that it executes at 12.5 million operations a second, comparable to a midrange mainframe in the West. Apparently, another fast computer, the Elbrus II, can execute 125 million operations a second, but Western observers have yet to see one in operation. Experts in the West are skeptical of these operating speeds, which they feel would require parallel processing in all ten of the computer's processors.

During the Twenty-Seventh Party Congress, Gorbachev confirmed his country's single-mindedness in developing high technology. He said:

> Machine construction, electrical engineering, microelectronics,
> computer technology and instrument making and the entire
> information industry—the true catalysts of acceleration in scientific
> and technical progress—will receive priority development.[67]

Many observers feel that the introduction of computers from the "bottom up," rather than the "top down" (the usual Soviet approach), and their integration throughout the economy is the only way the Soviets could come close to reaping benefits similar to those received in Western society. It is, however, highly unlikely that the bottom-up computerization of Soviet society will occur, because that would require a stronger economy and would dilute centralized government authority. Many more Soviets would need access to a computer, the supply of machines would have to increase, and software for making them useful would have to be readily available. More computers in individual hands would create a broader base of computer literacy and pressure from workers to incorporate these new tools into their workplace.

COMPUTERS AND EDUCATION

As a way of ensuring the success of his new initiatives, Gorbachev is concentrating on improving the Soviet Union's image both in the eyes of Soviet citizens and at all levels of the international community, including science and technology. A corollary objective of the national computer-literacy program is to forge links between schools and industry. At a relatively low risk, the national computer literacy program could generate enormous payoffs in key sectors of the Soviet economy. Although the worker incentive program will contribute most to an increase in Soviet innovation, the computer-literacy program could improve the quality of the work force by training a new generation of computer-literate workers and help modernize the existing industrial base by creating an environment for innovation.

The program began in March 1985 and produced a national curriculum on informatics in the fall of 1986. Ninth-grade students were the first to benefit from the program in 1985. One thousand personal computers were destined for use by these 64,000 high school students during the program's first year.[68] As of mid-1987, far from all the schools were participating.

Seymour Goodman, who visited one of the Soviet high schools participating in the program in 1986, felt that the students were struggling along with outdated hardware and minimal software. He thought that the textbook on computers—emphasizing mathematics, algorithmic thinking, and software—was adequate and would have been difficult for a U.S. student of the same age to understand. Its 150 pages were sprinkled with few illustrations. Called "Basics of Informatics and Computer Technology," it was published in two versions, one for use with a computer and another for use without one. Most students in the program had a textbook but no hands-on computer experience.

During his visit, Goodman observed a computer lab with two ponderous Soviet-made computers. Twelve students had access to them. Their almost unusable printer utilized thin, fragile paper. They had only rudimentary software—a BASIC interpreter and an elementary printing utility. The students were inputting programs out of a book, generating simple line graphics, and printing their work. Unaware of the official curriculum, they nonetheless enjoyed working with the computers.

Administrators of the computer-literacy program speak in grandiose terms about its success and bright future. When Professor Goodman asked his host about the program's future, he was told, "We will use it for all of our courses. We will take 20 percent off the time it takes for the average Soviet high school student to learn all required subject materials." Asked to explain how this estimate was developed, the host volunteered that it was the result of precise theoretical calculations.

The Soviets may have grand plans, but the gap between the two outdated computers in the schools Goodman visited and a room full of functional, modern personal computers needed to implement a massive computer-aided instruction system is wide indeed. The Agat, Elektronika 60, DVK Series, Yamaha, BK-0010, and a few locally produced personal computers are used in schools along with a few networked systems in which "dumb" terminals link to an enterprise mainframe. A few U.S. personal computers, such as IBM PCs and Apple Macintoshes, have appeared beside several Japanese models, while the Soviets attempt to design an indigenous personal computer to meet their ambitious goals.

The program aims so high that it may not be realizable. When it was announced, computers had not reached schools in any significant numbers; rather, they were concentrated within military circles and high-priority industries. The government became attuned to the gap between dream and reality and cut its projections drastically, stating instead in 1986 that it would probably introduce 100,000 to 200,000 personal computers in the schools by 1990. By comparison, U.S. schools already had 3 million computers in 1986.[69]

Before computers can penetrate Soviet schools in quantities approaching those in the U.S. educational system, the country's industry will have to mass-produce an inexpensive personal computer and its peripherals. The Soviets will also need software to support the informatics curriculum. Eventually, they will also require the infrastructure so visibly missing and so necessary for the development of computer literacy, including networks and inexpensive printers. New initiatives abound, though, and it appears that the computer-literacy program will receive a boost through purchases of Western computers, such as the IBM PC, and the ongoing Soviet efforts to develop a more advanced personal computer for schools.

SOVIET VISIONARIES

Although the Soviet government seems encumbered by both Russian tradition and its own ideological goals, influential levels of society could be transformed by the efforts of strategically placed individuals. Three men—Yevgeny P. Velikhov, Andrei P. Ershov, and Boris N. Naumov—may help shepherd the Soviet people, including the bureaucrats, into the computer age. Although Naumov died in June 1988, his ideas and vision will still have an impact on the future of Soviet computing. The new generation of advanced thinkers must recognize the huge task facing the Soviet Union if it wants to approach the West's level of computerization. But for that kind of undertaking, they must first gain positions in the hierarchy where they can make massive changes in the way the Soviets create and implement computer technology.

Yevgeny Pavlovich Velikhov may already have risen high enough to make a significant contribution, and he may well be at the helm of a Soviet-style computer revolution. Born in 1935, he has risen through the scientific community to be Gorbachev's right-hand man for science policy. He was appointed to the Soviet Academy of Sciences and became its vice president in 1981. By 1987, he had become chief of the Committee for Informatics, Technology, and Automation, and at 52 years of age, he was also the leading candidate to succeed Aleksandrov as head of the Academy of Sciences. (In 1987, he was passed over; Guri Marchuk, chairman of the GKNT, became the president.) A physicist by training,

Velikhov is a member of the Kurchatov Atomic Energy Institute and heads the Soviet-directed energy program that is part of the Soviet SDI.[70]

With science and technology at the top of Gorbachev's agenda, Velikhov is a person to watch. Ironically, a familiar figure in anti-SDI circles, he has condemned the U.S. program (although he oversees Soviet strategic defense research at the Atomic Energy Institute). He is also a self-proclaimed pacifist, and as chairman of the Committee of Soviet Scientists for Peace Against Nuclear Threat, he generally speaks out at Soviet and international peace conferences. In 1983, he wrote one of the first articles on personal computers published in the Soviet Union. Velikhov advocates the use of personal computers throughout the Soviet Union, an opinion that threatens old-guard scientists and bureaucrats.

In 1985, Velikhov met with David Hamburg, president of the Carnegie Corporation and a member of the U.S. National Academy of Sciences Committee on International Security and Arms Control, to discuss how nuclear war could be avoided. Velikhov promoted his concept that introducing computers into the schools was critical to avoiding nuclear war, and both men agreed that scientific cooperation was important. They departed from their meeting with an outline for a joint project on computers in early elementary education.[71] Velikhov's meeting with Hamburg, however, may also have been an effort to persuade the U.S. academic community to pressure the Reagan administration into loosening export restrictions on personal computers.

Lacking the usual inhibiting influence of the old guard, Velikhov's department at the Academy of Sciences includes more than 100 recent university graduates who are familiar with the latest technologies.[72] In a recent *Izvestia* interview, Velikhov expressed his enlightened and probably sincere views on personal computing.

> The arrival of personal computers signals a fundamental and revolutionary change. The machine ceases to be a sort of mystery, accessible only to professionals. The computer is a powerful amplifier of communications. Naturally, you need not idealize the machine; it will not replace a living being. Nevertheless, it dramatically increases the active acquisition of knowledge and the exchange of new information.[73]

Some may have difficulty matching Velikhov's effusive comments with Soviet realities, both technical and political. But Velikhov personifies his message by using a word processor and doing research on an IBM personal computer that he imported from the United States. He advocates establishing computer-game arcades throughout metropolitan areas as a means of familiarizing the populace with computers.[74] To keep up with U.S. computer developments, he often meets with Western computer vendors attending technical or trade conferences in Moscow. His colleagues say he is ambitious and adroit at using the Soviet political system to advance his scientific goals. Both the Soviet government and U.S. observers value his views, but whether he will remain a strong influence only in the academic arena or also become influential in politics and industry is not clear. Velikhov's presence at the December 1987 U.S.-Soviet summit in Washington underlined his role in the Soviet courtship of the U.S. computer industry. He attended a meeting between the Soviets and U.S. computer experts that included both Apple and Digital executives as well as representatives from key academic and technical research institutions such as MIT. The purpose of the meeting was to encourage business relationships that would result in the transfer of technology to the Soviet Union. (During the meeting, the U.S. National Academy of Sciences agreed to assist the Soviets with their program to place computers in schools.[75])

Andrei P. Ershov also bears watching. In perhaps his most notable achievement, he led computer scientists from Novosibirsk in designing the national computer-literacy program. After completing the project, he became disillusioned by the difficulties he encountered in trying to convince political leaders of the necessity for dramatic changes in both the research and the industrial base. Even so, Ershov wants to create a project that would result in restructuring the computer industry and changing the Soviet design and production process.

Ershov's radical thinking is exemplified by his belief that the Soviet Union must adapt to new technologies even if it means changing the structure of society.[76] Ershov believes that personal computers should be used by individuals, not kept within collective organizations—another opinion that threatens many centralist thinkers in the Politburo. Ershov's enlightened attitude is the result of his international travels as a world-class computer scientist. A fan of Apple Macintosh computers, he can carry on a lively conversation in English about computers on a level comparable with any avid U.S. Mac user.[77]

Even though Ershov is cosmopolitan and technically sophisticated, he turns down promotions that would transfer him to Moscow, preferring to live in an apartment in Novosibirsk. The Academy of Pedagogical Sciences will probably limit any global influence that he could have, wanting him instead to concentrate on the computer-literacy program. Ershov does not believe that capitalism is the answer. Instead, he thinks that Soviet pioneers in computer science will be motivated through professional recognition and a desire for collective benefits.

The late Boris Nikolayevich Naumov completes the troika of Soviet computer visionaries. In 1958, he was a visiting professor at MIT. Later, he was made responsible for developing the SM series, which includes minicomputers and personal computers, and became a member of the Academy of Sciences. More important, in 1983, he became director of the Institute of Informatics Problems, the Moscow organization of some 900 computer scientists charged with turning into reality many of the Twenty-Seventh Party Congress commitments to the computerization of Soviet industry. The institute reports directly to the Academy of Sciences.

In 1986, Naumov became director of the Intersectorial Scientific and Technological Complex for Personal Computers. The new organization is attempting to increase the number of personal computers in the manufacturing sector. Naumov beat the drum for technological progress and was particularly keen on joint ventures with the United States to help develop the Soviet computer industry. While acknowledging the strategic and security-related reasons for limiting American access to Soviet technology and vice versa, he was convinced that the two superpowers should cooperate in the area of personal computers. His ideas for U.S.-Soviet cooperation included joint development of personal computer-based computer-literacy software, computer networks to link data bases, and joint standards-making efforts for the development of new computer systems.

Naumov understood the benefits American firms could realize from expanding their personal computer sales to the Soviet Union, assuming their commercial ventures are truly profitable. But he also pulls no punches about Soviet objectives, stating, "If you are not prepared to join us, then excuse us, please, but good-bye. We will survive without you."[78] By "join us," Naumov probably meant a U.S. rapprochement with the U.S.S.R., bringing increased technical cooperation and sales of more sophisticated technology.

Although Naumov was an aggressive, modern thinker, he qualified his vision about personal computers by stating that they should remain independent, stand-alone machines to be networked only carefully for selected, state-approved purposes such as process-control applications.

Gorbachev is attempting to replace old-guard politicians with more progressive bureaucrats and technocrats, such as these three men, who are and were potentially more receptive to promoting technical innovation through political compromise and persistence. The Soviet computing community is already responding to the Gorbachev initiative for increased internal computer-technology capacity. With the need to improve industrial productivity as one of Gorbachev's top priorities, the quality and quantity of industrial robots and numerically controlled (i.e., by computers) machine tools have improved. The Soviets produced 13,500 industrial robots in 1985; their ambitious Five-Year Plan calls for annual production to increase to 28,600 in 1990.[79]

Statements from Gorbachev and the scientific community broadcast the Soviets' desire to develop a computer industry independent of the West. But most Western observers remain skeptical of their ability and intentions to do so. Although speeches at party congresses throughout this century have expounded the Soviet Union's will to rid itself of technological dependence on the West, realities within the country often steer it toward Western expertise and products. His initiatives, along with a dramatic increase in Western electronics and computer trade, could still bring the current Soviet Five-Year Plan closer to realization. But the Soviets appear to be falling short in all areas of their scientific and high-technology goals for 1990, signaling a guaranteed continuation of both the legal and the illegal technology-acquisition game.

NOTES

1. A method of welding rails by which the rail ends are heated to extremely high temperatures by "flashing" them with high currents of electricity.

2. David F. Feeley, senior vice president for operations, New York City Transit Authority: Interview, May 4, 1987.

3. U.S. Department of Defense, *The FY 1987 Department of Defense Program for Research and Development*, statement by the under secretary of defense for research and engineering, to the 99th Cong., 2d sess., 1986, Washington, D.C., February 1986, II-10, II-11. The report states that the United States is superior in computers and software, electro-optical sensors (including infrared), guidance and navigation, life sciences (human factors/biotechnology), microelectronic materials and integrated circuit manufacturing, production/manufacturing (including automated control), robotics and machine intelligence, signal processing, signature reduction, and telecommunications (including fiber optics). Although even with the United States in submarine detection, radar sensor, propulsion (aerospace and ground vehicles), and materials (lightweight, high strength, high temperature), the Soviets appear to be gaining in these areas.

4. *A Study of Soviet Science* (Washington, D.C.: Government Printing Office, 1985), p. 18.

5. "Gorbachev's Modernization Program: A Status Report," a paper presented by the Central Intelligence Agency and the Defense Intelligence Agency for submission to the Subcommittee on National Security Economics of the Joint Economic Committee, Congress of the United States, Mar. 19, 1987, 4-A (Fig. 3).

6. *Van Nostrand's Scientific Encyclopedia*, 6th ed., S. V. "Particles (subatomic)."

7. John Noble Wilford, "Shades of Sputnik: Who's Ahead in Space?" *New York Times*, Jan. 3, 1988, p. IV, 7.

8. Paulette Thomas, "Soviet Union Took Commanding Lead in Space Last Year," *Wall Street Journal*, Mar. 30, 1987, p. 26.

9. Wilford, p. IV, 7.

10. Louis Lavoie, "The Quality of Soviet Engineering," *Current*, March/April 1986, p. 35.

11. *Soviet Military Power, 1987*, 6th ed. (Washington, D.C.: Government Printing Office, 1987), p. 45.

12. William J. Broad, "The Secrets of Soviet Star Wars," *New York Times Magazine*, June 28, 1987, p. 24.

13. William P. Hoar, "Moscow's Strategic Defense Initiative," *Conservative Digest*, May 1987, p. 97.

14. Broad, p. 24.

15. *Soviet Military Power*, p. 51.

16. Lavoie, p. 35.

17. Len Lederman, Special Analytical Studies Section in the Division of Science Resources Studies, National Science Foundation: Interview, May 20, 1987; National Science Foundation, *International Science and Technology Data Update 1986*, p. 3. Included in the Soviet count are engineers and non-degreed technical workers.

18. Gary Taubes and Glenn Garelik, "Soviet Science: How Good Is It?" *Discover*, August 1986, p. 38.

19. Ibid., p. 40.

20. The Academy of Sciences was patterned after European research academies during the era of Peter the Great. His European perspective was reflected in the makeup of the first participants: It had eight students from Vienna, sixteen Western European members, and fifteen German scientists; its first president was Peter the Great's personal physician, also from Germany. (Source: Henri Troyat, *Peter the Great* [New York: E. P. Dutton, 1987], pp. 297, 306, and 332.)

21. Julian Cooper, "Technology in the Soviet Union," *Current History*, October 1986, p. 319.

22. As of March 1988, the Soviet government was continuing to consolidate and restructure its ministries; the number of ministries and their responsibilities may still be changing.

23. Speech by A. P. Aleksandrov, *Pravda: Organ of the Central Committee of the CPSU* (St. Paul, Minn.), Feb. 27, 1986, p. 5.

24. It can be argued that it takes the Soviets a great deal of creativity and innovation to copy Western technology.

25. Vera Tolz, "Aleksandrov's Speech to the Twenty-Seventh Party Congress: The Role of the U.S.S.R. Academy of Sciences," *Radio Liberty Research Bulletin*, RL 108/86, Mar. 5, 1986, p. 3.

26. N. C. Davis and S. E. Goodman, "The Soviet Bloc's Unified System of Computers," *Computing Surveys*, June 1978, p. 113.

27. Harley D. Balzer, "Is Less More? Soviet Science in the Gorbachev Era," *Issues in Science and Technology*, Summer 1985, p. 34.

28. Seymour E. Goodman, "Software in the Soviet Union: Progress and Problems," *Advances in Computers*, vol. 18 (1979), p. 266.

29. Grace Murray Hopper, Capt., U.S. Navy, ret., Arlington, Va.: Interview, Jan. 21, 1988.

30. Loren Graham, *Science, Philosophy and Human Behavior in the Soviet Union* (New York: Columbia University Press, 1987), p. 271.

31. Ibid.

32. Igor Reichlin, "How Dogma Cripples Soviet Science," *Science Digest*, March 1984, p. 101.

33. Mark Kuchment, Russian Research Center, Harvard University, Cambridge, Mass.: Interview, Dec. 28, 1987.

34. Mark Kuchment, "The American Connection to Soviet Microelectronics," *Physics Today*, September 1985, p. 45.

35. Taubes and Garelik, p. 37.

36. Ibid., p. 38.

37. Anthony C. Sutton, *Western Technology and Soviet Economic Development 1945–1965* (Stanford, Calif.: Hoover Institution Press, 1973), p. 319.

38. Kenneth Tasky, "Soviet Technology Gap and Dependence on the West: The Case of Computers," in *The Soviet Economy in a Time of Change*, ed. John P. Hardt (Washington, D.C.: Government Printing Office, 1979), vol. 1, p. 513.

39. Ibid., p. 512.

40. William K. McHenry and Seymour E. Goodman, "MIS in Soviet Industrial Enterprises: The Limits of Reform from Above," *Communications of the ACM*, November 1986, p. 1038.

41. Sutton, pp. 321–22.

42. Tasky, p. 510.

43. Richard W. Judy, *The Soviet Information Revolution: Some Prospects and Comparisons* (study sponsored in part by the National Council for Soviet and East European Research, March 1987), p. 6.

44. "Elektronika' u nas doma," *Izvestia*, Mar. 21, 1987, as cited in Viktor Yasmann, "Black Market Computer Games in Moscow," *Radio Liberty Research Bulletin*, RL 160/87, Mar. 27, 1987, p. 1.

45. Alex Beam, "Atari Bolsheviks," *Atlantic Monthly*, March 1986, p. 8.

46. Barbara Van, Dataquest Incorporated, San Jose, Calif.: Interview, Dec. 23, 1987.

47. Judy, p. 70.

48. According to *Webster's Third New International Dictionary*, a hacker is an expert at programming and solving problems with a computer; a computer whiz. The usage of the term "hacker" to include those who illegally gain access to computer systems by using a home computer does not apply here, particularly since the Soviet Union does not yet have the widespread use of telephones, not to mention modems.

49. Loren Graham, professor of science history at the Massachusetts Institute of Technology, Cambridge, Mass.: Notes to the author, Mar. 5, 1987.

50. Victor Yasmann, "Home Computers Have Gone on Sale...," *Radio Liberty Research Bulletin*, RL 407/85, Dec. 6, 1985, p. 1.

51. Joachim Kempin, vice president, OEM Sales, Microsoft Corporation, Redmond, Wash.: Interview, Apr. 30, 1987.

52. Sharon Hashimoto, Dataquest Incorporated: Interview, Dec. 23, 1987.

53. Maxine Pollack, "Playing Computer Catch-up Against Incalculable Odds," *Insight*, Mar. 16, 1987, p. 31.

54. Beam, p. 29.

55. Ibid.

56. Yasmann, "Home Computers," p. 1.

57. "V dobry: put 'Korvet,'" *Pravda*, Aug. 26, 1987, p. 4, as cited in Viktor Yasmann, "Personal Computers in the U.S.S.R.—Will Help Come From the West?" *Radio Liberty Research Bulletin*, RL 388/87, Sept. 23, 1987, p. 3.

58. Ibid.

59. Melcher, p. 41.

60. Alex Beam, *Boston Globe*, Boston, Mass.: Interview, Mar. 6, 1987.

61. Yasmann, "Personal Computers," p. 4.

62. William K. McHenry, "Computer Networks in the Soviet Scientific Community" (Paper prepared for a *Symposium on Soviet Science*, NATO, Scientific Affairs Division, Brussels, Sept. 24–26, 1986), p. 21.

63. Seymour E. Goodman, "The Information Technologies in Soviet Society: Problems and Prospects," July 29, 1986, University of Arizona, MIS/BPA, p. 27.

64. Ibid., p. 30.

65. Seymour E. Goodman and William K. McHenry, "Computing in the U.S.S.R.: Recent Progress and Policies," *Soviet Economy* (1986), p. 337.

66. Andrew C. Revkin, "Supercomputers and the Soviets," *Technology Review*, August/September 1986, p. 71.

67. Mikhail S. Gorbachev, "Program of the Communist Party of the Soviet Union," *Pravda: Organ of the Central Committee of the CPSU* (St. Paul, Minn.), Mar. 7, 1986, p. 5.

68. Maxine Pollack and Ross Alan Stapleton, "Why Ivan Can't Compute," *High Technology*, February 1986, p. 42.

69. Donald L. Rheem, "Soviets Try to Catch U.S. Computer Wave," *Christian Science Monitor*, Nov. 10, 1986, p. 3.

70. William Kucewicz, "Moscow's Bigger Star Wars Drive" (editorial), *Wall Street Journal*, Dec. 16, 1986, p. 22.

71. Both U.S. and Soviet scholars became enthusiastic about pursuing the project, including American scholars from the University of Massachusetts, University of California at San Diego, Hunter College, and Harvard University's Graduate School of Education. The Soviets and Americans discuss the subject via The Source, an information service linking subscribers by long-distance telephone networks. The Soviet Ministry of Education and the Institute of Pedagogical Sciences are also interested in the joint project. In another effort to assist the Soviets with their computer-literacy program, Rochelle Heller and Diane Martin of George Washington University went to the Soviet Union in 1985 to train teachers at four universities in how to use a computer textbook.

72. Paul Walton and Paul Tate, "Soviets Aim for 5th Gen," *Datamation*, July 1, 1984, p. 56.

73. Kim Smirnov, "Young Sciences, Young Scientists," *Soviet Life*, April 1987, p. 10.

74. Joyce Barnathan, "Computer Gamesman," *Newsweek*, Nov. 18, 1985, p. 56.

75. Tom Breen, "Academy to Give Soviets Computers," *Washington Times*, Dec. 9, 1987, p. A5.

76. Beam, "Atari Bolsheviks," p. 38.

77. During the fall of 1986, twenty-one Soviet computer students and their instructors, led by Ershov, visited the United States and stayed with American families to observe the U.S. personal computer scene. The visit's U.S. sponsors were the Institute for Conflict Resolution of the Holy Earth and George Mason University. To witness firsthand the American computer revolution, the Soviet group visited high-technology companies, including IBM, and university computer science departments. Before departing for the Soviet Union, an attempt was made to enable the Soviet students to take Radio Shack computers home with them, but they left empty-handed.

78. Paul Tate and David Hebditch, "Opening Moves," *Datamation*, Mar. 15, 1987, p. 42.

79. Cooper, p. 320. Note that in the Soviet Union the term *robots* is defined more loosely than it is in the United States and includes many automated devices not regarded as robots by the U.S. computer industry.

4

OF ESPIONAGE
AND DIVERSION

A twelve-year-old boy swings a 12-inch plastic model airplane high over his head, creating a looping flight path as he swoops up and down his family's driveway. The model airplane, made by the Testor Corporation, is said to be an accurate reproduction of the top secret F-19 "stealth" fighter jet. Testor came up with the design details by reading aircraft-industry trade journals and technical publications and by viewing a sketch of the fighter made by a commercial pilot who saw a test flight.

With technical details this easy to surmise, it is not surprising that the Soviets can obtain much of what they seek through legal channels. In light of the Testor model, it may come as a surprise that the Soviets have launched such a substantial effort to discover U.S. high-technology secrets by illegal means. Yet each year, the Soviet Union commits millions of dollars and thousands of men and women to stealing U.S. cutting-edge equipment and information, either by spying on private industry and the government or by a twentieth-century version of smuggling known as diversion. Recent media attention to Soviet-sponsored espionage, such as the Walker spy ring, and high-tech smuggling efforts, such as those conducted by Charles McVey, may have been focused only on the tip of an iceberg. It is difficult to say which of these activities are the more dangerous and which are the toughest to stop—the strictly illegal ones, detailed in this chapter, or the borderline-legal and legitimate efforts, covered in Chapter 5.

Spies and export diverters are similarly motivated, primarily by greed, but they have different modi operandi. Espionage concerns the theft of classified information or technology that bears upon national security. Export diversion, on the other hand, concerns the illegal shipment of technology that is restricted for export by the U.S. Commerce Department. Typically, the illegal shipment passes through several companies—some of them dummy or front enterprises—on its way to the Soviet Union from the United States. A diverter is often a businessman who operates from a foreign country. Both offenses, illegal exporting and spying, are punishable by U.S. law, although each has its own set of laws to support prosecutions. The Soviets use both methods aggressively.

The collection techniques used by the Soviets, discussed in this and the next chapter, range from the highly publicized spying missions to legitimate, ongoing, and unremarkable business relationships. It is essential—*glasnost* or no *glasnost*—to understand the organization of the Soviet effort and the techniques employed before formulating an effective, constructive response.

THE CHAIN OF COMMAND AND ITS TARGETS

Before the Soviets begin acquisition activities in the United States or elsewhere, a request for specific American technology must travel a complex and not always consistent pathway within the Soviet bureaucracy. Calls for military-related technology apparently move through the government bureaucracy according to a general protocol, but the details of the protocol are not always easy to discern. The following description is what various international intelligence services have been able to put together about the Soviet system for technology acquisition.

The two organizations primarily involved in collecting U.S. technology are the KGB (*Komitet gosudarstvennoy bezopasnosti*, the Committee for State Security) and the GRU (*Glavnoye razvedyvatelnoye upravleniye*, the Chief Intelligence Directorate of the General Staff, Ministry of Defense), both of which follow the lead of the VPK, the GKNT, the Ministry of Foreign Economic Relations, and the Politburo. In its 1985 report on Soviet high-technology acquisition practices, the CIA revealed that the GRU is as involved in acquiring Western technology as its better-known cousin, the KGB. The report notes that the GRU excels in its ability to obtain hardware, particularly that related to military technology.[1] With its roots in an organization called the Registration Department of the Red Army, which was founded in 1918, the GRU is highly effective at gathering Western intelligence and technology for military use. It performed some of the first espionage missions using commercial cover in the United States. A typical GRU officer has a technical background, usually a degree in electrical engineering or physics.

The KGB is the world's largest intelligence organization, apparently employing more than 700,000 people, although some low estimates indicate that it employs only 90,000 career officers supported by 150,000 technical and clerical workers. The annual budget of the KGB hovers around $12 billion.[2] The KGB's origins go back as far as the tsarist police force, but the organization has been known as the KGB only since 1954. Headed by Viktor M. Chebrikov, the KGB continues to be an extremely powerful organization in the Soviet government. (Chebrikov, a member of the Politburo, appears unenthusiastic about Gorbachev's *perestroika* program.)

KGB field operations are organized into at least four "lines": Line PR for political intelligence, Line KR for counterintelligence, Line N for the support of agents abroad illegally, and Line X (Directorate T), called Scientific and Technical, for the acquisition of U.S. technology. Directorate T is the most profitable arm of the Soviet intelligence community.[3] Founded in 1963 to target Western technology, it now has a contingent at the Soviet embassy in Washington, D.C., and at every Soviet consulate in the United States.[4] According to the KGB, Directorate T contributes as much to the Soviet economy as the Soviet government spends on maintaining its intelligence network.[5] Its operatives all concentrate on obtaining high technology, although they occasionally collect economic and political data as well.

As does the GRU, Directorate T tends to recruit from the Soviet scientific community and has representatives on the GKNT. Its members tend to be graduates of Soviet scientific and research institutes with engineering degrees. At least 1,500 GRU officers and more than 500 Directorate T agents (both conservative estimates;[6] in 1982, *Business Week* placed the total number of Soviet high-technology collection agents at 5,000) operate outside the Soviet Union. The FBI (again conservatively) believes that 30 percent of the 1,368 Soviet diplomats known to be in the United States in 1986 were officers of either one or the other organization.[7] Their targets consist of geographic regions, types of technology, academic institutions, specific companies, and government agencies. They are carefully prioritized by the Soviet government, which allocates major resources to the most important targets.

Regionals: In 1985, Representative Ronald C. Packard (R-Calif.) listed the top U.S. regions the Soviets focus on for technology acquisition. In order of priority they were the Santa Clara (Silicon) Valley, Calif.; Dallas/Houston, Tex.; the Chicago area; the Raleigh/Durham, N.C., Research Triangle; Phoenix/Tucson, Ariz.; and suburban Boston.[8] Other areas targeted by the Soviets include the Pacific Northwest, Long Island, and the region from Mission Viejo to Del Mar in southern California. As high-technology firms seek locations outside these areas, the Soviets will undoubtedly follow them.

Technologies: Based on their knowledge of Soviet computer science, of industrial and military objectives, and of recent technology-acquisition activity, most experts believe the top targeted technologies are computers (especially supercomputers) and microelectronics, computer-aided design/computer-aided management, fiber optics, metal powder compounds,[9] composite synthetics,[10] semiconductors (especially very large scale integrated, or VLSI, chips) and semiconductor manufacturing equipment, and robotics.

The CIA has prepared a comprehensive list focusing primarily on technologies that have military applications. These include all types of computers, microelectronics and microelectronic manufacturing equipment, signal-processing equipment, and a broad range of design- and manufacturing-related technologies, including systems for factory automation, precision testing, process control, communications, lasers, guidance and navigation, propulsion systems, acoustical sensors for underwater navigation, electro-optical sensors, and radar systems.

Academic Institutions: According to the CIA, the Soviets satisfy some of their technology needs by tapping the resources of about sixty American universities, including MIT, Carnegie-Mellon, Harvard, University of Michigan, California Institute of Technology, Princeton, Stanford, University of California at Berkeley, Cornell, and Illinois Institute of Technology. These academic institutions get on the Soviets' target list because of their research programs relating directly to the sought-after technologies. Between 1970 and 1980, the number of U.S. universities targeted by the Soviets increased from twenty to its present level.

Companies: It is no surprise that the top-priority companies pinpointed by the Soviets happen to be defense contractors. General Dynamics, McDonnell Douglas, Rockwell International, General Electric, Boeing, and Lockheed lead the list, which also includes some familiar computer and electronics companies: IBM, Unisys, AT&T, Texas Instruments, Motorola, Control Data, Fairchild Industries, Computer Sciences Corporation, Xerox, Hewlett-Packard, Varian Associates, and Digital Equipment Corporation.[11]

Many high-technology company employees are unaware of the determination and sophistication of a Soviet intelligence officer in pursuit of U.S. high technology. Most employees cannot imagine that charts and diagrams used in a company meeting about new products would be highly desirable information for a scientific institute in Moscow. It rarely occurs to them that interested and highly motivated recipients await their diagrams in the Soviet consulate in San Francisco. Items of interest to espionage officers penetrating a high-technology company include computer printouts and blueprints, formulas, letters and memos, facsimile transmissions, production models and prototypes, and charts. They also try to observe a company's operations and intercept company communications, electronic and verbal.

U.S. government agencies are most concerned about protecting government contractors, but the limited human resources of the FBI and local law enforcement agencies do not afford every high-technology firm appropriate protection. As a result, the CIA's list of companies targeted by the Soviets (and also by U.S. counterespionage efforts) often excludes medium to small high-technology companies that are not government contractors. The Soviets tend to focus on the smaller firms to learn of advanced technology trends or simply because they provide alternate, often easier sources for acquisitions. Clearly, the smaller companies are more vulnerable than the larger government contractors because they rarely employ adequate security procedures, often do not see the need for precautions, and have limited staff and resources to take preventive action.

Government Agencies: The KGB has one directorate dedicated to political intelligence gathering. Called Directorate P, this group centers its activities on congressional personnel. An example of Directorate P activity is the lobbying done routinely on Capitol Hill by Soviet representatives or KGB agents. They attempt, using mostly disinformation, to sway legislators' opinions in a way favorable to the Soviet Union. This political connection is of concern to high-technology industry executives when hearings are under way concerning legislation on government security, hostile espionage activities, export of high technology, trade policies, and corporate security. The KGB has a stake in turning these hearings in directions favorable to its technology-acquisition efforts.

One channel for technology-collection requests runs through the Ministry of Foreign Economic Relations (formerly the Ministry of Foreign Trade), whose FTOs are responsible for many diversion schemes and which in the past has been used primarily for requests to acquire manufacturing and test equipment for weapons production lines. High on the ministry's acquisitions list are computers, communications equipment, robotics, and diagnostic equipment. The requests sometimes start with the Council of Ministers and then travel to the ministry, which funnels them to those foreign-trade and intelligence organizations that can most effectively collect the technology, using legal or illegal methods—the KGB, GRU, and intelligence services of other Soviet bloc nations. A foreign-trade organization that actively collects foreign electronics and computer technology is Elorg, which exports and imports computers and electronics; its employees are stationed around the world, sometimes behind the façades of front companies. Elorg also participates in U.S.-Soviet joint ventures.

The other channel greatly concerns the United States because it focuses specifically on military technology. Requests for Western military hardware and know-how sometimes originate with the Central Committee's Politburo, the nation's top ruling body, but more often they come from the Military Industrial Commission (VPK) of the Council of Ministers, a state body, not directly related to the Communist party, also known as the *spetsinformatsiya* (special information) organization. However, members of the VPK are party members. The relationship between the VPK and the Central Committee, however, is close; some VPK documents are circulated as Central Committee documents, and communication between the two is ongoing. Requests for military technology are formulated by objectives set forth in the most recent Five-Year Plan, announced in 1986, in addition to intelligence reports regarding technology requirements for the Soviet military and industry. The VPK oversees military research and development, coordinates research and development with production of military-related goods, and represents military producers and users. As of February 1988, the VPK was headed by Igor S. Belousov, formerly the head of the Ministry of the Shipbuilding Industry.[12] The CIA estimates that in 1980 the VPK had an annual budget of $1.4 billion earmarked specifically for high-tech acquisition.[13] The VPK uses the KGB and the GRU to fulfill its requests for militarily significant technology. Other key players in this channel include the minister of defense, as of early 1988, Dmitri Yazov, and the chief of the Department of the Defense Industry, Oleg Belyakov. (The Department of the Defense Industry reports to the Military Industrial Complex, whose director is a secretary in the Central Committee secretariat.) The Ministry of Defense has its own military equipment production facilities and therefore is directly involved in the military technology development process. The Central Committee secretary for defense production may also serve on the VPK.

Dr. Philip Hanson, who is professor of Soviet Economics at the University of Birmingham, England, is an authority on the organization of technology acquisition and the activities of the VPK. While studying the organization, he analyzed secret Soviet documents on industrial espionage that for the first time made the significance of the Military Industrial Commission clear to the West. In 1983, French counterespionage agents received the documents from a Soviet double agent, code-named Farewell, inside Directorate T, the KGB's office for high-technology acquisition. Hanson studied a portion of these 4,000 documents while at Harvard University during 1987. The cache included a 1979 VPK paper on *spetsinformatsiya*, which contained a ninety-page report by Directorate T, and a list of acquisition requests for rocket and space technology during 1981–85.[14]

Most of what the West knows about the VPK comes from Hanson's study of these documents. He found that at least seventeen ministries, nine of which are industrial, have representatives in the VPK, which compiles an annual list of technology needs into a book apparently the thickness of a metropolitan telephone directory. Approximately 3,500 items appear on the list each year; one-third of these (both hardware and technical documents) usually show up in the Soviet Union by year's end.[15]

The compilation of such a list is the result of an organized effort on the part of the Soviets. A Pentagon report released in 1985, *Soviet Military Power*, states that

> guidelines for the introduction of advanced manufacturing systems
> involving computer-aided design include a constant monitoring of
> available Western technology. As new information comes in from
> the field, science and technology requirements are constantly
> updated by the KGB, the GRU, and the State Committee for Science
> and Technology.

The report describes the efficiency of the Soviet acquisitions team, indicating that the turnaround time for the receipt of either hardware or software from the list can be a matter of weeks once specific acquisition instructions are given.

The technology requests are processed and prioritized by an organization within the VPK, the Technical Center of the All-Union Institute of Interbranch Information (VIMI). VIMI also coordinates activities among the Soviet intelligence agencies and the Soviet defense-related ministries. The VPK then assigns responsibilities for each item on the list, complete with budgets to cover their acquisition, to the appropriate espionage agency. The list is also reviewed by the Ministry of Foreign Economic Relations, the Committee for External Economic Relations (GKES), the State Committee for Science and Technology (GKNT), and the Academy of Sciences. According to the CIA, the GKNT has five responsibilities: It maintains scientific relations with foreign countries, monitors internal scientific programs, coordinates scientific research, oversees the centralized scientific and technological information system, and looks for scientific developments—in the Soviet Union or in foreign countries—that can be introduced into the Soviet economy. Rarely does the VPK actually play a collection role.[16] After an intelligence, trade, or scientific organization fulfills a technology request, the materials find their way back through VIMI and the VPK to the original ministry that made the request.[17]

Aside from military-related technology requests generated via the VPK and the Ministry of Foreign Economic Relations, individual research institutes, design bureaus, and enterprises also issue requests for U.S. technology. These requests may be satisfied by the intelligence services or simply by sending an individual to the usually complete collection of Western technical literature at the library of an Academy of Sciences research institute.

THE SOVIET PRESENCE

Who or how many of the several thousand Soviet citizens who visit the United States each year are carrying out their country's high-technology acquisition desires? The State Department classified 3,003 of the 9,356 Soviets who came to the United States in 1986 as tourists, 1,774 as businesspeople, 1,491 as members of international organizations such as the World Health Organization (WHO), 1,368 as diplomats, and the remainder as exchange students, reporters, and temporary workers.[18] Although few may have been on direct spy missions, the FBI reasons that most were on implied spy missions. An implied mission takes place when, for example, a Soviet scientist is given an exit visa to attend a technical conference in the United States and at the same time is requested to file a report with the KGB or the GKNT upon his return, describing new technical developments. If the scientist does not cooperate, he or she may not be allowed to travel outside the Soviet Union. At the very least, future travel requests will not be granted.

Whether officially classified as tourists, diplomats, or students, Soviets entering the United States are monitored by the State Department, Defense Department, and the intelligence community. Visa applicants are screened for security risks and for possible connections to Soviet intelligence organizations. Experience has shown the U.S. government that it should never entirely dismiss the possibility that a Soviet visitor has some, albeit small and perhaps indirect, relationship with Soviet intelligence.

The FBI classifies Soviet intelligence personnel operating in the United States in four ways: legals, illegals, co-optees, and agents. Legals are intelligence agents in the United States under official cover. Gennadi Zakharov, the United Nations official arrested in 1986 for spying in order to get technical secrets, was one such legal operative.

Illegals are intelligence officers that enter the United States using falsified documents and do not maintain formal contact with the Soviet government once inside the country. An example of an illegal is Yuri Loginov, trained for almost eight years by his KGB peers in American ways and language before entering the United States for a role as a handler of other illegals and American agents. He never fulfilled his mission. He was captured in South Africa in 1967 while trying to create a background for his fictitious identity.[19] Co-optees are Soviet visitors, emigrés, and officials who are requested to do a specific task for the KGB or the GRU.

Agents, sometimes called false-flag agents, are the most difficult to spot and prevent. They are citizens of the United States or of nations friendly to the United States, such as Canada, Japan, or West Germany, who are recruited to operate on behalf of the Soviet Union. Americans are particularly susceptible to operations carried out by false-flag agents because they do not normally suspect Westerners, or those posing as friends of the United States, of complicity with the U.S.S.R. The "agents" category also includes anyone recruited in the field for the purpose of spying or supporting others engaged in espionage. The most notorious agent of the 1980s was undoubtedly John Walker, who headed the spy ring that delivered critical naval communications secrets to the Soviets.

The general public is most aware of Soviets in the United States through their diplomatic missions, especially the one to the United Nations, and the various consulates. Until 1986, the Soviets had about 250 diplomats in their mission to the United Nations, a controversial number because it is proportionately so much larger than that of other nations' delegations. In 1987, for example, France fielded a U.N. mission of 15 diplomats and 50 staff members; West Germany had 30 diplomats, 20 support personnel, and 10 local employees. U.S. officials have been concerned about the U.N. mission because the Soviets used it as a cover for illegal espionage activities. For many years, the departments of State and Defense grudgingly acquiesced to the Soviets' inordinately large delegation. But by the mid-1980s, it had become well known that many of its members (the most recent and infamous being Gennadi Zakharov) were pursuing technology-transfer assignments given by the GKNT, KGB, and other groups. Sometimes the delegates themselves were members of the intelligence organizations; as many as 25 to 30 percent of the delegates were KGB agents, according to the FBI. Others were "free-lancing" or taking "sick leave" to handle espionage activities in addition to carrying out diplomatic duties.[20]

As a result, in March 1986, then U.S. Defense Secretary Caspar W. Weinberger demanded that the Soviets reduce the size of their U.N. mission to 218 before October 1986 and to 170 by April 1988. In October 1986, the United States expelled 25 people from the Soviet mission, of whom 5 were thought to be KGB agents, and asked 56 others to leave. (In return, the Soviets expelled 10 U.S. diplomats from the Soviet Union.) The expulsions did not affect the almost 450 employees of the Soviet Foreign Ministry who work for the U.N. Secretariat on an on-loan basis. Even delicate diplomatic efforts, such as the signing of the Intermediate-range Nuclear Forces (INF) treaty in December 1987, did not deter Soviet espionage activities. One week after the treaty signing, the United States caught and expelled a Soviet diplomat at the United Nations because of alleged spying on a U.S. defense contractor. Because obtaining information of Soviet origin is difficult and because these employees are in the United States on loan, the United States sometimes cannot carefully check their background to see if any of them are Soviet intelligence officers. (To guarantee their choice assignments, these employees agree to send back to the Soviet government about $20 million in hard currency. Arkady N. Shevchenko describes the kickback system in his book, *Breaking with Moscow*. He tells how Soviet nationals employed at the U.N. Secretariat cash their paychecks before going to the Soviet mission's bookkeeper, to whom they turn in all their wages. The bookkeeper then returns to them their "salary." One Soviet officer received about $2,000 a month; he was required to return approximately $1,200 of it to the Soviet government, being allowed to keep only $800.[21])

The Soviet embassy also gives officials of the U.S. intelligence community sleepless nights. Many Soviet high-technology espionage missions have begun at the Washington embassy. Thomas Cavanaugh called the Soviet consulate in San Francisco and the embassy in Washington several times in 1984 and 1985 to establish contact with a Soviet official to whom he could sell his company's stealth bomber secrets for $25,000. In June 1986, Col. Vladmir Izmailov, a top-ranking Soviet Air Force officer assigned to the Washington embassy, was caught trying to steal military secrets. An FBI agent posed as a U.S. Air Force officer in a sting operation to thwart Izmailov. Before making the sting, the FBI watched Izmailov carefully. It closed the trap when the agent dropped off secret documents containing information about the SDI, the stealth bomber, the cruise missile, and the Trans-Atmospheric Vehicle, a hypersonic passenger jet, at a location in Prince Georges County, Md., where Izmailov had left $41,100. When he realized that his contact was in reality an FBI agent, Izmailov struggled briefly but succumbed to arrest. He was expelled from the United States.[22] The Soviets employ 225 diplomats in the Washington embassy and are hoping to move into a new embassy on Mt. Alto, whose elevated location will enable them to eavesdrop electronically on government buildings throughout the city.

The U.S.S.R.'s San Francisco consulate has also played a role in the theft of technology secrets. The building at 2790 Green Street has a sinister appearance, and its crown of antennas are particularly disconcerting: Only 35 miles away is Silicon Valley and some of the most sensitive technology in the United States. The antennas are also in the line of sight of

Oakland and downtown San Francisco, Marin County microwave installations, the Mare Island Naval Shipyard in Vallejo (a nuclear submarine
base), and a naval base on Treasure Island in the San Francisco Bay. The
size of the consulate was also reduced at the request of the U.S. government in late 1986; it now houses approximately twenty-six Soviet employees. State Department spokesman Charles Redman pointed out at the
time that the expelled Soviets were involved in "activities incompatible
with their diplomatic status."[23] Although law enforcement officers in Silicon Valley noticed a temporary decrease in technology-theft attempts after the consulate's reduction, it is likely that rerouting of acquisitions has
by now minimized any impact of the expulsions. The FBI believes that at
least one-third of the original thirty-eight member staff was affiliated
with Soviet intelligence services and thus involved in some aspect of illegal technology acquisition.

The San Francisco consulate has been used as a meeting place for
Americans acting as agents. Both A/1C Bruce Ott and former FBI agent
Richard Miller met their contacts there. In 1986, Ott, an administrative
clerk at Beale Air Force Base (Yuba County), attempted to sell information about the fast, high-flying SR-71 Blackbird reconnaissance aircraft to
Soviet agents. He was arrested when he tried to sell documents to FBI
undercover agents posing as Soviet spies in a Davis, Calif., motel. In
1984, Miller, the first FBI agent to be accused and convicted of espionage, was prosecuted for selling classified information to two Soviet
emigrés, Nikolai and Svetlana Ogorodnikov, in southern California for
cash and gold.

Soviet diplomats share with their colleagues of other nations im-
munity from U.S. prosecution for espionage, but they still have to be
cautious. And although it may seem irresistibly tempting to a Soviet
diplomat stationed in San Francisco to drive into Silicon Valley for a
closer look at, say, Dalmo Victor, it is unlikely that he will take the chance.
The U.S. government has made it clear that it will immediately expel any
Soviet found in the valley, one of several areas to which access by Soviet
citizens is restricted by the State Department.

Restricted areas comprise industrial zones throughout the United
States with a high concentration of technology companies, government
contractors, and classified activities. Defense-related activities in certain

areas also make them off-limits. The State Department publishes a detailed map of the United States with the restricted zones carefully outlined.[24] Congress, pointing to the close relationship between the Soviet Union and the Eastern European satellites, has turned up the heat during the past several years by attempting to make the areas off-limits to members of all Soviet bloc foreign missions.

SOVIET SPY RECRUITING

Given the caution Soviet diplomats must observe and the tendency of some American high-technology industry employees to turn against their employers (or seek free-lance wages), it seems natural that Soviet intelligence officers would recruit Americans to perform many of their illegal technology-collection missions. Such recruits shield the Soviets from discovery and potential banishment from attractive posts in the United States. Even more important, the Americans have greater access to the technological objects of Soviet desire.

Soviet intelligence officers look for employees who have a particular vulnerability or a character weakness. A combination of access to sensitive information and a potentially compromising personal situation is a most desirable profile for the object of recruitment. Many contacts occur at electronics industry conventions where confidential meetings are normally held for a variety of legitimate reasons. Military personnel and government workers are also targets of recruitment.

Among the Soviet intelligence officers present in the United States primarily to recruit Americans was Gennadi Zakharov. U.S. intelligence experts suspected him of being the leader of a large network of technology spies during his four years at the United Nations. He likely reported to Directorate T. A Ukrainian physicist and former GKNT member, he worked for $50,000 a year as a scientific officer at the United Nations' Center for Science and Technology for Development, which promotes technology transfer to Third World countries.[25] He was not an official member of the Soviet mission to the United Nations and therefore did not have diplomatic immunity.

The FBI arrested Zakharov as he met a contact, Keakh Bhoge, on a subway platform in Queens, N.Y., in 1986. Bhoge's story illustrates some of the methods used by Soviet agents to lure Americans into their employ. Zakharov first met Bhoge at Queens College in New York when Bhoge was a third-year student in computer science. Another student at the college mentioned to Bhoge that a Soviet professor, actually Zakharov, was looking for a researcher, and Bhoge signed on to do the research. In addition to asking for materials from libraries, Zakharov asked him if he could get classified material. He smiled when Bhoge declined.[26] Bhoge contacted the FBI and continued to work for Zakharov as instructed by his FBI handlers. Later, even when Bhoge didn't perform the requested research, Zakharov wanted to pay him for his efforts, a ploy designed to make Bhoge feel indebted to his employer. At one time, Zakharov asked Bhoge to sign a receipt for payment for a set of photocopies Bhoge had delivered. (Signed receipts provide blackmail material if an agent becomes difficult to handle.) At another time, he told Bhoge to drive his new car to Dover, N.J., and wait for another car and man to meet him there; the man never showed. Later, Zakharov explained that the incident was a test to see if Bhoge would be a reliable agent, capable of following directions. The recruitment was in full force.

After cultivating the relationship with Bhoge for two years, Zakharov convinced him to get a job with a U.S. defense contractor where he would have access to classified technical information, particularly in the field of artificial intelligence or robotics. Bhoge agreed, left Queens College after receiving his degree, and went to work for a company in Queens that manufactures unclassified components for use in military aircraft engines. Zakharov asked for and received microfiche relating to robotics and artificial intelligence.[27] In May 1986 Bhoge signed a formal ten-year espionage contract with Zakharov to provide classified information in return for monetary payment. But later, on the afternoon of Aug. 23, 1986, Bhoge met Zakharov on an elevated subway station platform in Queens to deliver an envelope containing classified documents. This time, however, Bhoge had planned his delivery to Zakharov with the FBI so that two FBI agents could arrest Zakharov as the exchange of documents for payment occurred. When he handed over the envelope, one agent arrested Zakharov. After Zakharov's arrest but before the United States could bring him to trial, he was returned to the Soviet Union in September 1986, when the Soviets released Nicholas Daniloff, a *U.S. News*

& World Report correspondent who had been apprehended by the Soviets
on spying charges.

Recruitment of Americans by Soviet intelligence agencies is a
refined art. The FBI obtained a copy of a 1962 KGB manual entitled
"Training for the Recruitment of Americans in the U.S.A. and in Third
Countries." Although the document is old, the FBI feels that its techniques are still used today. One section describes the exploitable characteristics of vulnerable company employees. Among the traits Soviet
recruiters are instructed to look for in their targets are: strong sympathy
with the Soviet Union; financial problems; a desire to seek revenge
against employer or country; vices and eccentricities; a feeling of intrigue
about being a spy; and an intense commitment to world peace. The KGB
document also tells agents to look for American scientists interested in
establishing contacts with their counterparts in the U.S.S.R. It outlines
how an employee's dissatisfaction with aspects of the U.S. government
can be a motivation for spying. Suggestions for identifying recruitment
opportunities take up several pages, as do techniques for payment of U.S.
agents. Blackmail is not often used these days, because Americans are
known to succumb easily to direct financial rewards. Also, spies
recruited by the use of blackmail are generally not loyal for long. Other
prime candidates for recruitment come from among the Soviet emigré
population in the United States. If they still have family in the Soviet
Union, the emigrés are often extremely vulnerable, especially if their rela-
tives' health and safety appear threatened. In a few cases, the Soviets
have sent bogus emigrés to the United States, knowing that they will be
drawn into American society and will sometimes obtain useful employment, perhaps with a high-technology company.

As illustrated by Keakh Bhoge's experience, Soviet intelligence
officers take several steps before successfully recruiting an agent. First,
they must position themselves in a location, with a credible cover, that
will give them access to potential recruits. For example, a KGB or GRU
officer may come to the United States as a visiting scholar at one of the
American universities that have strong programs in advanced technologies. Next, officers need to spot, screen, and select a potential recruit.
They use their knowledge of the exploitable characteristics outlined in the
KGB manual. To identify potential candidates, Soviet intelligence officers

peruse high-technology periodicals, rosters of those giving speeches at high technology-related conferences, and official biographies of U.S. government employees. A stage called "development" comes next— after the potential agent is identified but before he or she is actively recruited. The KGB officer then seeks ways to make the candidate feel indebted, such as doing small favors or paying for social events for the candidate and the candidate's family. During the development process, intelligence officers will often give a U.S. prospect their address and phone number in case of emergencies. They may also coach the potential spy in clandestine photography and surveillance techniques. At times, officers will attempt to interest candidates in traveling to a foreign country where they might speak more freely. In some cases, Americans are eager to follow this process simply because of the image of intrigue promoted by spy films and books. Intelligence officers take as much time as is needed; a successful recruitment will do much in Moscow to further an officer's career.

When Soviet intelligence officers feel that a candidate is ready for recruitment, they will attempt to get the American to state an interest in helping the Soviet Union. During development and recruitment, officers create the impression that their relationship is confidential. (However, officers surely inform their superiors of their recruitment efforts.) Recruitment actually occurs when the officer is successful in getting the potential agent to obtain either equipment or documents in return for payment.

Over the years, the motivation of an American who decides to collect technology for the Soviets has gone through some changes that may be instructive. During the 1950s, Americans either offered themselves or were recruited for ideological reasons. Disenchantment was rife; the U.S. government and the seeming injustices of a capitalistic society were but a few of the many objects of scorn by American malcontents. In the 1960s, the Vietnam War was added to the roster. Although a later example, Christopher Boyce, who worked for TRW in the 1970s while selling his employer's secret satellite plans to the Soviets, was angry about U.S. intelligence activities. Some American agents believed that Soviet socialism offered a better, more egalitarian society.

Since the 1970s, however, Soviet recruiters have been confronted with a less ideological, more content population; yet they have found holes in the new fabric of society and have wasted no time in increasing their size. Lower-level employees have succumbed to drug habits that require extracurricular financing. Others have been enticed by sex or have given way to basic greed. The Soviets have less need to use their own intelligence organizations for technology acquisitions because an increasing supply of Americans have been willing to spy for money. KGB officers have reportedly come up with an English acronym for a potential recruit's desirable traits: MICE (money, ideology, compromise, and ego).[28]

Recent cases of technological espionage in which money played an important role are those of Ronald Pelton (arrested in 1985, convicted in 1986) and the Walker family (1985). Pelton sold National Security Agency (NSA) communications and surveillance secrets worth billions to the Soviets. To Pelton, the $35,000 he received was a large amount of money. The Walker case involved substantially greater sums. John Walker, Jr., the leader of the family spy ring, and his son and brother eventually ended up in prison for selling classified information to the Soviet Union. John Walker served in the U.S. Navy from 1955 to 1976, for ten of those years as a radioman, deputy director of the radioman school in San Diego, Calif., and communications officer. During that time, he had access to thousands of classified documents and top secret encryption codes. In the late 1960s, Walker began selling his prize booty to the Soviet Union, apparently because of financial difficulties resulting from a failing business. In 1968, his wife inadvertently became aware of his illicit dealings by discovering some papers on his desk.

While in San Diego as an instructor for the navy in 1969, Walker met another radioman, Jerry A. Whitworth. Because Walker planned to retire from the navy soon, he regarded Whitworth as a possible collaborator and successor.[29] Sometime between 1970 and 1975, Whitworth began to work with Walker, providing him with additional top secret cryptographic information. When Walker left the service in 1976, he started an investigative service business in Norfolk, Va. During the time the two worked together, Walker paid Whitworth cash amounts ranging from

$6,000 to $100,000. By the time he was arrested in 1985, Whitworth had received $332,000.

Walker's brother, Arthur, a retired navy officer, began to smuggle classified navy documents to John in 1980. Walker's son, Michael, an enlisted man in the navy, began to work for his father while aboard the aircraft carrier U.S.S. *Nimitz* during 1983. He brought his father classified information and in return received $1,000 from him. Finally, in 1985, the FBI arrested John Walker by following him to a drop site in Maryland where he was attempting to deliver a bag of documents to his Soviet contact. Federal prosecutors in San Francisco estimate that John Walker received almost $600,000 for his espionage activities.[30]

COMMERCIAL COVER: TECHNOLOGY FOR TRADE'S SAKE

KGB officers as well as other gatherers of technology, such as GRU operatives, also use trade relations between the United States and the Soviet Union to gain access to high-technology secrets. Because foreign trade is essential to the management of a capitalist, free-trade economy, Americans find it difficult to refuse links between the two countries that might translate into business contracts for U.S. companies. And these trade links enable the Soviets to establish legitimate footholds in the United States in a nonthreatening way.

Soviet trade officials can contact U.S. companies and meet individual executives under the pretext of improving or establishing trade relations with the Soviet bloc, when in fact they may be fulfilling high-technology requests of their government. Also, the Soviets often acquire technology through commercial fronts, which sometimes take the form of companies employing Western or American personnel. Unlike Soviet diplomats' activities, which are carefully proscribed, these representatives' movements are not restricted, and they operate in the United States with more freedom. They can peruse at will U.S. corporate and scientific libraries and lunch with American scientists, all within the context of furthering trade contacts. The FBI counts approximately thirty Soviet com-

mercial visitors in the United States each month.[31] The GRU has made
frequent use of commercial covers for espionage ever since the 1920s.[32]

The oldest and strongest Soviet trade foothold in the United States is
the Amtorg Trading Corporation (*Amerikanskaya torgovaya*). Amtorg acts
as a liaison between Soviet foreign trade organizations and U.S. companies and related trade associations. It represents the Soviet Union in
contract negotiations with the United States and monitors the execution
of contracts between the U.S.S.R. and U.S. firms but does not initiate business between the two. Amtorg often sends corporate representatives
from the United States to the Soviet Union and enables Soviets to visit
U.S. companies.

Thought to be the earliest U.S. base for Soviet espionage activities,
Amtorg has housed some of the most active Soviet intelligence officers in
the United States, a number of whom have admitted their Amtorg ties in
congressional hearings or during FBI interrogations. Examples of the
company's connections with KGB and GRU officers abound. A GRU
officer, Moishe Stern, directed military espionage from 1927 to 1931 while
working out of the Amtorg office. Before returning to the Soviet Union in
1937, where he was subsequently executed, he tried to recruit an employee at Arma Corporation in New York City to gain access to Arma's
classified work. According to William R. Corson and Robert T. Crowley
in their book, *The New KGB*, at least forty Soviet intelligence officers have
been associated with Amtorg since its establishment in the United
States.[33] In January 1980, the U.S. State Department established a ceiling
of sixty-nine for Soviet commercial trade representatives, with thirty-
nine of those at Amtorg. In 1988, the FBI suspected that 30 to 40 percent of
the employees working in the New York Amtorg office were members of
Soviet intelligence agencies.

Amtorg was the first organization established by the Soviet government in the United States. It was incorporated in 1924 in the State of New
York with specific provisions for the location of its office in Manhattan
and its existence until 2024. Henry Ford was responsible for a major portion of the business transacted through Amtorg during its first three
years, when he sold tractors to the Soviets; in 1929, Ford agreed to build
an automobile plant in the Soviet Union. The plant, whose existence was
made possible by negotiations through Amtorg, eventually produced

$30 million in revenue for Ford. Armand Hammer, who received the first concession for business with the Soviets in 1921, has continued to do millions of dollars' worth of transactions with them, some of which has come from contracts negotiated with the help of Amtorg.

Amtorg was heavily involved in U.S.-Soviet trade negotiations during 1924–1933 while the United States assisted the Soviets in implementing their first Five-Year Plan (1928–33). By 1930, 86 percent of U.S.-Soviet business was transacted through Amtorg.[34] During World War II, when the Lend-Lease protocols were being administered, Amtorg also played a major role, carrying out all U.S.-Soviet transactions under the law until its end in 1947. As part of its activities, Amtorg sent representatives to U.S. factories to accept materials; they were in charge of shipping the materials to the Soviet Union. Between 1927 and 1949, the Soviets had uninhibited access to U.S. patents via Amtorg, either through direct contact with the U.S. Patent Office or through a publishing company operating on behalf of the Soviet government called the Four Continent Book Company.[35]

During the 1930s, when Soviet-U.S. business ties were at a peak, Amtorg employees and sponsored representatives numbered more than 1,000. By requiring that contracts between the United States and the Soviet Union provide for the admission of Soviet inspectors into U.S. companies, Amtorg could justify increasing its staff. In July 1930, it employed 578 such inspectors. A survey of factories on the U.S. Government's Procurement Planning and Industrial Mobilization Lists enabled the Soviets to gain firsthand knowledge of U.S. technology with the cooperation of the American firms, which were eager to court the Soviets as business prospects.[36]

Today, Amtorg continues to play an important role in East-West trade. Recent Soviet efforts to promote U.S.-Soviet joint ventures are channeled through the company, which keeps Soviet officials apprised of interested U.S. businesses. Among the Soviet trade organizations it represents are Elorg and Licensintorg; the latter specializes in the exchange of scientific and engineering ideas. In addition, part of Amtorg's official mission is to conduct market research on U.S. companies. Its employees study various industries and become familiar with both public and private firms, their products, and key personnel.

Because of the increasing number of proposals from U.S. companies, effusive optimism colors the comments of the Amtorg employees seeking technology-related joint ventures. In late 1987, Sergei Frolov, senior economist at Amtorg, expressed this enthusiasm when he said, "We're excited, trying to push them all [i.e., the venture proposals] forward." He also pointed out that the new joint ventures would "build new links between Soviet organizations and U.S. companies."[37]

Other Soviet commercial fronts can be trade delegations, offices where trade officials work, or such organizations as the news service Tass and the airline Aeroflot. These fronts provide the means by which Soviet intelligence operatives may gain both legal and illegal access to high technology in the United States. Two other front organizations are Intourist, a Soviet tourist agency, and the U.S.S.R. Chamber of Commerce and Industry, which has a representative in New York. In 1980, the CIA published a directory identifying 129 Soviet trade officials working in the United States. (By comparison, fewer than 10 per country served the rest of the world, except for Cuba and India.) The FBI located 130 trade officials in 1987. The count, though, is controversial and subject to different methods of calculation. For example, the FBI stated that 230 trade officials served in the United States in 1985. But as of February 1988, the State Department counted only 65 Soviet commercial and trade representatives in the United States, including those who worked for Aeroflot, Amtorg, Intourist, and other Soviet companies. Tass apparently brought along 40 additional Soviet employees.[38]

That Tass provided a front for KGB activities was indicated in 1981, when a KGB officer who worked for Tass in Holland, Vadim Leonov, was expelled. He supported the activities of the Dutch peace movement, which at that time was using violence against U.S. military installations. Before he left the country, he said, "Do you know how you can get 50,000 demonstrators at a certain place within a week? A message through my channels is sufficient."[39] According to the FBI, nine of eleven Aeroflot employees in the United States during the 1970s were GRU officers.

The Soviets are continually seeking ways to increase their presence and access to American know-how. Financial links can be a subtle way for them to obtain Western equipment and technology—unless they are discovered. They were in 1975, when they attempted to acquire three northern California banks and interests in a fourth: the Peninsula National Bank of Burlingame, the First National Bank of Fresno, Tahoe National Bank of South Tahoe, and Camino California Bank of San Francisco. The KGB sent $70 million in letters of credit through the Moscow Narodny Bank to a Singapore businessman, Amos Dawe, via Panama and Tennessee. He was in the process of using the money on behalf of the Soviets when he was found out by the CIA; the transaction failed. The bank acquisition would have given the Soviets access to Silicon Valley companies that held loans and placed investments through the banks, because any company seeking loans or investors must provide to a bank many confidential details of its business and give it the opportunity to tour its facilities. Also, if the Soviet-owned banks had become investors in a high-technology firm, they could have gained additional inside information.

Another trade-related front for the Soviets is the U.S.S.R. Chamber of Commerce and Industry, mentioned before. In a January 1987 report, the U.S. State Department outlined the intelligence-gathering activities that take place from this Soviet organization. Its methods include the use of international trade exhibitions to gather technical information and the falsifying of information on export license applications to enable U.S. equipment to enter the Soviet Union. The FBI maintains that the GRU is represented in the organization and uses it to collect information relating to high-priority technology, such as robotics. In addition to being on the board of the U.S.-U.S.S.R. Trade and Economic Council, KGB Lt. Gen. Yevgeny P. Pitovranov has been active as an officer of the chamber.

One of the chamber's most successful means of technology collection is its use of inspectors who check equipment ordered by the Soviet Union before it leaves the U.S. factory. Sometimes the Soviet inspector can stay at the factory for months, gathering unauthorized access to technical information and perhaps using the position to recruit scientists and engineers as agents. U.S. intelligence officials also suspect that the chamber's computers (an IBM 370 and a Digital PDP 11/70) tap into U.S. on-line data bases.[40]

CORPORATE GOLD MINES

The competitive environment of America's high-technology industry can well serve the needs of Soviet agents searching for eyes and ears in the U.S. technical community. Also, the number of thefts of high-technology equipment points to the industry's vulnerability. Many corporations seem to leave themselves wide open to industrial espionage—by competitors or by the Soviet Union.

The American corporation and its employees play important roles in the Soviet technology-supply network. Rather than casting a broad net, Soviet intelligence officers typically set their sights on specific areas, companies, and individuals. (The KGB, however, will not turn down technology an agent collected simply because it wasn't officially targeted.) Silicon Valley, an area south of San Francisco with more than 1,300 firms dedicated to making high-technology products, has been the target of many well-known Soviet spies and smugglers. Millions of dollars' worth of chips and other computer components were stolen from the valley each year, some of it ending up in Soviet hands. Most of the chips, however, reach the Soviets through overseas diversion schemes. Spying and thefts also occur in other areas of the country where high-technology companies are clustered, such as the Route 128 belt around Boston, and southern California, North Carolina, and Colorado.

Sometimes a Soviet agent will reap technical benefits from a falling-out between employer and employee. In 1986, Allen John Davies, an employee at Ford Aerospace & Communications Corporation in Palo Alto, Calif., sought revenge for being involuntarily released by the U.S. Air Force two years previously. During the two years, he fought with the air force as it attempted to collect his reenlistment bonus. Using the "secret" clearance he had obtained in the service, he tried to retaliate by giving the Soviets details of an air force reconnaissance project. The Soviet "officer" he contacted turned out to be an undercover FBI agent.

In 1978, James Catanich was terminated from his job at National Semiconductor Corporation because he was suspected of stealing chip designs and passing them to Peter Gopal, a Silicon Valley entrepreneur accused in 1980 of selling those designs to the Soviet bloc during the late

1970s. Before leaving the company building for the last time, the angry Catanich copied the plans for seven devices onto a computer tape, put the tape under his ski jacket, and walked out, marveling at how easy it was to take with him some of the company's most valuable assets. He was caught in 1978, tried in 1980, and sentenced in 1981.

San Jose (Calif.) police Lieut. Tim W. Skalland, in charge of the Burglary Prevention Unit, is often embroiled in Silicon Valley technology thefts. He notes that almost one-half of the large truck thefts in Silicon Valley in 1987 involved high-technology products. In one such theft, in March 1987, a trailer full of Paladin Software Company's (now VisiCorp) latest word-processing software sat in a trailer truck near its shipping dock in Santa Clara. James Fred Delgado, a mobile-telephone installer, stole the trailer from the parking lot, taking the $1.9 million worth of software to a warehouse. There he and his partners in crime were in the process of finding buyers when the San Jose police caught them. Delgado had advertised the software, and undercover detectives posing as insurance adjusters contacted him. Skalland points out that most of the software thieves in Silicon Valley know that their booty becomes obsolete quickly, so they are always ready to sell quickly and cheaply.

In 1979, Intel discovered that 10,000 chips had been stolen from its production line. Because the chips had not gone through the testing procedure, the company had not yet placed its logo on each chip, providing any future recipient with a clean surface for other marking. The chips ended up in teletype machines in West Germany, but high failure rates enabled authorities to trace the theft. The largest chip theft in Silicon Valley was in 1981, when almost $3 million worth of chips were stolen from Monolithic Memories, eliminating 20 percent of its chip inventory.[41] Whether the chips ended up in the Soviet Union is unknown, but the incident illustrates the security dilemma facing many companies that deal in potentially critical high technology.

Chip heists and other thefts are made easier in Silicon Valley and other such areas by the inbred nature and the close proximity of high-tech firms to one another. Furthermore, employees, particularly engineers, move from one company to another, carrying with them corporate high-technology secrets.

U.S. corporate security—or, more often, the lack of it—can also abet the Soviet effort. Many corporate records are now contained in computer data bases, which makes them an easy target for snoopers, particularly Soviet agents who tap corporate microwave communications. Most high-technology companies do not employ sophisticated data encryption systems (unless they are government contractors working on classified projects, and then they are required to use KY-7 scrambler phones) and electronic mail systems; entire chip or computer design records are free for the taking by those able to gain access to corporate computers.

Even shipments of technology, either products or documentation, through express couriers present export-law enforcers with a dilemma. The inspection of the U.S. mail or of a private carrier is generally an illegal procedure, and thus this threat to corporate security continues to exist. In the past, the problem did not exist because computers were too big to be sent in a Federal Express or an Airborne package. But now that technology theft can be of software, documentation, and small electronic components, diverters in Vienna can receive valuable semiconductors overnight for only $35.

Even though the government issues security-procedure requirements for companies engaged in classified work, not all are careful about following the recommendations. The Lockheed Corporation, for example, became the subject of concern in 1986, when it could not locate more than 1,400 classified government documents at its Burbank, Calif., plant, which was working on the F-19 fighter jet that uses stealth technology. The government was so incensed at Lockheed that it threatened to cut off contract payments, insisted on new security procedures for the company, and pulled some clearances.[42] In October 1987, the Defense Investigative Service reported that other government contractors probably had similar security problems.[43]

In 1985, a senior U.S. intelligence official responsible for protecting sensitive government information told the media that Soviet agents used electronic surveillance on a number of large U.S. corporations. During the late 1970s and early 1980s, high-technology firms were making so much money so quickly that they grew lax about security, but difficult times in the industry during the mid-1980s caused many corporations to take security more seriously. Major oil companies, for example, encode seismological and drilling data when they transmit it electronically.[44] Some companies now routinely shred unused documents, lock rooms, issue computer passwords, and require security personnel to make regular reviews.

Janitorial services, however, fall outside these procedures and can be potential channels for high-technology theft. Maintenance personnel have access to corporations at night when the premises are unsupervised. Some corporations contract with outside services, whose employees then have access to corporate records and computers, not to mention the material in wastebaskets. Janitorial personnel are not paid high wages and could conceivably, for modest pay, be persuaded to provide whatever they might otherwise throw away—say, drawings of chip designs—to competitors or to Soviet or Eastern bloc agents. Some companies, Digital for one, are attempting to plug this security loophole by using their own internal janitorial service. The same goes for security services. Outside security firms are also privy to corporate secrets, and although the firms themselves may be above suspicion, their employees come and go. Some corporations prefer to provide these services internally to improve security. But when companies cut administrative budgets, their own janitorial or security services often suffer. For example, in the fall of 1986, Intel trimmed its costs by laying off 150 people from its internal security staff, opting instead to hire an outside firm.

U.S. high-technology companies might also unknowingly give the Soviets access to corporate technical secrets through telephone voice and data lines. Most use unsecured telephone lines linked by terrestrial microwave and satellite dishes. Some semiconductor firms download mask design data to their overseas factories through unsecured telephone lines. It is well known that the Soviets eavesdrop on U.S. telephone lines from their Washington, D.C., embassy, from their San Francisco consulate, from receiving towers in Lourdes, Cuba, from offshore AGIs (intelligence-gathering ships), and from clandestine spy satellites. The Soviet listening facility in Lourdes was begun in 1960 and is now maintained by 2,100 technicians. Communications between the ground station there and Moscow are practically instantaneous.[45] The KGB can also employ a more mundane and inexpensive technique for corporate spying: the use of American recruits to listen to transmissions from corporate satellite dishes. Although U.S. government agencies will not confirm such occurrences, it is worth considering how open most high-technology firms leave themselves to theft of secrets by their competitors and especially by the Soviets.

DIVERSION: HIGH-TECH SMUGGLERS

The most widely known technique employed by the Soviets for dual-use technology acquisitions is espionage, but probably the more common is diversion or, in the vernacular, smuggling. An article in the Aug. 12, 1985, issue of *U.S. News & World Report* stated that diversionary schemes account for 75 percent of all illegal high-technology shipments to the Soviet Union.[46]

The art of export diversion is practiced at various levels of sophistication and complexity. A pure and simple form of diversion takes place when a Soviet representative (an American agent or front company, for example) purchases a computer from a U.S. manufacturer and illegally exports it to Moscow. Such a purchase usually involves obtaining an export license by providing fraudulent information to the U.S. Commerce Department or shipping the goods without an export license. Another form of diversion occurs when the Soviets purchase an American-manufactured computer from a European distributor. The distributor illegally ships the goods to Moscow after informing the U.S. Commerce Department that the equipment will stay in Western Europe.

The Soviets benefit from more complex diversion schemes that involve a network of front (or fake) companies. A Soviet trade organization will send a purchase order to a Soviet-sponsored purchasing company in Western Europe. A contact in the United States will then ship the equipment to the European company, which in turn will send it to the customer in the Soviet Union, often through at least one or two other intermediary destinations to confuse anyone tracking it. Many shipments leave the United States through Los Angeles, Boston, or New York City for destinations in Western Europe, South Africa, or Asia, ultimately to be diverted to Moscow.

Well-worn paths also exist from such U.S. manufacturing centers as Silicon Valley and New Jersey, to intermediary destinations such as West

Germany, and then to Moscow. A typical diversion plan might begin at an electronics trade show where a KGB agent approaches an American semiconductor sales representative. The agent, claiming to represent a small manufacturing company in West Germany, indicates an interest in purchasing a small number of semiconductors. The agent and the sales representative exchange business cards, and the agent takes product literature and proposes that they meet later for drinks. The agent brings a briefcase to the next meeting and opens it, discreetly revealing its contents: several rolls of $100 bills. By this time, the agent has proposed to pay for the semiconductor order in cash, provided that the sales representative ships the chips as soon as possible and in the strictest confidence. The agent gives instructions for sending the chips to a seemingly innocuous destination in one of West Germany's shipping centers, labeling them as costume jewelry, and packing them in shipping materials that will not reveal the actual contents or the identity of the sales representative's firm. If all goes well during the conversation, the agent may allude to future orders, larger and even more lucrative than the initial one. The chips are sent to the company in West Germany, actually a Soviet front managed by the KGB, which then immediately ships the chips to the requestor in Moscow.

As it does spies, greed motivates diverters. For example, in 1981, Hughes Aircraft Company received a $637,070 cash-in-advance order for electronic testing equipment. Hughes reported the suspicious order to the Customs Service and, after an investigation, learned that the products were destined for Bulgaria and the Soviet Union. A group of American and European businessmen had agreed to purchase the equipment and to resell it through the Bulgarians to the Soviets for $5 million, a handsome markup.[47]

One of the best-known high-technology diverters is Richard Müller, who has, up to this time, eluded the grasp of the U.S. Customs Service, the Commerce Department, and the Justice Department, the agencies that enforce export controls on dual-use high-technology products. A West German, Müller started his lucrative smuggling career in the 1970s but first came to the attention of U.S. officials in 1983, when he attempted to divert a $1.5 million Digital VAX 11/782 computer and $9 million worth of state-of-the-art semiconductor manufacturing equipment to the Soviet Union.

The computer is popular in the Soviet Union because it can be used in military guidance systems and in the design of semiconductors. Müller set up at least six front companies in South Africa that would receive crates of VAX components from the United States. For this particular diversion, he used the Microelectronics Research Institute (MRI) in Cape Town. He then planned to ship seven 40-foot containers carrying the restricted equipment plus a variety of nonrestricted items to two locations: Four were to go to Sweden and the rest to West Germany. In November 1983, the U.S. Department of Justice and the Customs Service requested that the Germans seize the equipment in West Germany, but the semiconductor manufacturing equipment got through to the Soviets. Müller is at large in Europe, a fugitive from U.S. justice. In January 1988, a federal grand jury indicted him for illegally shipping computer equipment to South Africa between 1980 and 1983. Müller could receive a fine of as much as $10 million or spend a maximum of 30 years in jail. The U.S. government will attempt to extradite Müller to the United States to stand trial.[48] His name and the names of his known front companies are on the Commerce Department's denial list, meaning that any application for a license to export goods to him or his firms is immediately denied and usually investigated. Müller and three business associates, Sven Olof Håkansson (who in 1984 was sent to jail in Sweden for almost two years and is now free), Jim Nissmo, and Brian Möller-Butcher, however, are also still operating in Europe.[49]

In mid-1985, a Soviet intelligence officer arranged to have a middleman purchase computerized side-scan sonar devices, which are restricted for export, from a New England manufacturer. These devices detect and locate objects in the sea, particularly submarines. First, the Soviets had attempted to buy the instruments directly by contacting the manufacturer in New Hampshire. The U.S. Commerce Department refused the U.S. company an export license. The same manufacturer then received an order from a Japanese company and was again denied a license because of the recent Soviet order. Soon, another U.S. manufacturer received a similar order from a Norwegian company—in fact, the Soviet middleman. The U.S. company was finally issued an export license. From New England, the sonar devices traveled west to Louisiana and back east to New York, from where they left the United States for

Norway. From Norway, they were shipped to Sweden and on to Japan, where officials seized the containers, which were marked "ship parts," before they could depart for the Soviet Union on a trawler.[50]

An American, Charles J. McVey, Jr., allegedly took millions of dollars' worth of computer equipment from the United States to the Soviet Union through Switzerland. In addition to computers, McVey diverted satellite image processing systems and oscilloscopes, all without export licenses. In some cases, he shipped equipment from his companies in Orange County, Calif., to West Germany, on to Switzerland, and then finally to Moscow. He also allegedly sold IBM computer equipment to the Soviets and later sold them training courses for the machine.[51] His two accomplices were a representative of the trade organization for computers in the Soviet Union, Yuri Boyarinov, and a freight agent in Switzerland named Rolf Lienhard. As they were Bruchhausen's, former employees were McVey's nemeses. Two of them informed the U.S. Customs Service of his dealings with the Soviets. Customs then seized a McVey shipment of electronic gear bound for the Soviet Union.

Indicted in 1983, along with two accomplices, for the illegal export of state-of-the-art computers and peripherals to the Soviets through Switzerland, McVey had already been on the U.S. Customs Service most-wanted list for several years. The twenty-three-count indictment handed down in Los Angeles charged that he sold the restricted computers to the Soviets, starting in 1979 and ending in 1982, through a number of California-based front companies, such as Land Resources Management Inc., Facilities Management Ltd., and Vangard International Ltd. On Oct. 13, 1983, the Commerce Department put McVey on temporary export denial order; the order became permanent in 1986. The Commerce Department also fined the companies a total of $1,240,000.[52] McVey was indicted again in November 1987 for allegedly selling computer equipment in the Saxpy case.

McVey remained at large until one day in August 1987, when his life as a multimillionaire fugitive came to an abrupt end. By shifting his residence between houses in Switzerland and Malta, he had managed to elude capture. A fruitful piece of intelligence came to light when U.S. Customs agents learned that McVey took periodic fishing trips to the Yukon Territory in Canada. They alerted the Royal Canadian Mounted

Police that he might again enter their jurisdiction and distributed his photograph throughout their stations.

That August day, Royal Canadian Mounted Police Corp. Daniel Fudge was sitting in a restaurant in Teslin, Yukon, wondering if the elderly man opposite him was the man in the photograph on his office wall. McVey's 300 pounds were not easy to miss. Fudge left the restaurant and went to his office, where he verified his hunch. He returned to arrest the sixty-four-year-old McVey, who quietly submitted.[53] But McVey continued to be elusive. Law enforcement officials were appalled to discover that the warrant for arrest had been issued improperly and was thrown out by a Canadian judge. So, for 24 hours, McVey was again a free man, only to be recaptured to await extradition to the United States on the basis of making false statements. In June 1988 a Canadian court ruled that he could not be extradited because of inconsistencies between U.S. and Canadian extradition treaties.

Industrial espionage and illegal diversions such as McVey's have caught the attention of the American public, and if these were the Soviets' only means of obtaining cutting-edge equipment and know-how, the job of policing the flow of controlled high technology would be far more straightforward than it is. The Soviets can avail themselves of myriad legal methods to obtain the very equipment they sometimes resort to stealing or smuggling. As discussed in the next chapter, an irony of U.S. society is that one of its greatest strengths—its openness—can also be a weakness.

NOTES

1. Central Intelligence Agency, *Soviet Acquisition of Militarily Significant Western Technology: An Update* (Washington, D.C.: 1985), p. 16.

2. Robert A. Manning, with Steven Emerson and Charles Fenyvesi, "Casey's CIA: New Clout, New Danger," *U.S. News & World Report*, June 16, 1986, p. 24. No one really knows the exact numbers, which are highly sensitive Soviet state secrets. It is also unclear whether any numbers cited in the press include the large contingent of border guards.

3. U.S. Department of Justice, Federal Bureau of Investigation *Focus on KGB Espionage in the United States* (Washington, D.C.: 1987), p. 6.

4. John Barron, *KGB: The Secret Work of Soviet Secret Agents* (New York: Reader's Digest Press, 1974), p. 76.

5. Ladislav Bittman, professor, Boston University, Boston, Mass.: Interview, Nov. 6, 1987. Same, *The KGB and Soviet Disinformation—An Insider's View* (McLean, Va.: Brassey's International Defense Publishers, 1985), pp. 205–6.

6. Ibid.

7. U.S., Congress, Senate, Select Committee on Intelligence, *Meeting the Espionage Challenge: A Review of United States Counterintelligence and Security Programs* (Washington, D.C.: Government Printing Office, 1986), p. 20.

8. "Reports Soviets Are Increasing U.S. High-Tech Penetration," *Electronic News*, Aug. 5, 1985, p. 10.

9. Metal powder compounds, such as an alloy of aluminum with lithium, are used in the production of rods and structured bars for airplanes. (Source: Joel P. Clark and Merton C. Flemings, "Advanced Materials and the Economy," *Scientific American*, October 1986, p. 56.)

10. For example, graphite-epoxy composite material for aluminum alloys used in aircraft fuselages and fiberglass-reinforced plastics. (Source: Clark and Flemings, p. 56.)

11. *Soviet Acquisition*, pp. 18–19.

12. Jane Lester, Radio Liberty Research, Washington, D.C.: Interview, Feb. 23, 1988.

13. *Soviet Acquisition*, p. 3.

14. Philip Hanson, "Soviet Industrial Espionage," *Bulletin of the Atomic Scientists*, April 1987, p. 26.

15. *Soviet Acquisition*, p. 6.

16. *Soviet Acquisition*, pp. 20–21.

17. Philip Hanson, professor, University of Birmingham, England: Interview, Jan. 11, 1988.

18. Pamela Chavez, U.S. State Department, Statistics Branch, Washington, D.C.: Interview, Sept. 30, 1987.

19. Barron, p. 21.

20. Tom Morganthau, "Moscow's Prying Eyes," *Newsweek*, Sept. 30, 1985, p. 30.

21. Arkady N. Shevchenko, *Breaking with Moscow* (New York: Alfred A. Knopf, 1985), pp. 131–32.

22. "The U.S. Boots Out One Spy, Convicts Another, and Gets a Soviet Defector," *Christian Science Monitor*, June 23, 1986, p. 7; U.S. Department of Defense, "Recent Espionage Cases," August 1986, p. 17.

23. "San Francisco's Soviet Consulate Long Suspected as Home for Spies," United Press International, Domestic News, PM cycle, Oct. 22, 1986.

24. After World War II, the United States complained to the Soviet Union about the travel restrictions placed on Americans in the Soviet Union. To motivate the Soviets to open up areas for travel, the United States set up its own restricted areas to Soviet travelers in 1955. (Source: Carey Cavanaugh, U.S. State Department, Washington, D.C.: Interview, November 1987.)

25. Mary Anne Weaver, "U.S. Investigates Soviet Spying," *Christian Science Monitor*, Aug. 29, 1986, p. 9.

26. Michael Daly, "I Spy," *New York Magazine*, Apr. 6, 1987, p. 39.

27. Affidavit for an Arrest Warrant and Search Warrant, U.S. District Court of New York and Southern District of New York, United States against Gennadi Fyodorovich Zakharov, Appendix E. U.S., Congress, Senate, Select Committee on Intelligence, *Meeting the Espionage Challenge: A Review of United States Counterintelligence and Security Programs,* pp. 138–39.

28. U.S., Department of Justice, Federal Bureau of Investigation, *Framework for Understanding the Soviet Union Soviet Intelligence Organization, Training, Deployments, and Operations Focus on KGB Espionage in the United States* (1987), p. 18.

29. James Bamford, "The Walker Espionage Case," *Proceedings/Naval Review,* 1986, pp. 111–19.

30. Leida Schoggen, Assistant U.S. Attorney, San Francisco, California (prosecutor in the Walker/Whitworth case): Interview, May 4, 1987.

31. Sue Schnitzer, FBI, Washington, D.C.: Interview, Dec. 28, 1987.

32. William R. Corson and Robert T. Crowley, *The New KGB, Engine of Soviet Power* (New York: William Morrow & Co., 1985), p. 279.

33. Ibid., pp. 465–78.

34. Sergei Frolov, senior economist, Amtorg Trading Company, New York City, N.Y.: Interview, Mar. 25, 1987; Amtorg, "60th Anniversary, 1924–1984," (brochure), p. 3.

35. Corson and Crowley, p. 465. The Four Continent Book Store was acquired by Victor Kamkin Bookstores Inc. in 1983. Kamkin is located in Maryland with one outlet in New York City. Kamkin imports books from the U.S.S.R. and sells them along with U.S. books. (Source: Kamkin Bookstores, Rockville, Md.: Interview, Jan. 13, 1988.)

36. Ibid., pp. 298, 317, 465.

37. Sergei Frolov: Interview, Dec. 29, 1987.

38. Richard Johnson, U.S. State Department, Washington, D.C.: Interview, Dec. 28, 1987.

39. John Barron, *KGB Today, The Hidden Hand* (New York: Berkeley Publishing Corp., 1985), pp. 230–31.

40. U.S., Department of State, *Intelligence Collection in the U.S.S.R. Chamber of Commerce and Industry,* (Washington, D.C.: 1987), pp. iii and 2.

41. "Monolithic Discloses Theft of $2.7 Million in Integrated Circuits," *Wall Street Journal,* Dec. 3, 1981, p. 18.

42. Tim Carrington, "Lockheed Concedes Security Lax at California Site, Sets Auditor Probe," *Wall Street Journal,* July 25, 1986, p. 4.

43. Tim Carrington, "Pentagon Finds Lack of Secrecy in Defense Jobs," *Wall Street Journal,* Oct. 1, 1987, p. 4.

44. David Burnham, "Experts Study Effect on Law of Latest Electronic Services," *New York Times,* Mar. 18, 1985, p. 17.

45. Senator Daniel Patrick Moynihan, *Congressional Record,* Jan. 6, 1987, S262.

46. Robert S. Dudney, "How Soviets Steal U.S. High-Tech Secrets," *U.S. News & World Report,* Aug. 12, 1985, p. 33.

47. Robert Lindsey, "Need Joins Greed in Schemes to Smuggle U.S. Technology," *New York Times,* Feb. 4, 1986, pp. A1 and A7.

48. Joseph E. Digenova, U.S. District Attorney, District of Columbia: Press release, Jan. 28, 1988, pp. 1–3.

49. Brooks Olsen, Office of Export Enforcement, U.S. Department of Commerce, San Jose, Calif.: Interview, Dec. 18, 1987.

50. Dudney, p. 33.

51. William Fahey, U.S. District Attorney, Los Angeles: Interview, Feb. 24, 1988.

52. U.S., Department of Commerce, "Commerce Imposes $1.2 Million Fine, 30-Year Denial of Export Privileges for Illegal Export to Soviet Union," *Commerce News*, Aug. 11, 1986, p. 1.

53. "High-Tech Fugitive: The Big One Who Didn't Get Away," *San Jose Mercury News*, Aug. 21, 1987, p. 8F.

5

FREE SOCIETY, ALMOST FREE TECHNOLOGY

The open nature of U.S. society permits much high technology to flow legally to the Soviet Union. The FBI estimates that most of the American know-how and equipment that reaches Moscow does so through legitimate channels or through apparently legitimate channels turned to nefarious purposes by Soviet agents. This very openness affords anyone else in the world countless opportunities to study our most advanced technology. Consequently, our law enforcement agencies do not expend much effort watching all the legal pathways through which high-technology information flows. Given the Soviet Union's stated desire to obtain Western technological know-how and given the persistence of its intelligence-gathering network, it is only logical that the Soviets take advantage of the accessibility of U.S. high technology. Soviets in the United States enjoy the same access to information as U.S. citizens, with only few exceptions: Specific regions are restricted for travel because of their great concentration of high-technology and defense industries, and certain information is restricted by U.S. export laws. Whether it is researched by students on an exchange program or by KGB agents on a technology-gathering mission, unclassified high technology in the public domain is free for the taking.

Soviet scientists wander in and out of some U.S. research facilities and high-technology companies to learn of new developments, to understand technological trends, and to anticipate where new technical breakthroughs might occur. Soviet exchange students, trade delegates, diplomats, and some KGB officers (or their American recruits) at times have just as easy access to the same data. High-technology information then travels to the Soviet government, enabling it to develop new acquisition requests and assisting with setting priorities for military and civilian research and development projects.

The individuals involved in these collection efforts may be U.S. citizens, Soviet bloc emigrés in the United States, citizens of hostile foreign countries, Soviet bloc citizens with visas, or sometimes illegals (Soviet bloc citizens who come to the United States using false passports, become naturalized, and blend into American society). Whatever their vocation, those intent on passing U.S. high technology to the Soviets have a plethora of sources.

Legitimate Computer Sales to the Soviets

Those who follow the headlines about technology espionage and export diversion may be surprised to learn that some U.S. computer companies sell their products directly to the Soviet bloc in complete compliance with U.S. export laws. Obviously, if the Soviets could have their way and were not so concerned about the drain of hard currency, they would purchase all their high technology, such as advanced computers, instead of illegally acquiring it, because an official transaction would allow them to have open and continuing contact with the manufacturers for parts, maintenance, and enhancements. IBM has done business with the Soviets since the 1930s; more recently, many other U.S. computer firms, including Apple Computer, have sought markets in the U.S.S.R. In most cases, electronics companies sell outdated equipment not restricted by U.S. export laws or equipment that the Soviets are able to obtain through other sources. Soviets wishing to purchase U.S. equipment, usually those in a research institute or in an industrial enterprise familiar with U.S. computer literature, initiate contacts with the United States. They find the product they need and submit its name to their superiors for inclusion on their organization's technology requirements list. If the product is approved for purchase, the hard currency required for it accompanies the approval. In some cases, transactions are based on barter: The Soviets will buy $X worth of computers from an American firm in exchange for an equivalent amount of vodka or another commodity. This system was used widely in the 1950s and 1960s and may again find use in the late 1980s and 1990s as many U.S.-Soviet joint ventures develop.

In some cases, a U.S. computer company deals directly with a Soviet FTO, which can easily shield the identity of Soviet military purchasers who wish to use a U.S. computer. In most cases, the Department of Commerce allows the export of unrestricted technology only to those who will use it for civilian purposes. The FTO sometimes requests the U.S. company to purchase a Soviet product in return for its purchase of the American product, but U.S. firms prefer hard-currency transactions.

High-technology companies are hesitant to say much about their business relationships—past, present, and future—with the Soviet bloc because of their interest in maintaining close relations with the Commerce Department and the Customs Service. They fear that if they become known as major exporters to the Soviets that Commerce and Customs may suspect them of selling restricted technology in addition to unrestricted products and will investigate their legitimate export operation. Also, a company may be hesitant to reveal details of its sales to the Soviet bloc for political and public relations reasons. American firms are, in general, also more cautious in the 1980s than they were before. After all the fanfare the Soviets created in the 1970s about potential business in the Soviet Union was followed by the tightening of restrictions on trade with the Soviets, U.S. computer companies are more realistic about obtaining significant contracts. Although these hesitations are dissipating, they still color most corporate comments about sales to the Soviet bloc.

The experience of Digital Equipment Corporation in dealing with the Soviets is typical of many U.S. firms. Digital began selling computers to the Soviets in 1972. It sold its now outdated PDP-11, a 16-bit minicomputer, through systems integrators, which sell computer systems made up of various manufacturers' equipment. In Digital's case, one such system, used for medical administration, was built around the PDP-11 hardware. The Soviets bought several PDP-11s with accompanying peripherals. In the early 1970s, Digital also sold a number of PDP-8 12-bit minicomputers to the Soviets; in 1973, it sold a PDP-10 36-bit machine, considered a mainframe at the time, to a Soviet physics research institute. Furthermore, manufacturers of cloned PDP-11s often sell their equipment to the Soviet bloc from Europe. Digital would have sold more, but the Soviets wanted the manufacturing rights instead. Even though Digital refused to sell those rights, the Soviets manufactured their own reverse-engineered PDP-11 about five years later.

U.S. export laws usually require service and parts for computer systems to be covered under separate transactions, which require separate export licenses, but 1987 revisions of the export regulations allow American firms to provide for six to twelve months of parts and service with the sale of equipment. As do all U.S. companies that sell to the Soviet bloc, Digital has had to consider the difficulty of servicing its equipment abroad. Digital used to inspect its equipment during occasional on-site visits. During the 1970s, its service personnel worked out of a thirteen-person office in Vienna. Although a system integrator would procure export licenses and sell the equipment to the Soviets, Digital would provide service and support. But now, the integrator handles both service and support. As a backup, the Soviets purchase large quantities of parts to maintain their Digital equipment.

Since Digital's founding, it has probably done $2 million in sales with the Soviets and an equal amount with other Soviet bloc countries.[1] All transactions have been accomplished through cash payments or through letters of credit. At the time of the Soviet invasion of Afghanistan, Digital ceased selling to the Soviets, but company representatives continue to appear at trade shows in the Eastern bloc.

Because Digital computers, particularly the VAX line of 32-bit computers, have been the machine of choice for many Soviet scientists, Digital has not emerged from years of export controls unscathed. In 1983, according to Jeffrey Gibson, Digital's corporate information manager, Digital sold its VAX equipment to a West German company, Deutsche Integrated Time, indirectly controlled by Richard Müller. Digital shipped the equipment, which, according to Gibson, was not on the Commerce Department's export denial list at the time. Just as the equipment arrived in South Africa on its way to West Germany, the Commerce Department alerted Digital to the connection between Deutsche Integrated Time and Richard Müller. Digital then told Commerce of its transaction with the company. In Germany, U.S. Customs agents seized the equipment before it went on to Sweden and, ultimately, to the Soviet Union. Digital cooperated with Commerce and Customs officials but was fined $1.5 million in 1984, a punishment reduced to $1.1 million when it provided information (equipment serial numbers and other records pertinent to the sale) to investigators.

After the 1985 Geneva summit meeting between President Reagan and General Secretary Gorbachev, during which the Soviet national computer-literacy program was discussed, Digital made several presentations to the Soviets. Obviously, the Soviets were looking at alternatives for fulfilling their promise of manufacturing hundreds of thousands of computers for use in schools by 1990. A Soviet ministry contacted the Commerce Department to inquire about purchasing personal computers. With the support of the Commerce Department, Digital responded by making presentations to Soviet ministry officials and academicians, as did IBM and Apple Computer. Because the Soviets were unable to commit to a transaction in hard currency, no purchases were made.[2]

IBM has had a much longer relationship with the Soviets than Digital. Before 1936, the Soviets leased IBM equipment through Amtorg. After 1936, requisitions were passed through the Bureau for the Import of Calculating Machines and Typewriters, which attempted without success to convince IBM to sell rather than to lease its equipment. IBM kept a technical staff in the Soviet Union that was paid for by the Soviet government. In 1958, IBM approached the Soviet Union with the idea of holding an exhibition of computers in Moscow.[3] The exhibition, which opened later that year, featured computers programmed to answer questions about the United States in several languages. The long lines of Soviets anxious to see this impressive example of U.S. technology proved embarrassing to Soviet officials, and U.S. press representatives were not allowed to send home photographs of the long queues.

Export of IBM equipment is restricted on the same basis as all other advanced computers; equipment with military use and especially advanced technology is usually denied export to the Soviet Union. During the early 1970s, IBM sold the Soviets the 360 and 370 series, which were the basis for the Soviet Ryad I and II mainframes, in compliance with U.S. export laws. Since 1979, IBM has sold typewriters, copiers, small computers, and a few PCs to the Soviets. Under 1988 export law revisions, IBM can sell its 16-bit PC without an individual export license and its European-manufactured computers, shipping them from West Germany. Sales of its mainframes, however, are no longer permitted.

To honor its service warranties to the Soviet Union, IBM maintains a small office in Moscow, staffed as of 1987 by one full-time employee and a small group of locally contracted Soviets. When warranties expire, Soviet customers assume service responsibility. As does Digital, IBM receives payment in U.S. dollars.

Hewlett-Packard also makes sales to the Soviet Union. Like IBM and Digital, HP employs its own representatives in Moscow. At the Soviet-sponsored Exhibition of Science, Technology, and Culture at New York City's Coliseum in 1959, David Packard saw copies of Hewlett-Packard testing equipment, the HP model 410 voltmeter, among the Soviet electronic testing equipment.[4] In its early years, the HP logo first appeared in the Soviet Union via the HP calculator. The Soviets attempted to reverse-engineer the calculator and, in effect, simply placed their own cover on HP electronics while touting their nonexistent engineering feat.

During the 1970s, HP too was inundated with Soviet interest in its computer equipment. Its sales staff rushed samples and literature to Moscow and made what seemed like endless sales presentations—without much resulting business.[5] They did manage to sell several HP 3000 computers and some calculators and medical and chemical analysis equipment. Currently, HP sells its 8-bit personal computers, the only category of its computer line that is not restricted by U.S. export laws. Products are shipped out of the company's Vienna warehouse to the trading organizations in the Eastern bloc.

Apple Computer's experience selling to the Soviet Union is limited, although the Soviets want to bring Apples into their national computer-literacy program. An Apple subsidiary in Sweden has sold computers to the Soviet Union, as has a distributor in Finland. The Apple IIe was decontrolled for export by the Commerce Department in 1987. The Apple II is also unrestricted by U.S. export laws. Although the basic Macintosh is on the restricted list if sold in large quantities, Apple can sell it in groups of six or fewer if the sale is approved by Cocom. On one occasion, Apple sold twenty Macs to the Soviets in several batches.[6] If the Soviets wanted fifty Macs at once, though, Apple would need a Cocom exception and special license approval by the U.S. Commerce Department. So cumbersome does Apple consider the procedure of receiving separate licenses for service and parts sales to the Soviet Union that it simply does not provide service for its equipment once it arrives there.

Although Apple's vice president and secretary, Albert A. Eisenstat, stated in June 1987 that his company had no joint venture in the works with the Soviet Union, Apple will probably follow in the footsteps of other U.S. companies engaged in joint ventures with the Soviets.[7] John Sculley, its current president, was hired from PepsiCo, one of the most active U.S. companies in the Soviet Union. He remains a good friend of Donald M. Kendall, chairman of PepsiCo, who advocates closer trade ties with Moscow. In addition, Apple was the only U.S. computer manufacturer to send representatives to a "science summit," sponsored by the National Academy of Sciences, during the Reagan-Gorbachev summit held in December 1987 in Washington, D.C.[8] Considering the Soviets' intense interest in providing their schools with personal computers, they will probably try to arrange a business venture with Apple.

Judging from the computer companies contacted by the author, sales to the Soviet Union do not appear to be expanding at any significant rate. Clearly cognizant of the paperwork involved in arranging for licenses, of the difficulties of getting hard-currency payments, and of the problems surrounding service contracts, the firms are wary of Soviet overtures. Although the thought of increasing international sales via

Soviet bloc customers may be enticing, the price of doing business is delaying an enthusiastic U.S. response. This may change if the Soviets continue making overtures to American companies and especially if the U.S. government loosens the export laws, removing restrictions on higher-level technologies.

Still, U.S. computer companies are leaving the door open for business contacts with the Soviets, who show no sign of becoming disinterested in American computing equipment. Beginning in June 1987, a U.S. exhibit called Information USA traveled to Moscow and eight other cities, including Kiev and Leningrad, to display U.S. personal computers with performance capabilities that conform to U.S. export regulations. Activities such as this are creating demand in the Soviet Union for IBM, Digital, HP, and Apple computers as well as other U.S. electronics equipment.

PAYING THE PRICE FOR A FREE SOCIETY?

If the Soviets do not wish to steal U.S. technology, cannot afford to buy it, or are not allowed by the United States and Cocom to import it, they can usually find out about it through unclassified, publicly available information, 90 percent of which reaches the Soviet Union legally. Because this information is not classified, it escapes the access restrictions that the U.S. government places on sensitive information. Even though the transfer of unclassified information may seem harmless, it has led to significant Soviet advances. For example, although some design similarities are inevitable, the Soviet space shuttle is a copy of the American one; the Soviet TU-4 bomber was a copy of the U.S. B-29.[9]

Soviet agents sometimes pose as market researchers, telephoning companies about market projections, product characteristics, and new developments. Some top U.S. market research and consulting firms, including Arthur D. Little, have been alerted to this practice by the FBI, but their normal business practices do not include determining whether a client is affiliated with the Soviets. Complicating the detection of Soviet efforts to use American consultants to gather information, the Soviet intelligence officer may hire a third party to contact the American company. When large U.S. consulting firms do business through their offices in Europe and Asia, where controls, laws, and loyalties are more uneven, the situation becomes still more complex. If American firms will not take on the work, the Soviets can always turn to European research organizations. One of these is the International Institute of Applied Systems Analysis in Vienna, which locates and provides technical and computer science-related information for interested Soviets.[10] A multinational analytic organization, it employs scientists from North America, Eastern and Western Europe, and the U.S.S.R. to work on problems of common interest to East and West. Dr. Henry Rowen of the Hoover Institution on War, Revolution, and Peace believes that the KGB has penetrated the Vienna institute.

Soviet agents, however, satisfy most of their assignments for information by perusing U.S. unclassified documents, libraries, and any number of publications. Excellent sources of information on the latest U.S. technology are readily available technical media such as *PC WEEK, PC World, Byte, Aviation Week & Space Technology,*[11] academic and technical papers, product specifications in corporate sales literature, employment ads in technical publications, congressional hearings proceedings, and on line research data bases. U.S. technical and scientific publications, translated into Russian, fill the libraries of Soviet research institutes and military and intelligence organizations. The huge Soviet research community obtains thousands of international publications each year.

Contacts with people who manage a few of these technical publications reveal that they are unaware of any efforts by the U.S. government to control who, in terms of nationality and politics, may subscribe to them. *Aviation Week & Space Technology,* an excellent source of technical information about U.S. military and space activities, reaches readers in 124 countries, including the Soviet Union, Romania, Czechoslovakia, Poland, and Bulgaria. The total number of Soviet bloc subscribers to the magazine is 146.[12] The Soviet embassy in Washington, D.C., also subscribes. The Association for Computing Machinery publishes a magazine, *Communications of the ACM,* containing leading-edge technical papers. James M. Adams, director of ACM membership and professional services, says that the association has several members from the Soviet bloc and two from the Soviet Union, including Andrei Ershov, the visionary cited in Chapter 3. But Mark Mandelbaum, the ACM's director of publications, states that the ACM refrains from officially exchanging information with the Soviet Union. Before the invasion of Afghanistan, the ACM exchanged complimentary copies of its magazine with the state-owned Soviet technical publication, *Mir*. Representing a new relationship between Soviet readers and U.S. technical publications is a publishing joint venture signed in April 1988. IDG Communications Inc. (Framingham, Mass.) agreed with Moscow-based publisher, Radio I Sviaz, to publish a Russian-language version of *PC World* magazine. Scheduled to begin publication in July 1988, the magazine will have one-third of its articles written by Soviet journalists. IDG plans a circulation of about 50,000. At first the publication will appear quarterly, but it will evolve to a monthly. Advertising purchased by Western computer companies provides most of the magazine's revenue, 51 percent of which the Soviets will retain. Because the revenue comes from Western sources, it will be in hard currency and therefore easy to repatriate.

If the Soviets aren't satisfied with their access to Western print media, they can turn to electronic means of obtaining technical data. The Soviet Academy of Sciences is a particularly avid user of international computerized networks. The academy sends representatives to the United States to utilize on-line data bases at universities and other research institutions. Furthermore, although no specific incidents are documented or unclassified, the Soviets can probably tap U.S. and Western European data bases via telephone and satellite networks.

The National Technical Information Service (NTIS) provides to the public previously unpublished, unclassified research material produced by federal laboratories, contractors, consultants, and agencies, both in electronic and paper form. Its files include more than 1.5 million titles, nearly half of which were produced through the Department of Defense.[13] That origin alone makes the information contained likely to be sensitive. By accessing the NTIS files, an interested Soviet research scientist can find out about nuclear explosions and devices, electronic and acoustic countermeasures, supercomputer applications, and missile tracking systems, among many other developments. The only steps taken so far to restrict this source have been to give some government agencies the right to determine what is to be released to NTIS.[14]

Starting in 1986, government agencies, including the National Security Agency, began to ask data-base services for subscriber lists.[15] The inquiries were part of a government study to assess damages if the Soviets made significant use of technical information available from commercial data-base vendors. Their objective was also to learn what information subscribers were getting. Although much of the information is not classified, offering it to countries hostile to the United States may be risky.

Private data-base vendors, such as CompuServe (a major data-base supplier in Columbus, Ohio) and Mead Data Central, are worried about increasing government control over commercially available information. One solution to their concern is the Department of Defense's concept of "compartmentalizing." Certain categories of information—for example, nuclear fusion or rocket motor design research—could be designated as off-limits to foreigners. Implementing such a plan is a problem, though, because most data-base vendors are hesitant to place any obstacles in front of their customers. Some have even threatened to boycott official information services if the government becomes too insistent on controls and access to subscribers. Instead of waiting for onerous federal restrictions, data-base vendors are thus beginning to police themselves. Mead Data Central has removed the sensitive NTIS file from its service.

The government is looking at other ways of heading off U.S. companies that sell data-base information to foreign countries. In the fall of 1986, NTIS proposed that companies selling Energy Department data stop dealing with foreign countries, but the proposal was quickly withdrawn. Other government information services have attempted to restrict access to their data bases. Although NASA has broadened access to its aerospace research, it has developed a list of thirty-four companies suspected of selling information abroad, plus embassies, consulates, and representatives of foreign companies, that are not allowed to purchase NASA data. An example of one such company is University Microfilm International in Ann Arbor, Mich., which sells reprints to foreign customers.

Dave Kishler, a spokesman for CompuServe, points to problems of restricting electronic data bases such as the CompuServe Information

Service, which is available to personal computer owners on a subscription basis. He feels that although companies like his own do not determine what is and is not sensitive they often protect what they know to be sensitive. Because data-base companies are in the business of disseminating information to the widest possible community, inserting restrictive procedures in such publicly available services is counterproductive. Also, they are not well equipped to do the necessary investigative work that would be required to screen out unwanted users. They do have security measures, such as encryption software, for those data bases that contain sensitive information. Still, Soviet scientists can access CompuServe (or other such data-base services) simply by connecting to its mainframe computer, assuming that they have an account and can pay in U.S. dollars. Calls to CompuServe from abroad usually go through access sites close to but not always at the originator's location, making it difficult to know the call's origin. A system operator would also be hard-pressed to go through the manual checks necessary to track down and monitor calls from a particular point of origin. Needless to say, the costs of doing so would have to be passed on to all users of the system. Even if they could perform such an investigative task, "we don't feel we should play the role of censor, judge, or jury," says Kishler.[16]

SOVIET SCHOLARS IN AN OPEN SOCIETY: THE ACADEMIC CONNECTION

The cornerstones of America's open society, that is, its major centers of learning, also provide the Soviets with access to leading-edge technology. The CIA estimates that 20 percent of all Soviet high-technology information collections take place at trade, business, and academic conferences. Indeed, American academia may give the Soviets a vast amount of significant technical information.

The CIA has studied how the VPK—the Soviet Military Industrial Commission mentioned before—uses the U.S. academic community as a source for collecting high-technology research and for confirming the results of Soviet research and development. It lists U.S. universities by the number of visa applications made by Soviet bloc scientists to come to the United States for study and research. The list, prepared in the early 1980s, indicates the actual number of visits made by Soviet bloc scientists working in areas related to Soviet military technology. MIT heads the list, followed by Carnegie-Mellon University, Harvard University, University of Michigan, California Institute of Technology, and Princeton University.[17]

Universities with strong programs in targeted technologies often receive applications from an eager group of Soviet bloc scholars. The CIA lists sixty-three universities and colleges, including Duke University, University of Michigan, George Washington University, Stanford University, Clemson University, and Iowa State University.[18] During the 1970s, some 5,000 Soviet bloc students entered the United States each year. Soviet exchange students and visiting delegations are particularly interested in an institution if it has a strong math, physics, engineering, computer, or biology department. During the late 1970s, practically every Soviet student entering the United States for study was interested in lasers, a sought-after resource for Soviet military developments at that time.

The average Soviet exchange scholar is a 35-year-old scientist or engineer with an equivalent of a Ph.D. and eight years of practical experience in a science-related specialty. Some members of Soviet academic delegations in the United States and "students" are also members of the GKNT—the State Committee for Science and Technology—or one of the Soviet intelligence organizations. If the purpose of the Soviet visitor is not to study U.S. science, it may be to recruit scientists as agents. A 1976 Senate Intelligence Committee report stated that 25 percent of all Soviet students who entered the United States between 1965 and 1975 were themselves Soviet intelligence agents.[19] Soviet intelligence organizations have found that recruitments on college campuses are generally effective, because they can find technically competent students in need of money who later on are likely to work for a technology-related company. Libraries, such as the math library at Columbia University, that specialize in technical literature, are also preferred recruiting locations. New York FBI officers visited librarians of technical libraries in 1987 to gain their cooperation in spotting and reporting Soviet recruitment activities, causing many librarians to unite in protest against what they believed to be an intrusion on the rights of their patrons.

Since 1968, American universities have had assistance from the International Research & Exchanges Board (IREX), which receives funds from various government agencies, including the Department of State and the U.S. Information Agency, in communications and exchanges with Eastern European countries and the Soviet Union. Founded by the American Council of Learned Societies, IREX promotes research exchanges between the United States and socialist countries. With a budget of about $5 million for the year 1985–86, IREX funded U.S. academic exchanges with the Soviet Union, Bulgaria, Czechoslovakia, the German Democratic Republic, Hungary, Poland, Romania, and Yugoslavia.[20] During that period, fifty exchanges occurred between U.S. and Soviet scholars, including a Working Meeting held in Moscow in 1986 between Yevgeny Velikhov, the previously mentioned proponent of Soviet computerization programs, and Judah L. Schwartz at MIT and Harvard on the subject of the use of computers in education. Several exchanges included large groups of academicians from each of the superpowers.

IREX reviews applications to U.S. institutions from Soviet bloc graduate students and refers them to the State Department, which in turn consults with the Committee on Exchanges (COMEX), a government organization that consists of representatives from the U.S. intelligence agencies. (In addition to IREX, the National Science Foundation [NSF] and the National Academy of Sciences [NAS] support academic exchanges with the Soviet bloc.) COMEX advises the State Department on the acceptability of visa requests for study in the United States, and the State Department processes the visas requested by IREX, the NSF, or the NAS.

The United States does not place any quotas on the number of exchange students allowed in from Eastern European countries and the Soviet Union but does require that a reciprocal number of U.S. scholars be allowed into Soviet or Eastern bloc countries. U.S. universities try to match the technological strengths of countries with which the United States exchanges students with the research needs of the other countries or of the United States. If, for example, a U.S. university is behind in growing crystals, it will look for qualified Polish students, because they are known for their advanced work in that field.

In 1986, President Reagan created the U.S.-Soviet Exchange Initiative to spur academic exchanges. The initiative is already having an effect: In the IREX annual report for 1985–86, Allen Kassof, the board's executive director, noted that applications for the 1987–88 research exchanges with the Soviet Union were up 25 percent after ten years of decline. Kassof also pointed out that although exchanges would likely continue and probably increase, a difference remained between U.S. and Soviet objectives, the United States being concerned with history, social sciences, and literature, while the Soviets were still preoccupied with technology and applied science.

During the May–June 1988 summit in Moscow, Reagan and Gorbachev agreed on increasing the number of high-school exchange students between the two superpowers. The agreement proposes an increase from 50 students to 1,500 students a year. As of late June 1988, details were still being negotiated. The United States wants U.S. exchange students to live in private Soviet homes, an arrangement so far unacceptable to the Soviets.

THE GOODIES: COMPUTERS AND RESEARCH

U.S. officials argue about two points regarding Soviet students in the United States. One is the broad issue of whether attendance at U.S. universities by Soviet bloc students should even be allowed. The other is the more specific issue of whether they should be allowed access to computers, particularly supercomputers, computer data bases, and, especially, research itself.

Regarding the issue of Soviet students' access to computers in American universities, the Department of Defense recommends that Soviets be denied the use of supercomputers, both in and out of academia. A network of supercomputers set up by the NSF, linking Cornell University, the University of Illinois at Urbana, the University of California at San Diego, Carnegie-Mellon University, Princeton University, and MIT, has caused particular concern to Defense Department officials. The U.S. academic community, however, opposes any such intrusion and prefers not to police the nation's supercomputers. Those in charge of university computer programs argue that any out-of-the-ordinary use of a computer would attract their attention. Use of the supercomputers for encryption or weapons-design analysis would be noticed immediately, they say, because such lengthy jobs far exceed a normal student's research needs. At the John von Neumann National Computer Center in Princeton, N.J., one of the centers in the NSF network, prospective users of the supercomputer, a Cyber 205, must fill out a request for use of the system. The request form asks the applicant for personal data and the name of a project sponsor; the applicant must also be able to pay the $1,000-per-hour usage fee. The center is aware of all research being performed using the supercomputer, and none of the research is classified.[21] (Of course, a Soviet visiting the United States could gain access to a supercomputer's capabilities outside academia through a commercial service bureau if armed with a corporate account number.)

The Defense Department can cite few instances of errant Soviet bloc exchange students in support of its argument for controlling access to the computers. One case occurred in 1978, when a Soviet scientist in the United States on exchange, Vladimir Aleksandrov, used a Cray supercomputer at the National Center for Atmospheric Research in Colorado for climate modeling. (Apparently, he had also tried to access it by phone from Moscow.) Although climate modeling in itself is not a closely guarded U.S. technology, the software to perform the task and the Cray's performance are considered sensitive technologies and cannot be exported to a Soviet bloc country. Through a computer network originating at Oregon State University, the Soviet scientist later used a second Cray for the same purpose.[22] This incident and a limited number of others like it have not inspired U.S. lawmakers to address the situation.

Conscious that such access could one day lead to problems, the NSF and the universities are attempting to work out a solution that would provide some monitoring without initiating a cumbersome program that would needlessly restrict the academic community. The Defense Department has asked that the State Department decide whether to allow specific exchange students access to supercomputers before it grants them visas. Notations appearing on the student's visa could indicate his or her level of security clearance. The NSF staff has not explained how this could be enforced or if the universities would check visa notations.

SECURITY CONTROLS ON ACADEMIC RESEARCH

While debate continues in the U.S. policy-making community about Soviet students' access to American schools' science programs and computers, universities already receive the special attention of U.S. security agencies.

Sponsored by the National Academy of Sciences, the Department of Defense, and several private foundations, the Panel on Scientific Communication and National Security, along with the Committee on Science, Engineering, and Public Policy, conducted a significant study of the control of academic research in the early 1980s. The group, made up of representatives of UCLA, Cornell, Cal Tech, Stanford, and other universities, met to determine how technology-related export controls should ideally affect the academic community. Its report, issued in 1982 and officially titled *Scientific Communications and National Security* but also called the Corson Report after the panel's chairman, Dale Corson, president emeritus of Cornell University, advised against any restrictions on academic institutions unless they undertake research in a field of technology that has one or more of four specific traits: (1) if it is fast-developing, (2) if it has identifiable military applications, (3) if it would result in clear near-term military advantage for the Soviets were it transferred to them, and (4) if it is available only in the United States.[23] The report also commented on a wide range of related topics, supporting only limited export restrictions on academic research, encouraging U.S.-Soviet scientific exchanges and calling on universities to control access to their high-technology research on a voluntary basis. Generally, the panel was in favor of preserving the free exchange of ideas rather than place restrictions on universities. But the report's recommendations are unlikely to become part of U.S. export law, because the task of defining the restricted research presents insurmountable complexities. The Department of Defense decided that access restrictions should remain on classified fundamental research.[24]

The U.S. government has at least three mechanisms for determining the type of restrictions placed on the dissemination of research information. First, the U.S. government classifies much of its information according to the impact on national security. Such classifications include the designations TOP SECRET and SECRET. Only U.S. citizens with specific security clearances that relate to their need to know are permitted access to classified information. For example, if the U.S. government funds a classified research project at a university, access to any information related to the project is restricted to those with appropriate security clearances.

Second, the U.S. export-control laws restrict dual-use technology-related information. The export regulations view the dissemination of information to foreign nationals as an export of information. If academic research is related to technology restricted by export regulations even though it is not classified, access by foreign nationals is restricted.

The Freedom of Information Act (passed in 1966) gave individuals the right to receive a wide range of information from the federal government. Problems arose when the Defense Department, as well as other government agencies, noticed that a loophole in the act allowed anyone, including visiting Soviets and even criminals sitting in foreign jails, to gain access to government information. For that reason, the Defense Department controls access to unclassified military information when it withholds from public disclosure any information that would likely receive an exemption from U.S. export control. By restricting the dissemination of Defense Department–funded research to those specified in a research contract, the Defense Department also has the right to restrict access to conferences where papers prepared under such contracts are presented. Export controls do not restrict fundamental research that is publicly available unless it is classified or restricted through a research contract.

The 1984 defense authorization bill, along with the Defense Department Directive 5230.25, enabled the U.S. government to restrict access to some Defense-sponsored research, usually directly related to military research. (Fundamental research, however, remains unrestricted.) According to National Security Decision Directive (NSDD) 189, issued by President Reagan in September 1985, no restrictions are placed on Defense-funded fundamental research unless "there is a likelihood of disclosing performance characteristics of military systems, or of manufacturing technologies unique and critical to defense."[25]

The directive also called on the Defense Department to provide its research to government contractors only if it required the contractors to comply with U.S. export-control laws by not putting the research into the public domain.[26] Under directive 5230.25, Defense has asked private technical societies and organizations that provide forums for the exchange of information based on Defense-sponsored research to consider limiting attendance to those who can prove that they are not representatives of the Soviet bloc.

The Strategic Defense Initiative has been responsible for a surge in on-campus military research. In 1986, Department of Defense–sponsored university research totaled $1.2 billion, up from $650 million in 1980.[27] Most research is in the fields of computer science, electrical engineering, and particle physics. Universities under contract, which include Stanford and MIT, seem caught between their wishes for research funding and the obligation to maintain academic freedom and openness. Even though security problems can be avoided if a university has separate laboratories for classified research, such as the Johns Hopkins Applied Physics Laboratories, some researchers are already feeling crowded by security restrictions. When a researcher at the University of California at Berkeley attempted to publish his work, the Pentagon delayed the paper several months because some of the information appeared to have applications for the SDI.[28] Some universities refuse to sign research contracts that restrict student access to research.

Most institutions would prefer that Defense contract proposals stipulate whether the result of the research would be subject to controls. If they did so, universities could turn down contracts containing restrictions instead of struggling with the regulations after the research was in progress. The department does advise the university if research is classified but will not determine if the research is controlled by U.S. export laws: Such determinations are made by the Commerce Department. The general feeling among universities is that their research should not be subject to the export laws (and most is not). They argue that too much is being made of the national security implications of Soviet access to U.S. academia, but they are willing to cooperate in any efforts to establish criteria to evaluate research that might be subject to controls. University officials do not dispute that critical information on new technologies could flow to the Soviets via university channels. But until specific evidence indicates that U.S. national security is being jeopardized from within the halls of America's colleges and universities, they oppose any government restrictions on unclassified academic pursuits, citing their staunch commitment to academic freedom.

SCIENTIFIC CONFERENCES: ANOTHER OPPORTUNITY

Like American universities, scientific and industrial conferences provide opportunities for Soviet high-technology gatherers. Determining the extent to which the Soviet Union exploits these opportunities is extremely difficult. Conferences are subject to specific federal controls on classified, sensitive information. The Defense Department provides access guidelines for classified material, and the Commerce Department administers control over the access by foreign nationals to restricted information. Conference presenters are responsible for any illegal exportation of information. Export regulations covering unclassified conference material are almost never followed by private industry groups, and Commerce rarely enforces them. If, however, a scientific conference presents material that is in the public domain but based on Defense Department–sponsored research, other regulations come into play.

The Defense Department decides how much of its own research information it will provide a conference presenter based on the presenter's willingness to cooperate with conference access restrictions. (The department has agreements on sharing technical data with certain friendly nations such as Britain.) When, for example, the Association for Computing Machinery or the Institute of Electrical and Electronics Engineers sponsors technical conferences and seminars covering Defense-sponsored research, they must consider the national security implications of their subject matter. Brochures advertising conferences on such topics as weapons technology often inform potential participants that the relevant information will be classified and that participants must be cleared before they can attend. In October 1984, the Society for Advancement of Materials and Processing Engineers required conference attendees to submit proof of U.S. citizenship to gain access to four of its seminars, even though none of the society's research is classified. Conference organizers posted security guards at the doors of these restricted sessions.[29] Also, the Society of Manufacturing Engineers held a conference in September 1986, and the Defense Department had to turn away a group of French researchers because the organizers had not followed government guidelines for presentations covering restricted information.

These efforts to control access by foreigners to Defense-sponsored research, however, are not consistently maintained throughout the conference business. In the past, clearances have been secured by providing only a driver's license number and an office phone number, although the Defense Department officially requires attendees at classified conferences to present government identifications or certificates verifying that they are U.S. citizens or resident aliens using the information for specific purposes.

Industry associations have not always taken kindly to the Defense Department's requirements. The Association for Computing Machinery takes a strong position against restricting attendance at any of its conferences. It will not cosponsor one that limits participation for any reason other than the size of the conference hall. Although it sponsors many international conferences, it will not sponsor any conferences in the Soviet Union. The ACM Conference Board chairman, Frank Freedman, has the impression that visitors from the Soviet bloc have never attended an ACM conference in the United States, and he does not recall any contact by the U.S. government expressing concern over the association's conference admission policy. But Dr. Lara Baker, a scientist at Los Alamos National Laboratory, recalls at least one incidence of Soviet attendance: At the ACM conference in 1969 in San Francisco, several Soviets were present, including Andrei Ershov who presented a technical paper.[30]

The Department of Defense has developed its own procedures to allow presenters who are either federal employees or work for government contractors to reveal controlled information at seminars. They must first submit their papers to the department, which screens them for information that is classified or restricted by the export-control laws. Papers not sponsored by the government may still be subject to restrictions by U.S. export laws, and therefore the author needs an export license for distributing it to foreign nationals. The issue of the control of technical information is extremely controversial, complex, and still unresolved. It is unclear whether the government will develop a simplified, clear policy on information access or whether our society can tolerate controls necessary to restrict access by the Soviet Union.

A CAMPAIGN OF DISINFORMATION

In addition to specific and direct efforts to acquire U.S. technology, the Soviets have launched a more subtle, long-term campaign to obtain high-tech equipment by influencing U.S. trade policy. One goal of Gorbachev's efforts to open and restructure Soviet society is, at least in part, to interest Americans in doing business in his country and to break down official barriers to the transfer of high technology to the Soviet Union. In all probability, the Soviets regularly pass on so-called disinformation to the U.S. public, government, and press and to U.S. allies to nudge U.S. trade laws toward a more pro-Soviet stance. Apparently, the Soviets have used disinformation for at least fifty years to manipulate U.S. and other Western states' foreign policies or for even more sinister purposes, such as the character assassination of key political, scientific, and industrial figures.[31] Disinformation is the deliberate planting of false or misleading political information to influence either public or elite opinion. This definition, published in one of a series of articles in the *Christian Science Monitor* in 1985, properly emphasizes the premeditated planting of information. By 1959, the Soviet Union had had such success with disinformation campaigns that it formalized its activities in a section of the KGB called Service A.[32]

Disinformation comes into play in the effort to acquire U.S. technology when the Soviets plant information intended to get the United States to relax export controls. For example, they may try to convince Americans that the Soviet Union had developed certain high-technology products so that U.S. export controls will be removed. In the 1950s, Khrushchev undertook a similar plan, which was unequivocally revealed to have been a disinformation campaign. First, he downplayed Soviet technological capabilities so that the United States would not feel threatened by Soviet progress. He then emphasized a Soviet interest in "peaceful coexistence" and an ardent abhorrence of nuclear war. He recruited Soviet scientists to interact with U.S. colleagues as a means of getting U.S. support for this campaign. That these efforts were disingenuous was confirmed by Soviet defectors, such as Arkady Shevchenko, who acknowledged that such events as the 1957 Conference on Science and World Affairs, held on Cyrus Eaton's estate in Nova Scotia, were sponsored in part by the KGB.[33]

Today's disinformation efforts may be getting important support from Anatoly Dobrynin, who heads the International Department of the Soviet Communist Party Central Committee. Equipped with his valuable experience as Soviet ambassador to the United States for many years, Dobrynin works closely with Service A. Stepped-up disinformation activities under Dobrynin's guiding hand include an effort to portray the United States as the developer of acquired immune deficiency syndrome (AIDS) as part of a biological warfare plan.[34]

Whether the Soviets gather technology through illegal or legal methods, their techniques are well thought out. Americans tend not to suspect that citizens of other countries would intentionally deceive or harm them. Such overriding optimism colors foreign policy and general attitudes toward the U.S. defense posture and the Soviet intelligence-gathering community. A sober realization of the varied and sophisticated techniques employed by the Soviet bloc to steal and otherwise acquire technology does not mean that American optimism must be sacrificed but rather that Americans must continue to construct intelligent and informed ways of implementing foreign policy, developing defense systems, controlling exports, and conducting corporate activities. Only then will their valuable high technology be protected.

NOTES

1. Ted Johnson, former director of sales (1965–80), Digital Equipment Corporation, currently a venture capitalist and consultant with his firm, Prelude Management Inc., Concord, Mass.: Interview, Apr. 8, 1987.

2. Jeffrey Gibson, manager of corporate information, Digital Equipment Corporation, Maynard, Mass.: Interview, May 5, 1987.

3. William Rogers, *Think* (New York: Stein & Day, 1969), p. 259.

4. Bruno O. Weinschel, "Russian Test Equipment and Ours," *Electronic Design*, Aug. 17, 1960, pp. 65–66.

5. Tom Christiansen, manager of international trade relations, Hewlett-Packard Company, Palo Alto, Calif.: Interview, Mar. 2, 1987.

6. Guy Palmer, import-export manager, Apple Computer, Inc., Cupertino, Calif.: Interview, June 21, 1987.

7. Albert A. Eisenstat, vice president and secretary, Apple Computer, Inc., Cupertino, Calif.: Interview, June 22, 1987.

8. Paul Freiberger, "Soviets Want to Upgrade Computers in Schools," *San Francisco Examiner*, Dec. 13, 1987, p. D5.

9. Testimony by Dr. Jack Vorona, assistant director of scientific intelligence at the Defense Intelligence Agency, in the Senate Committee on Government Affairs, permanent subcommittee on investigations, *Transfer of United States High Technology to the Soviet Union and Soviet Bloc Nations*, 97th Cong., 2d sess., 1982, p. 6.

10. Bill Dooley, "Some High-Tech Information Too Easily Available?" *Management Information Systems Week*, Mar. 2, 1987, p. 12.

11. Often called "Aviation Leak" by those concerned about its role in disseminating U.S. technology.

12. *Aviation Week & Space Technology*, Business Publication Publisher's Statement, for 6 months ended Dec. 31, 1986.

13. Diane Fountaine, director of information systems, Office of the Assistant Secretary of Defense, Command and Control Communications and Intelligence, in a draft speech for the National Information Policy Forum, Dec. 17, 1986, p. 4.

14. Ted Agres, "Documents Unveil Soviet Methods of Obtaining Western Technology," *Research and Development*, June 1985, p. 48.

15. Bob Davis, "Federal Agencies Press Data-Base Firms to Curb Access To 'Sensitive' Information," *Wall Street Journal*, Feb. 5, 1987, p. 25.

16. Dave Kishler, CompuServe Incorporated, Columbus, Ohio: Interview, Jan. 13, 1988.

17. Central Intelligence Agency, *Soviet Acquisition of Militarily Significant Western Technology: An Update* (Washington, D.C.: Government Printing Office, 1985), p. 23.

18. Ibid., p. 22.

19. Ladislav Bittman, *The KGB and Soviet Disinformation—An Insider's View* (McLean, Va.: Brassey's International Defense Publishers, 1985), p. 208.

20. International Research and Exchanges Board, Annual Report 1985–86, p. 27.

21. Doyle Knight, president, John von Neumann National Computer Center, Princeton, N.J.: Interview, Dec. 28, 1987.

22. Andrew C. Revkin, "Supercomputers and the Soviets," *Technology Review*, August/September 1986, p. 72.

23. National Academy of Sciences, *Scientific Communications and National Security* (Washington, D.C.: National Academy Press, 1982), p. 65.

24. "Fundamental research" means basic and applied research in science and engineering, the results of which ordinarily are published and shared broadly within the scientific community. It is distinguished from proprietary research and from industrial development, design, production, and product utilization, the results of which ordinarily are restricted for proprietary or national security reasons. (Source: "National Security Controls and University Research,

Information for Investigators and Administrators," prepared by the Association of American Universities for the Department of Defense—University Forum, Washington, D.C., June 1987, p. 5.)

25. Richard DeLauer as cited in *Science, Technology, and the First Amendment, Special Report, Congress of the United States, Office of Technology Assessment* (Washington, D.C.: U.S. Government Printing Office, January 1988), p. 61.

26. Frank Sobieszczyk, chief of research programs in the Defense Technology Analysis Office, U.S. Department of Defense, Washington, D.C.: Interview, Jan. 5, 1988.

27. Timothy Aeppel, "Pentagon-Campus Ties," *Christian Science Monitor,* Dec. 29, 1986, p. 3.

28. Ibid., p. 5.

29. Gary Putka, "U.S. Blocks Access of Foreign Scientists to High Technology," *Wall Street Journal,* Jan. 25, 1985, p. 1.

30. Lara Baker, staff member, Los Alamos National Laboratory, N.M., manuscript review notes, January 1988.

31. The earliest case of disinformation was about 1900, when the Russians circulated the "Protocols of the Learned Elders of Zion," a document that contended there was a Jewish conspiracy to enslave the Christian world. The *Times* of London revealed in 1921 that this document was taken from a nineteenth-century anti-Semitic novel, but the Russians had already used the story to blackmail Jews in World War I. Hitler picked up on this line of thinking to justify atrocities he committed during World War II. (Source: Elizabeth Pond, "There's a Trojan Horse Built Every Minute," *Christian Science Monitor,* Feb. 26, 1985, p. 16.)

32. Ibid.

33. Jan Sejna and Joseph D. Douglass, Jr., "Soviet Ambitions and the Lure of Western Technology," *World and I,* February 1987, p. 110.

34. John Hughes, "Lies About the U.S." (editorial), *Christian Science Monitor,* Oct. 6, 1987, p. 12.

6

THE
INTERNATIONAL
CONNECTION

Although the United States is the main target of Soviet efforts to acquire high technology, other nations have also become embroiled in the controversy over technology transfer to the Soviets. According to the French intelligence service, nearly 40 percent of Soviet high-technology acquisitions between 1976 and 1980 came from countries other than the United States, including U.S. allies West Germany, France, Great Britain, and Japan.[1]

Western Europe's industrialized countries are channels for U.S. technology traveling both legally and illegally to the Soviet Union; they can be havens for smugglers and spies, as well as alternative sources for technology. Even though the United States often influences the trade policies of its allies, other nations' self-interest sometimes conflicts with current U.S. trade policies. Nonaligned nations and neutral countries operating outside the influence of U.S. trading and foreign-policy objectives create further problems. The United States, thus, has limited choices for controlling the flow of technology to the Soviets once it has left American shores.

Stephen Walton, director of strategic investigations at the U.S. Customs Service, has observed a move away from export diversions within the United States to international diversion points. Because of the increased international awareness and human resources devoted to the prevention of illegal technology exports, diverters now seem hesitant to ship out of such U.S. ports as Newark and Elizabeth, N.J., or San Francisco. The "insulation process," as Walton calls it, is becoming more sophisticated. Diverters are finding new and more sophisticated ways to insulate or protect themselves. They are adding more intermediate stop-off points and more intermediaries, sometimes three or four, to increase the distance between themselves and international law enforcement agencies.

The trend is also toward using diversion points in the Far East. In addition to the already popular countries of Austria, West Germany, and England, the number of illegal exporters is increasing in Hong Kong, Singapore, South Korea, Taiwan, and Malaysia. This shift is largely a result of increased diligence in some European countries and U.S. pressure on Cocom.

COCOM

Founded in 1949, Cocom, or the Coordinating Committee for Multilateral Export Controls (a sixteen-member group), acts as the international clearinghouse for East-West export-license applications and is the only multilateral mechanism for restricting exports from its member countries to the Soviet bloc. Cocom is not a formally decreed organization bound by treaties, nor is it under the aegis of any other internationally recognized organization. Bound only by agreement among its members, Cocom oversees member countries' licensing and enforcement procedures, which are theoretically the same as those in the United States. Its membership comprises the United States, Britain, France, Italy, the Netherlands, Belgium, Luxembourg, Norway, Denmark, Canada, West Germany, Portugal, Japan, Greece, Spain, and Turkey.

Four events prompted the former World War II allies to lay the groundwork for this gathering of concerned nations: the split between the Yugoslavian Communist leader, Marshal Tito, and Stalin (1948), the Berlin blockade (1948), the creation of the People's Republic of China (1949), and the first explosion of a Soviet atom bomb (1949). These international events each signaled global instability and the polarization of communist from noncommunist countries. Those nations that signed the North Atlantic Treaty Organization agreement in 1949 also formed the core of the group that was determined to limit exports of militarily significant technology to the Soviet bloc.

Today, Cocom meets rather secretly in Paris each week in a building near the U.S. embassy, rarely publicizing its proceedings. Its activities are treated as diplomatic functions and so are managed on the United States' behalf by the State Department. Because delegates are from the diplomatic corps, they seldom have any training in the high technology whose fate they determine. The reason for Cocom's confidentiality is elusive. A State Department spokesman, Paul Pilkauskas, explains it by pointing to the sensitive diplomatic situation created as member countries give up a degree of their sovereignty to allow other countries to influence their exports. Cocom's deliberations are also confidential, so companies cannot find out that a competitor was denied an export license and then attempt to go after its business. In addition, the State Department feels that if the Soviets were to find out which technologies were restricted by Cocom (the group's lists of controlled commodities are secret) they would be able to learn which of them had reached high levels of sophistication and then target them.[2] Whether these reasons justify Cocom's cloak of secrecy is unclear, but its closed-door tradition makes auditing its effectiveness difficult.

Cocom's agenda consists of reviewing applications from companies seeking licenses for exports. Applications from U.S. firms would have already gone through the Commerce and State departments' review processes. These agencies contribute to the U.S. position regarding a particular export. Commerce determines if a license needs Cocom approval; the U.S. requirements for Cocom review are outlined by the federal law restricting exports, the Export Administration Act (EAA), as amended. When seeking an exception to Cocom rules, the State Department delivers a U.S. position statement to its Cocom delegate in Paris, who then presents it at a meeting.

Three lists occupy Cocom members, one for munitions, another for atomic energy-related products, and a third, called the General Industrial List, covering dual-use technologies, computers, and electronics—all three of which together are referred to as the International List. Although the list controls a range of products, the group's activities focus on high technology, particularly products and know-how that would enhance the receiving country's military capability. Fewer embargoed items are on the list than are in the equivalent U.S. Commerce list, but apparently overlap is substantial. Member country representatives decide which technologies should be placed on the list in the first place and whether to make exceptions when evidence supports a more lenient position.

A member country can request that an export be reviewed by Cocom. The country is responsible for presenting its case to the other member countries before recommending a specific action. Member countries often differ widely about whether to grant exceptions or to include or exclude items on the lists. As a result, the requirement for unanimity for granting exceptions to its embargoes can limit Cocom's effectiveness, at least from the business point of view. The United States has put pressure on the group to change this and other aspects of its operations. In 1985, Cocom agreed to change the way it compiles its list. Reviews, previously made all at once every three years, are now made annually, with one-fourth of the list emended each year to make it more enforceable. This procedure results in a yearly new list and a completely revised one every four years. In addition, as a result of the highly publicized Toshiba and Kongsberg affair, in which the Japanese and Norwegians illegally exported high technology to the Soviets, the United States is putting pressure on Cocom members to tighten their controls, beef up enforcement, and impose stringent fines. Since mid-1987, the United States has been reassessing Cocom's effectiveness, but it is not clear that any significant changes will occur. Some observers feel that the organization needs more money to operate and a more professional staff. Member nations contribute about $500,000 a year to its budget, and it employs approximately five staff members.

Even with Cocom's current weaknesses, the U.S. commitment to its efforts remains firm. The 1985 amendments to the EAA outline an agreement to improve the international control list as well as the staffing, computer services, and facilities of the committee. They also reinforce the U.S. Cocom position, which tends to be more conservative than other nations', by favoring a limitation of exceptions to the list. For example, the United States generally votes against an exception, while other members usually vote to allow the export of the technology.

To strengthen Cocom, the United States wants increased cooperation from nonaligned countries, such as India. The United States hopes to bring India in line with the organization's principles. A closer relationship between Cocom and India, however, raises the prospect of India (or any other such country) learning the details of what technologies are considered too sensitive to export; it could then pass these details on to the Soviets. If the United States can bring nonaligned nations into the Cocom fold, it may be able to move away from many of its unilateral controls and rely more heavily on multilateral agreements to restrict technology exports to the Soviets. This arrangement would be in keeping with the recommendations made in the 1987 National Academy of Sciences report, which argued that the United States should seek to reconcile its tight trade restrictions with the more open approach of the Cocom allies. But the inclusion of these countries could complicate efforts to tighten cooperation within Cocom, because many of the nonaligned countries do not agree with U.S. national security concerns. Since 1982, Switzerland, Sweden, and Austria have signed agreements to tighten Cocom controls on U.S. technology entering their boundaries. They did not, however, tighten any controls on exports of their own technology. In return for this increase in cooperation with the United States, the Commerce Department will loosen controls on U.S. technology exported to these countries if it is not reexported.

Even if efforts to broaden the group come to fruition, Cocom will be far from a perfect solution. Stephen Walton points out that, as committed as the other members become to export controls, the United States will always shoulder an inordinate portion of the enforcement burden. Furthermore, he does not expect other nations to rewrite their export laws in the American image. As he says, "For any one nation to take any action at all, there had to be a legal basis for them to do it. And in some cases, these countries don't have the laws, or their laws are too weak."

In late January 1988, Cocom members met in Paris to discuss shoring up Cocom's enforcement efforts. At the urging of U.S. officials, member countries agreed to remove items from the list that for one reason or another could not be realistically controlled, strengthen controls on the remaining items, and tighten enforcement. Eventually, the United States may reduce licenses for products destined for Cocom countries by 36,000 each year. The United States loosened controls on 16-bit computers, such as the IBM XT, to go to the Soviet Union as of January 1988. In return, Cocom members agreed to recommit themselves to the organization's goals while considering U.S. proposals for stepped-up enforcement. The United States wants Cocom to increase enforcement personnel within member countries and exchange intelligence data that would assist in catching illegal exporters.[3] Paul Freedenberg, assistant secretary for export administration, says that "what we have tried to do is get Cocom to be more effective, get coordination of enforcement, and get coordination of negotiations with non-Cocom members."[4]

Several European countries are moving to enact more restrictive high technology-export laws, but the process is proving extremely slow. In Europe the subject of technology controls is politically controversial, just as it is on Capitol Hill. Some European Cocom members who are receptive to trade with the Soviet Union hold the opinion that the illegal export of technology is not as critical an issue as the United States believes and that the national security issue is simply an excuse for the United States to control European markets. The Soviets are intent on getting the Western European countries to give them increased access to their high-technology items. Some companies are vigorously pursuing a Soviet market for their products and hope that Cocom will be generous when considering their export requests.

THE ALLIES: TRADING PARTNERS OR PROFITEERS?

Even though U.S. allies cooperate with the United States in protecting U.S. high technology, many have export laws different from those of the United States. Thus, if someone violates U.S. export laws while in a foreign country such as Great Britain, the person may not be breaking that country's law, and the country may not allow extradition of the person to the United States.

Britain has hosted various smugglers, who have used the country as a way station for U.S. technology bound for the Soviet Union. In 1985, Daniel J. O'Hara was indicted for illegally shipping $500,000 worth of chip manufacturing equipment to East Germany via Britain.[5] On Oct. 24, 1986, O'Hara, a resident of Nevada, pled guilty and was sentenced to eighteen months in prison. Charles McVey, awaiting extradition in Canada, had operations in Britain and used the facilities to arrange for computer sales and training for the Soviets.

The Federal Republic of Germany balances its relations with the West with its delicate political and economic ties with the German Democratic Republic (East Germany) and other Soviet bloc countries. The West Germans are willing to trade with the Soviet bloc to enhance relations with their eastern neighbors: As a result of the creation of the Berlin Wall in August 1961, Germany has gingerly managed its relations with the Soviet bloc to ease travel restrictions across the wall since the 1970s. Also, its highly developed industrial economy places unrestricted trade high on the political agenda. West Germany sells more goods to the Soviet bloc than any other Western industrialized country. However, because of the United States and West Germany's strong post-World War II relationship, the Germans look at export restrictions as necessary but difficult to administer.

West Germany has been home base for some of the best-known technology diverters. Because so much trade occurs between Germany and the Soviet bloc and because Germany is a highly industrialized nation, technology smugglers can easily operate without detection. Furthermore, diverters can operate in Germany knowing that the government will not allow them to be extradited to the United States to face a trial for violating export laws. Werner Bruchhausen and Richard Müller hail from West Germany, and many Soviet fronts and warehouses used to transship illegal exports have West German addresses.

Germany is also the target of new Soviet overtures for increased cooperation. In January 1988, Soviet Foreign Minister Eduard Schevardnadze went to Bonn to sign three cooperative agreements and ask Germany to pressure Cocom to ease its export restrictions, something Germany has already been doing.[6]

France takes another stance regarding the flow of Western technology to the Soviets. It strongly criticizes Soviet political and economic policy but is willing both to trade with the Eastern bloc and to subsidize interest rates on loans to those countries. Still, France cooperates with the United States on its campaign to restrict high-technology exports and shares the U.S. commitment to keeping strategic and militarily critical equipment out of Soviet hands. In 1981, the French government created a commission for the protection of its own advanced technologies.[7] As a result, France has its own licensing procedure for high-technology exports and also audits U.S. goods that arrive there. Still, because compliance with Cocom rules is voluntary, France removes items from Cocom consideration and is free to act independently.

As part of its commitment to restrict the transfer of high technology, France has begun to look into its own role in illegal sales to the Soviets. During the summer of 1987, when the Toshiba affair was sorting itself out, Japan accused France of having made illegal shipments of critical technology to the Soviet Union, an accusation echoed by Norway later in the year. Toshiba said that it proceeded with its illegal sale only after learning that a French firm had sold critical technology to the Soviets many times in the mid-1970s. As of fall 1987, the French were investigating these charges but without coming to any conclusions; the French firm in question, Ratier-Forest, had gone bankrupt.[8] Also in the fall of 1987, the French magazine *L'Express* revealed that Accessoires Scientifiques sold semiconductor manufacturing equipment to the Soviets in 1985. The equipment was produced by the U.S. company Veeco Instruments Inc. Accessoires Scientifiques, owned by the French bank Société Générale, had already been reprimanded by the United States, which had denied it access to U.S. exports after learning that the company had violated U.S. export laws.[9] Well into 1988, the French were arresting company executives who allegedly sold restricted technology to the Soviets. In April 1988, four men were arrested for breaking a French counterespionage law even though their crime involved illegal shipments rather than spying. The technology, embodied in machinery used to produce turbine blades for jet engines, was sold by Machines Françaises Lourdes, S.A., from the early 1970s to the present. The French government's use of a counterespionage statute as the basis for the charges indicates that the French government wants the United States to know of the increased French efforts to enforce Cocom agreements.[10]

Soviet espionage has long been prevalent in France, a legendary haven for technology spies, in addition to West Germany and Switzerland. In 1983, forty-seven Soviet spies, most there to acquire Western technology, were asked to leave by their previously tolerant French hosts. The Parisian newspaper *Le Monde* reported that these agents' technology acquisitions had saved the Soviets almost $56.5 million in research and development costs in 1979 alone.[11] This housecleaning effort, however, by no means eliminated KGB and GRU personnel from France. In the same year, a new KGB resident arrived in Paris. Vladislav Nichkov, born in New York in 1947, had been a specialist in trade and scientific-technical cooperation between the Soviet Union and the West. In 1979, he was appointed first secretary of the Paris embassy, responsible for a section of the Soviet GKNT.[12] His arrival in France was evidence that the Soviets viewed the expulsions as only a temporary delay in their high-technology espionage activities in the French capital.

JAPAN

In 1980, Igor A. Osipov, a KGB officer and vice president of a Soviet foreign-trade organization called Tekmashimport, entered the Moscow office of a Japanese trading company, Wako Koeki. The Japanese trading firm had been in business since 1952, selling Japanese products to countries such as China and Vietnam. Osipov,[13] who had previously shown an interest in purchasing products whose export is forbidden by Western laws, requested equipment for making large ship propellers, indicating that the possession of this equipment would shorten the time it takes the Soviets to make quiet propellers for submarines. Cocom restricts the export of milling equipment with more than three axes;[14] the equipment requested by the Soviets had nine.

Working on Osipov's behalf, Wako located the best suppliers for the deal: Toshiba Machine Company, a subsidiary of Toshiba Corporation; C. Itoh & Company, Toshiba's regular export broker; and a Norwegian firm, Kongsberg Vaapenfabrikk, a state-owned defense company now on the brink of bankruptcy. The machine, model MBP-110 in the Toshiba sales brochure, cost more than $4 million. Two contracts were signed in Moscow on Apr. 24, 1981. One, between C. Itoh and Tekmashimport, was for the machines from Toshiba; the other, with Kongsberg Trade, a marketing arm of the Norwegian firm, was for the computers to control the machines. Negotiations for Kongsberg were handled by Bernhard John Green, a British national who was its sales manager. The Soviets wanted four of the machines, worth nearly $17 million.

Toshiba no doubt knew it was violating Cocom export restrictions when it built the four machines and prepared the export-license application for them. On the other hand, it had on its side the Japanese tradition of low-key enforcement of export controls, including an honor system of compliance, weak penalties for violations, and a brief statute of limitations. In preparation for shipping the equipment to the Soviet Union, both Kongsberg and Toshiba falsified information on the license applications. Toshiba stated on the appropriate line that the machines were the model TDP 70/110, which has only two axes and is not represented in the Toshiba sales brochure, instead of the MBP-110. Furthermore, the company said the equipment would be used to improve an electric power utility in Leningrad.

In December 1981, Toshiba began shipping its machines to Leningrad; Kongsberg shipped its software to Leningrad and its computers to Toshiba in 1982. By the summer of 1983, the Soviets had the equipment in place in their Baltic shipyards. Toshiba and Kongsberg engineers went to the site six times to assemble and fine-tune the machines, a process that involved secretive, intense sessions with Soviet technicians surrounded at all times by KGB guards. The Soviets, convinced they were on to a good deal (they had even received a five-year service agreement), ordered and received four additional machines in 1984, making their total purchase worth more than $25 million, not an inconspicuous transaction. (This second transaction, involving less expensive models, was revealed in June 1987 in confessions by two Toshiba executives after the statute of limitations expired, making them immune to prosecution.)

Not until 1985 was official attention drawn to these illegal sales, although word spread privately about the deal the year it was consummated. A former employee of Wako, Kazuo Kumagai, who had been involved in Japanese-Soviet trade for twenty-two years, wrote a letter to Cocom explaining what had happened. Kumagai admits that he was partially motivated by not being promoted for his efforts as an interpreter for the Toshiba technicians in Leningrad. (Another view is that Kumagai himself was a KGB agent and that his letter to Cocom was an attempt to upset Japanese-American relations.) Later, he also said Wako had been associated with the KGB during his entire tenure with the company.[15] After writing the letter, he was dismissed from his job in April 1986. Cocom followed up on the information by contacting Japan's Ministry of International Trade and Industry (MITI) but found its officials unresponsive and unwilling to investigate the affair. Later that year, then Defense Secretary Caspar W. Weinberger learned of the deal, and he took the matter up with the Japanese defense minister in December 1986. The Japanese began investigations in early 1987. In May 1987, the public first learned of the illegal sale.

Even though Toshiba executives at first protested and said that the sales were legal, they eventually admitted their crime. The president of Toshiba Machine Company and two other executives resigned. Two others were arrested for the first shipment of machines to the Soviets. The president and chairman of Toshiba Corporation also resigned and later received suspended sentences. Bernhard Green was arrested in Norway, and the Tokyo District Court fined Toshiba Machine Co. $15,750.

After much international publicity and pressure from U.S. lawmakers, the Japanese government promised reforms in its export-control process. It proposed to increase the number of export inspectors, to extend the time period for the statute of limitations, and to increase criminal penalties. In addition, Toshiba accepted offers made by the Commerce

Department for an audit of its licensing procedures. It also promised to increase its financial contribution to Cocom. Toshiba procured the legal services of Washington lawyer Leonard Garment (former legal counsel to President Richard M. Nixon) and in July 1987 ran full-page ads in U.S. national magazines and newspapers with the headline TOSHIBA CORPORATION EXTENDS ITS DEEPEST REGRETS TO THE AMERICAN PEOPLE, apologizing for its transgressions and enumerating the reforms it was undertaking.

Norway's government officials have proven somewhat less cooperative. They say that the transaction was the work of one employee isolated from management, the British expatriate Green. However, the Norwegian prime minister, Gro Harlem Brundtland, sent President Reagan a letter promising to tighten her country's procedures for exports to communist countries. The government launched an investigation of the sale during the summer of 1987 but took no tangible action before the statute of limitations expired. The Toshiba affair caused several European countries to point accusatory fingers at one another and argue that many members of Cocom routinely violate its export restrictions. In late 1987, Norway stated that West Germany, Italy, France, and England were guilty of Cocom violations far greater than those committed during the Toshiba affair. The Norwegian government provided names of machine-tool companies in all these countries that it felt had transgressed Cocom controls.[16]

The effect of the sale could be devastating to U.S. security. Department of Defense officials, many of whom already felt that the technical capability of the Soviet navy surpassed that of the U.S. Navy, say that the purchases will make it easier for the Soviets to manufacture propellers that can only be detected from within ten miles. (Previous Soviet propellers are detectable from a distance of 100 miles.) The diverted technology will likely enable more Soviet submarines to get so close to American shores that their missiles, if fired, could arrive in U.S. cities within ten minutes of launch.[17] Cost estimates for recapturing the lead in antisubmarine warfare vary from $1 million to $30 billion during the next fifteen to twenty years. Former Navy Secretary John F. Lehman, Jr., stated that the Soviets gained seven to ten years of research and development by purchasing the equipment. Some skeptical observers, such as Donald A.

Weedon, a Washington-based lawyer specializing in export controls, note, however, that the Soviets were previously gaining on U.S. submarine technology through their own technical advances and that these two sales only assisted them in closing an already narrowing gap.

This incident is an example of Japan's past dealings with the Soviets and displays its lack of commitment to safeguarding critical high technology. An earlier transgression came to light in 1982 when U.S. intelligence learned via spy satellite photographs of an 80,000-ton floating dry dock sold to the Soviets by the Japanese that was being used to repair the Soviet aircraft carrier *Minsk*. Since 1983, five Japanese trading companies have been caught violating Cocom regulations. Kazuo Kumagai, the Wako employee who alerted Cocom to the Toshiba sale, alleges that fifty other companies have traded with the Soviets in violation of Japan's and Cocom's export rules, although his allegations have not been confirmed.[18]

During the months that Japan was being scrutinized for its sale of milling equipment, Americans learned of the intensity with which Japanese companies pursue new customers. So desirous of increased sales are the Japanese that export-control agreements, respect for their American ally's concern for national security, and their sense of fairness in industrial competition can take a back seat to the profit motive.

The U.S. electronics industry has been overcome with concern about Japan as a serious threat to its competitive status in the world marketplace. The Japanese edge in nonmilitary-related, lower-technology items, such as audio and video equipment, is shocking enough. For example, few people realize that as of early 1987 Japan had manufactured more than 12 million videocassette recorders, the United States none at all.[19] Recently, the Japanese have also begun to invade what were previously American strongholds in high-technology items.

In one such area—semiconductor manufacturing—the Japanese have taken the lead. A report prepared jointly by the Defense Department and the Central Intelligence Agency indicates that one reason for the American loss of semiconductor market share to the Japanese is the frequent licensing of advanced U.S. chip technology to the Japanese.[20] The Japanese have capitalized on U.S. generosity at the expense of American industry's health. On the other hand, the U.S. chip industry may have stifled itself through inordinately aggressive profit-taking and the failure to reinvest in research and development.

The impact of Japan surpassing the United States in semiconductor manufacturing centers directly on U.S. ability to maintain a lead in military technology against the Soviets, because much of contemporary military technology depends on semiconductors. Already, some U.S. agencies are beginning to rely on Japan for chip technology advances. For example, the National Security Agency (NSA) now uses customized chips from Japan in its military communications equipment. U.S. dependence on the Japanese semiconductor industry might one day compromise the NSA (not to mention the military space program) and any agency using a supercomputer, especially if Japan makes the chips that run this equipment available to the Soviets.

Industry watchers have theories and plans for giving U.S. electronics companies a renewed impetus to make them internationally competitive vis-à-vis the Japanese. The government has now entered the debate in an effort to open up the Japanese market to U.S. electronic components, specifically semiconductor chips.[21] These actions have so far been motivated by economic necessity and by the fear that the Japanese could threaten U.S. national security. The Toshiba affair, however, has added a new element of suspicion to U.S. deliberations over the issue of Japanese competitiveness.

Japanese businesses continue to pursue U.S. technology from multiple angles. Japanese corporations have been buying interests in venture capital firms, banks, and high-technology companies with the goal of increasing their access to high technology, which they will then be able to sell internationally. The number of acquisitions of U.S. companies by the Japanese is steadily increasing; it went from thirteen in 1984 to twenty-one in 1985 and fifty-nine in 1986.[22] Japanese banks in the United States are often the link between a U.S. high-tech firm and a Japanese buyer. Japan gains access to advanced technology by funding start-up companies in high-technology centers such as Silicon Valley. California First Bank Venture Capital Corporation, owned by the Bank of Tokyo, is one such funding conduit; in 1984, it had a $3.2 million stake in a California biotechnology company along with eight other Japanese firms.[23] Orien

Ventures of New Canaan (Conn.) is a venture capital company formed jointly by U.S. and Japanese investors with the purpose of investing in high technology. As of October 1987, it had bought into sixteen high-technology companies, including some developing semiconductors and lasers.[24] U.S. firms that develop militarily critical technology are somewhat protected in Japan by an agreement signed in 1988 between Japan and the United States. The agreement provides the United States with Japan's guarantee that Japan will deny general access to patents of militarily critical technology by keeping such U.S. patent applications in a confidential file in the Japan Defense Agency. Moves such as this will bring controls over access to critical technology more in line with those in the United States.[25]

Despite the notable exceptions and the current hue and cry, Japan has generally maintained an export policy compatible with that of the United States and Cocom to ensure the future of its American security umbrella. The exceptions to its cordial dealings with the United States have occurred when it has sold technology to the Soviet Union as a diplomatic insurance policy and a guarantee that Soviet natural resources—including lumber, iron ores, and oil—will be available.[26] As a result, trade relations between the Soviet Union and Japan have been close. By 1979, Japan was the second most important nonsocialist trading partner, after West Germany, with $4.4 billion worth of trade between the two countries.[27] The Soviet Union has enjoyed a most-favored-nation status with the Japanese, who have given it lenient terms concerning exports. Japan's need for this relationship was evident when it only temporarily suspended trade with Afghanistan in 1980 rather than imposing other countries' decisive long-term suspensions. Between 1972 and 1977, Japan ranked as the top supplier to the Soviet Union of three high-technology commodities, and as second of five.[28] In 1986, Japanese trade with the Soviet bloc reached $3.8 billion.[29] Gorbachev, in his quest for high technology, needs the Japanese to help his sagging economy. Even though Russian tradition generally precludes relinquishing land, some observers have speculated that the Kuril Islands, now in Soviet hands, might become Japan's again as a quid pro quo for guaranteed Soviet access to technology and investment if the Japanese promised they would not militarize them.[30]

The basis for Japan's export controls is its Foreign Trade Control Law of 1949, which allows for the "normal development of foreign trade." This act controls the "necessary foreign exchange, foreign trade, and other transactions in order to maintain a favorable balance of payments, the stability of Japanese currency, and the most efficient expenditure of reserves."[31] The law does not mention military or national security reasons for restricting exports. The Japanese Diet did enact the Government Export Trade Control Order, which restricts sensitive items recognized by Cocom, but its list is much shorter than that used by the United States. The restrictions apply only to Japanese companies in Japan.[32] The Japanese see high-technology exports as the key to their economic growth strategy. Generally speaking, the government expects industry to use the equivalent of an honor system to control high-technology exports.

Although the restrictions appear in the Japanese law books, and the MITI, which grants export licenses, has the power to enforce them, it has only recently exploited its power to do so. The penalties—rarely used— for exporting items on the short control list are similar to those in the United States: fines, delays in exporting, and revocation of export licenses. Instead, the MITI has chosen to allow private enterprise to police itself, with occasionally dire results. A memorable event in export-control self-policing history occurred in 1982, when the Japanese sold the Soviets the dry dock with potential military uses.

Japan has not been above using espionage to advance its high-technology industry, which presents some complicated problems for U.S. lawmakers and lawyers. About 85 to 90 percent of Japan's intelligence-gathering resources are applied toward enhancing its economic and technical status. The MITI manages an intelligence network that operates worldwide to collect economic and technical information. In Japan, as in the United States, industrial espionage is not illegal unless patents are violated, and many companies spy on their competitors without hesitation.[33] Some Japanese managers hone their spying skills by attending company-sponsored courses on industrial espionage, which are often called "competitive analysis" seminars. The courses teach executives how to obtain company secrets legally.[34] When Japanese executives come to the United States, they no doubt avail themselves of the opportunity to gather company secrets.

As an example, between 1981 and 1982, several executives from the electronics company Hitachi illegally purchased secret information about IBM's 3081 computer and disk drives. The executives came to the United States every few months to pay a consulting firm for IBM's proprietary information. The FBI, alerted to Hitachi's activities by the owner of the consulting firm, monitored these transactions while one of their undercover agents observed each transfer of information. A representative from IBM security also attended some of the meetings between Hitachi officials and the consulting firm. At one time, Hitachi was eager to pay $525,000 for a large amount of information on the 3081. Finally, in June 1982, the FBI arrested nine Hitachi executives. In late 1983, two of them pleaded guilty; they were each fined $10,000 and placed on three years' probation. Hitachi and IBM settled out of court for an estimated $3 million to cover legal expenses. Later, in 1986, the agreement was revised and the payment reduced.[35] IBM was given the right to inspect future Hitachi products as insurance against copyright violations resulting from the information theft. In 1984, Mitsubishi Electric Corporation also admitted to stealing secret information from IBM and was fined $10,000.[36]

Shizuka Kamei, a member of the Japanese Diet, has called his country a "paradise for spies."[37] In June 1983, the first secretary of the Soviet embassy was expelled after it was discovered that he was directly involved in high-technology theft.[38] And in 1987, it came to light that four Japanese spies allegedly sold the Soviets technical data on U.S. military aircraft, including the F-16 fighter and a new Boeing AWACS radar plane, for $714,286. The four, one of whom had worked at a U.S. air base, were arrested for spying for the Soviet Union and China. One of them was caught trying to pass technical data to V. B. Aksyonov, a Soviet trade officer in Tokyo; some of the others sold data to Igor A. Solokov, a first secretary at the Soviet embassy.[39] Also in 1987, Minoru Shimizu, a Tokyo aircraft industry executive, sold several million dollars' worth of technical information about a computerized flight management system, among other items, for only $65,000 to a couple of Soviet intelligence officers. One worked at the Soviet embassy, and another was a manager for Aeroflot in Japan.[40]

Japan's loose attitude toward company secrets raises an interesting issue concerning its participation in the U.S. Strategic Defense Initiative. In late 1986, it was announced that Japanese companies and some public research institutions would undertake aspects of SDI research.[41] Defense Department critics are concerned about giving the Japanese access to critical military technology, because they have demonstrated a willingness to sell it to the Soviets. It thus seems imperative that the Japanese begin to take a more conservative approach concerning the protection of company secrets.

Although former Prime Minister Yasuhiro Nakasone attempted to pass legislation that would punish espionage with life imprisonment, he failed to do so. The Japanese people are hesitant to accept any restraints on their freedom because of their history of military regimes. One step taken to date has been the MITI's advice to Japanese companies that they limit employee access to those areas of their plants containing restricted technologies. Also, in an effort to placate the United States, Japan is becoming more aggressive in policing its exports of high technology. In April 1988, the MITI charged two trading houses, Kyokuto Shokai Co. and Shinsei Koeki Co., with illegally exporting high technology to China. In the same month, the Japanese government stopped an illegal shipment of 500 Nippon Electric Company (NEC) personal computers to North Korea.[42]

ISRAEL

Israel fits uncomfortably into the U.S. export-control policy puzzle. Although it enjoys a privileged relationship with the United States, cemented with $3 billion in U.S. aid every year, Israel has come to be a grievous source of U.S. high-technology leaks through espionage.

Jonathan Jay Pollard, a former U.S. Navy intelligence analyst, pleaded guilty in June 1986 to charges of spying on the United States for Israel; his actions provided Israel with classified military information, including U.S. intelligence on the Palestine Liberation Organization headquarters in Tunisia (which was later bombed by the Israelis), Pakistan's atomic weapon program, the identities of U.S. agents in the Middle East, satellite photos, and message traffic relating to Israel. Court testimony revealed that top Israeli officials were involved in Pollard's spying, indicating that it was not an isolated occurrence. One of the Israeli coconspirators was Rafi Eitan, a former intelligence official who some believe had previously headed Lekem, a government intelligence unit specializing in the collection of scientific and technical information worldwide.[43] A 1979 CIA report highlighted Israeli intelligence-gathering abilities, stating that the Israeli spy network is, next to the Soviet Union's, the most active in the world.[44] The Pollard affair has caused many a diplomat on both sides to shuffle around the issues.

The Israelis have apparently made still other efforts to acquire U.S. technical secrets through questionable means. In 1986, the U.S. Customs Service and Justice Department investigated charges that Israel obtained U.S. cluster-bomb manufacturing technology and equipment from a private U.S. defense contractor.[45] In 1982, direct export of cluster-bomb technology was denied Israel when U.S. officials learned that Israel was using the bombs in Lebanon. In 1985, U.S. Customs discovered that Israel illegally attempted to purchase electroplating equipment for use on tank-cannon barrels.[46] In 1986, Israeli agents were charged with attempting to steal an airborne spy camera system from an Illinois defense plant.[47] These events and others continue to put wrinkles in U.S.-Israeli relations and create mistrust and doubt concerning Israel's respect for U.S. law. They also illustrate that Israel is willing to take great risks to get U.S. high technology.

What these incidents do not make clear is whether Israel is leaking its stolen technology secrets to the Soviets. In late 1987, U.S. intelligence sources revealed that Mosaad, Israel's intelligence agency, had been penetrated by the KGB, raising the possibility that critical U.S. high technology in Israel's hands, received either through spies, such as Jonathan Jay Pollard, or through direct legal sales, may be finding its way to the Soviet Union. The United States became aware of the KGB connection when the CIA traced Pollard's information about U.S. weapons technology to the Eastern bloc.[48] With its flourishing arms industry shipping its product to countries hostile to the United States, Israel may knowingly or unknowingly leak U.S. technology to the Soviets through intermediaries such as its arms customers. On the other hand, Israel is playing a high-stakes game if it is willing to jeopardize its U.S. aid with potential discovery of its role in leaking critical military technology to the Soviets.

NEUTRAL AND NONALIGNED STATES: HOW RELIABLE ARE THEY?

Neutral countries such as Sweden, Austria, and Switzerland are intent on, even a little desperate about, maintaining their ability to purchase U.S. technology. Companies in these countries depend on U.S. high-technology products for their business operation or combine American equipment with their own products. The United States has made it plain to these governments and to specific company executives that if they do not support U.S. export controls they may lose their access to American high technology. Sweden, Austria, Finland, Singapore, and Switzerland are eligible for general export licenses from the United States although they are not members of Cocom.

The effort emanating from the Pentagon to garner greater respect for U.S. export controls by neutral nations has three purposes: first, to encourage the protection of technology exported to neutral countries; second, to persuade neutral countries to prevent technology diversions within their borders; and third, and most difficult, to prevail on them not to sell high-technology products that they manufacture to the Soviet bloc.[49]

SWEDEN

Sweden and the United States reached an agreement during 1981 and 1982 that called for the Swedes to be more vigilant in preventing illegal diversions in return for keeping the right to import U.S. technology. Sweden was anxious to sign the agreement because several of its companies had already been caught acting as way stations for high-technology products, particularly American computers, on their way to the Soviet Union. Even after the agreement, the Swedish firm ASEA AB paid a $440,000 fine to the Commerce Department in May 1986 for sending nine U.S.-made computers to the Soviet Union and Czechoslovakia between 1980 and 1983. U.S. officials negotiated the 1981–82 agreement quietly when Sweden feared losing access to U.S. technology as a consequence of its slack enforcement of U.S. rules.[50]

One infamous case is the Datasaab affair, in which the partly state-financed electronics firm sold air traffic control equipment containing illegally obtained U.S. chips to the Soviet Ministry of Civil Aviation. In 1976, the Swedish company, then called Stansaab, had applied to the U.S. Commerce Department for a license to reexport to the Soviet Union the $3.1 million worth of U.S. equipment for use in an air traffic control system. In 1977, Commerce rejected the application, and Datasaab reapplied, this time assuring that it would conform to ten conditions outlined by Commerce to minimize any possibility that the sale would jeopardize U.S. national security. By late 1977, the Commerce Department and Cocom had approved the license, and the Swedish firm purchased the U.S. equipment.

According to the Commerce Department, by 1980 it was obvious to its Office of Export Enforcement that the terms of the license were being violated by Datasaab, and it began to investigate the affair. Although Datasaab had assured Commerce that it would not sell a radar digitizing feature of the system to the Soviets, it became evident that the company had indeed done so. Furthermore, although it was agreed that the equipment was only to be used for civilian purposes, Commerce found that the Soviets were using the equipment to improve their military air defense system. At one point, in 1981, Commerce asked the Swedish government to investigate Datasaab, only to be informed that government officials felt the company was innocent. In the meantime, Datasaab was acquired by L. M. Ericsson Telephone Company, which had launched its own investigation. It finally concluded that Datasaab had violated the terms of the export license. In 1984, the United States charged Datasaab with violating its export license and imposed a $3.12 million fine.[51]

U.S. efforts to receive assistance from Sweden have been paying off. In September 1987, the Swedish Riksdag (parliament) voted to adopt stricter export controls, particularly concerning arms shipments. Furthermore, the United States reinforces its strong bargaining position with Sweden whenever it can. In 1981, Defense Secretary Weinberger offered them technology from Lear Siegler Inc., Teledyne, and Honeywell in return for increased diligence on their part concerning illegal exports. At the time, they needed the technology to develop a fighter-bomber.[52] Swedish customs officials also provided essential evidence to the U.S. government during the investigation of a case involving the illegal export of U.S. microprocessors.

Still, a Polish citizen, Marek Cieslak, and a Canadian citizen, Andrzej Schmidt, were caught illegally exporting microprocessors from a southern California company to Sweden between June 1985 and May 1987. U.S. Customs officials arrested the two men as they were about to board a plane to Stockholm, attempting to carry $46,000 worth of microprocessors out of the country in their hand luggage. Federal investigators found that Cieslak and Schmidt had shipped hundreds of Intel microprocessors to Sweden and on to Poland. They were indicted in May 1987 and convicted in October 1987.[53]

AUSTRIA AND SWITZERLAND

Just as the Swedes are increasing their cooperation, neutral Austria has made a commitment to tighten controls. By the end of 1987, its lawmakers finally responded to U.S. pressure to firm up its export laws, agreeing to allow temporary seizure of goods in transit in suspicious cases. Such goods pass through one country on their way to another and are stored temporarily in a secured area. The area is usually in a warehouse supervised by the transit country's customs officials. Goods in transit avoid customs fees.

The change had been a long time coming; Austria has the highest number of companies and individuals to whom exports have been denied by the Commerce Department. Until only recently, Austrian customs officials would not inspect or stop technology shipments moving through their jurisdiction to other destinations.

In the past, Stephen Walton of the U.S. Customs Service saw Austria as simply a revolving door for illegal diversions. The Austrian government indicated that it intended to crack down on the problem, and in January 1988 it passed legislation that tightened its own enforcement of export controls. With the changes, Austrian customs officials can now enter the customs-free zones to intercept suspect shipments. The U.S. government, specifically the Department of State, was instrumental in convincing the Austrians to fall in line with U.S. policy.[54]

Austria's new interest in cooperating with the United States stems from its dedication to gaining access to U.S. high technology. Previously, the United States underlined its concern over Austria's lax attitude by depriving three Austrian companies of the right to sell U.S. products. Of the three companies, Betriebs & Fianzierungs Beratungs GmbH, Bollinger GmbH, and Vrablicz & Co., two are freight forwarders and one is a management and financial consulting company. While investigating these companies, the U.S. Customs Service and Department of Commerce turned up a link with Dietmar Ulrichshofer, the infamous Werner Bruchhausen's Austrian colleague, who is one of the owners of Betriebs & Fianzierungs Beratungs GmbH.[55] Also, in Alexandria, Va., in 1985, D. Frank Bazzarre, an engineer, was given a term of one year in prison, 700 hours of community service, and a $110,000 fine for illegally exporting chip manufacturing and test equipment to Austria with the intent of then sending it to the Soviet Union.

As late as 1986, the Austrians provided the venue for a significant illegal shipment of several million dollars' worth of U.S. computers. The shipment left Belgium for a Vienna warehouse, where a Turkish buyer stored it for the Belgian company until he could send it on to the Soviet Union. Although U.S. Customs officials did not reveal the contents of the shipment, in 1986 the *Wall Street Journal* stated that the shipment contained equipment from Tektronix Inc. of Beaverton, Ore.[56]

Despite its mixed track record of leniency and cooperation, Austria received assurances in March 1988 that the United States would expand Austria's access to U.S. high technology. The encouraging remarks had not been followed by specific actions on the part of the United States or Cocom as of May 1988.

Switzerland, like Austria, is under pressure from the United States to tighten its export controls and to cooperate more fully with U.S. Customs officials to track down illegal shipments. Its government recently agreed to stricter in-transit controls. Historically, the Swiss have turned the other way when obvious diversion schemes have been carried out within their borders. In 1983, for example, Perkin-Elmer received an order from a Swiss company, Favag S.A., for two chip manufacturing-related machines. Favag received the equipment after the United States approved the export license on the condition that the equipment not be exported to the Soviet Union. Favag shipped the equipment to another Swiss company, Eler Engineering, which in turn sent it to the Soviet Union via France.

INDIA

India is among the nonaligned countries being pressured by the United States to stand behind its and Cocom's regulations. For the first time since the early 1960s, the United States is seeking closer ties with India and has permitted sales of restricted high technology there as a means of drawing the two countries closer. This new trend began in 1986, when Control Data sold $500 million worth of computer equipment to India after its government assured the United States that it would tighten security for U.S. high-technology goods used in the country.[57] In December 1986, India initiated the purchase of a Cray supercomputer from the U.S company, stating that the $8.3 million computer was to be used to help forecast monsoon rains. The XMP-14, Cray's low-end model, has dual-use capabilities that had many export watchers and the Pentagon concerned about its security once it reached the customer and wary that the technology might find its way to India's increasingly friendly neighbor to the north, the U.S.S.R. But by the fall of 1987, the United States had received enough assurances from the Indian government to persuade officials to permit the sale through a memorandum of understanding on export controls.[58]

The United States has ample cause for concern, however. The Soviet Union manufactures or comanufactures more than two-thirds of India's military hardware.[59] India is the only non-Warsaw Pact nation that is actively engaged with the Soviet Union in joint ventures for the production of Soviet military equipment such as the T-72 tank.[60] According to the Defense Department, the Soviets leased a nuclear submarine to India in 1988, and India has given the Soviets rights to use a naval base on the eastern coast of India. The submarine transaction was the first instance of a country transferring a nuclear warship to another country.[61] India, therefore, is likely to maintain its friendly, nonaligned political posture vis-à-vis the Soviets, especially since it knows that the United States has sold technology to its enemy, Pakistan. Consequently, the United States should not expect any compromises in return for the increase in technology export. At best, it could hope to maintain an open, status quo relationship as a short-term insurance policy for U.S. security interests in the region.

CARIBBEAN BASIN AND SOUTH AMERICA

Because the Soviet Union seems bent on widening its influence throughout Latin America, the likelihood of U.S. high technology falling into the hands of Soviet agents and personnel via the United States' southern neighbors will only increase without vigilance. In 1985 and 1986 a Cuban government agent, a Venezuelan middleman, and a U.S. businessman sold $1 million worth of IBM equipment to Cuba through a front company in Panama. The sale was discovered during a U.S. government inquiry into violations of the U.S. trade embargo against Cuba. The U.S. businessman and the Venezuelan middleman were arrested in the spring of 1987, but the Cuban government agent remains out of reach because the United States lacks an extradition treaty with Cuba.[62] This incident, along with heavy gray-market traffic of U.S. computer goods to the area through Miami, makes Central and South America a region to monitor closely for the illegal exportation of U.S. high technology.

THE ASIAN CONNECTION

The countries of Asia have moved within the purview of U.S. government agencies charged with controlling the export of critical technologies. During the 1960s and 1970s, most of the major technology diversion and espionage cases involved Western Europe. But during the 1980s, Asia became an increasingly active conduit for U.S. high technology on its way to the Soviet Union.

CHINA

China could become a significant source for the illegal transfer of technology to the Soviets, but U.S. foreign-policy interests currently complicate any resolution to this potential problem. As China has undergone economic liberalization and reforms, the United States has felt compelled to encourage and take advantage of those moves by increasing trade and investment there. As a result, the United States liberalized its export controls for China, even though China trades openly with the Soviets. The U.S. interest in closer ties comes from the potential for U.S.-Chinese cooperation in many areas, including joint intelligence efforts targeting the Soviets. Since 1981, the Chinese have apparently allowed the United States to operate listening posts targeted at the Soviet Union in the Xinjiang Uygur region in western China.[63] The United States may be sharing the listening data with China. These interests result in a risky and complex trade policy.

Since the normalization of U.S.-Chinese relations in 1979 and the subsequent shift in China's government toward a more open and capitalistic economy, the United States has happily rushed in with goods, services, investments, exchanges, and joint ventures in an attempt to open a new market and nurture the apparent changes. In 1979, the Chinese government indicated a greater interest in liberalizing its economic structure by announcing a new joint venture law to entice foreign investment. In September 1983, the government published the law, finally providing the terms and conditions for setting up foreign joint ventures.[64] In 1984, China created fourteen "special economic zones" to lure foreign investors.[65] That same year, the United States signed an agreement that gave U.S. companies in China credits for taxes they paid on interest and royalties.[66] In addition to attracting investment, the Chinese have opened wide the doors to trade with the West. By March 1988, they had signed 5,000 joint ventures with foreign companies, and in April further codification of private-sector activities, specifically joint ventures involving foreign investment, was enacted.[67] U.S. trade with the Chinese in 1986 was about $8 billion.[68] But this growing relationship is not without serious risks.

China and the Soviet Union have long competed for dominance of Asia and have seriously disagreed over their shared border and the Soviet presence in nearby countries. Still, they continue to trade goods and services. On Mar. 10, 1983, Soviet and Chinese ministers signed a trade and payments agreement intended to stimulate trade transactions between the two countries. The results were immediate: Trade volume increased from $300 million in 1982 to $800 million in 1983.[69] In 1986, trade between the Soviet bloc and China amounted to more than $2.6 billion;[70] by 1986, high-technology trade had increased to $1 billion from $144 million in 1982.[71]

The Soviets and Chinese reached other agreements in the 1980s as well. One, signed in China on Dec. 21, 1984, during a rare visit by a high-level Soviet leader, First Deputy Prime Minister Ivan Arkhipov, contained three important commitments: economic cooperation, scientific and technological cooperation, and the establishment of a Sino-Soviet committee for promoting trade and scientific cooperation. In the five-year agreement, both countries called for the "exchange of scientific and technical information and documentation, specimens of products and materials, 'knowhow' and licenses."[72] Other signals from Moscow, including continuing visits by Soviet dignitaries to China, indicate that a further rapprochement between the two countries is in the making. The Soviets are also attempting to resolve the border disputes and have offered troop withdrawals from strategic regions along the China-Mongolia border.

Changes in China's leadership also signal a potential increase in the transfer rate of technology between the two countries. In 1987, Li Peng was named acting premier of China, and he was confirmed in that post in April 1988. He has been a powerful force in China's economic reform program. Viewed as an influential technocrat, he was trained as an engineer in the Soviet Union at the Moscow Power Institute and is fluent in Russian.[73] Furthermore, he cochairs a Chinese-Soviet committee on technical, scientific, and economic cooperation. His interest in U.S. high technology was apparent when he visited Silicon Valley in 1985.[74] U.S. observers will be watching Li to see if he moves China toward more technical exchanges with the Soviets, a move that may jeopardize the existing flow of American high technology to China.

While attempting to stabilize its relations with the Soviet Union, China has also engaged in an effort to gain access to U.S. high technology. The Reagan Administration concluded trade pacts with China, allowing it to purchase U.S. strategic weapons, munitions, and some high technology. In February 1980 President Jimmy Carter had given China most-favored-nation status, which brought with it access to many U.S. trade items previously not permitted to travel to the communist nation. In a controversial move in 1983, the Department of Commerce began to make exceptions to its list of controlled commodities, allowing certain items to be shipped to China. Even after learning that China had sold its Silkworm missiles to Iran, Commerce widened the door to high-technology trade in June 1987 by allowing two more previously restricted products to be sold to China with only a departmental review.[75] Cocom also agreed with the liberalization of export policy. In addition, Commerce raised the maximum processing data rate for computers that could be exported to China to 285 Mbit/s from 155, enabling the Chinese to gain access to faster U.S. computers. The United States relaxed its trade restrictions in part because of its desire for an ally in Asia to counter the increasing Soviet presence and instability in surrounding countries.

China seeks the revitalization of its economy that a carefully orchestrated infusion of Western know-how, investment, and equipment can bring about. The list of sophisticated U.S. goods available to the Chinese in 1987 included a variety of computers, semiconductor equipment, nuclear processing equipment, satellite-tracking stations, and nuclear reactors. The United States offered China some choice equipment at the time denied to the Soviets and to most nonaligned countries.[76]

The Chinese also receive U.S. high technology through academic exchange channels. Compared with other nonaligned or Eastern bloc countries, China has placed a large number of students in American universities with strong technology programs. A dramatic increase in these numbers coincided with the liberalizing of the U.S. trade policy. After 30 years of suspension, China and the United States resumed educational exchanges in the mid-1970s, the United States giving the Chinese the opportunity to train at top U.S. universities and allowing them access to some sophisticated university computing centers such as those at MIT, Carnegie-Mellon, Cal Tech, and Stanford. According to the State Department, at least 40,000 Chinese students were attending American universities in 1988. Michael Marks, assistant director for global technology, Office of Science and Technology Policy (part of the Executive Office of the President), points out that the U.S. government does not always carefully screen Chinese students for technology transfer concerns.

In addition to attending such universities as Cal Tech and MIT, the Chinese students often participate in special programs at research labs such as the Lawrence Livermore National Laboratory and Los Alamos National Laboratory.

Although U.S. students studying in China concentrate on Chinese cultural studies, languages, history, and archaeology, Chinese students in the United States tend to target courses on technology, engineering, and sciences, particularly classes in microelectronics, computers, and advanced materials. Approximately two-thirds of the Chinese students studying in the United States between 1979 and 1983 were enrolled in technology-related courses. Students are selected and sponsored by the Chinese government, which helps determine what a Chinese student will study. About one-quarter of the Chinese students in the United States report monthly to their government on their progress and activities. In addition, some Chinese students are required to remit to their work units at home a specified portion of U.S. money that comes into their hands as a result of American-funded scholarships for Chinese students.[77]

Chinese students in this country receive the same treatment as that accorded U.S. students. They are given access to all computers, courses, and research laboratories, unless their work is classified by the government. U.S. students in China, however, often cannot take certain courses. The Chinese government charges them fees for research materials, and access to some libraries is prohibited. U.S. scholars often find some research documents classified, even though they have no bearing on Chinese national security interests. A few U.S. students have also discovered that they are not welcome at some archaeological sites.[78]

The FBI suspects that many Chinese students play a role in carrying back advanced U.S. technology to the Chinese government. But because the trading doors between the United States and China are currently so open, acquiring U.S. technology clandestinely may not be necessary, although evidence continues to surface indicating ongoing illegal exporting activity. In 1984, two Chinese, Zheng Da-chuan and sister-in-law Zhang Jing-li, and three Chinese Americans were arrested for illegally shipping computer equipment to China. All five were apprehended before the equipment left the United States. The military-related electronics equipment included traveling wave tube amplifiers used in radar guidance systems.[79] The three Chinese Americans ran a front company in Lincraft, N.J., called Eastar Corporation, for shipping the equipment out of the United States. One of the three Americans, Kuang-shin Lin, was the chief U.S. contact for Zheng and Zhang and was also a computer expert at AT&T. The five were caught after a Customs official infiltrated their group as a broker interested in selling 100 transverse wave tube amplifiers valued at $1.25 million.[80] Zheng Da-chuan was fined $10,000 and given two years' probation; charges were dismissed for Zhang; the three accomplices were fined $5,000 each and given two years' probation.[81]

Other incidents of illegal diversion have involved the Chinese. Chipex Inc., a San Jose, Calif., company owned jointly by China and Hong Kong, was founded in 1981 as a conduit for U.S. high technology, particularly semiconductor know-how, to China. It pleaded guilty in November 1983 to charges of the illegal export in May 1981 of silicon wafers into Hong Kong. During 1981, Commerce had canceled all export licenses enabling U.S. companies to ship to Hua-Ko Electronics Company Ltd., a Hong Kong company, because it learned that Hua-Ko owned Chipex jointly with individuals in China. Chipex was formed as a subsidiary of Hua-Ko, a direct representative of the Chinese. Hua-Ko had sent Chinese engineers to Chipex to locate technology and to learn certain high-technology processes. Between 1981 and 1983, Customs agents seized seventy-five wafers leaving the United States from San Francisco airport in the hands of Chipex representatives. Commerce, Customs, and FBI investigators observed companies that did business with Chipex, an effort that resulted in convictions and fines of two consulting firms, Pacific Enterprise Inc. of Cupertino and HSC MOS Inc. of Fremont, both in California. They pleaded guilty to illegally exporting related technical data. The U.S. government alleged that the company was a front for training Chinese engineers in chip manufacturing, a far more serious charge implying that China was launching its own high-technology espionage effort. Chipex was fined $50,000.

In 1985, five individuals related to the Chipex case were indicted in San Jose, Calif., on twenty-four counts of unlawful export. Philip Teik-Jan Tai (a California resident and Hong Kong national) of American Semiconductor Inc., Chi Pak Lui of Hong Kong-based Micro Mass Systems Corporation, and Walter Loi Shing Chiu and son of Hua-Ko Electronics

Company Ltd. were the key defendants. Philip Teik-Jan Tai entered a guilty plea to criminal charges, received a $50,000 fine and was required to perform 200 hours of community service. The other defendants are still at large. The original indictment was for the illegal transfer of electronic equipment to Hong Kong. The group of businessmen had been negotiating for the illegal sale of $6 million worth of equipment. When the Customs Service apprehended them, they had already procured $4 million worth, and equipment representing part of that amount had reached Hong Kong. Customs seized a $461,000 electronics testing system that was later forfeited by the defendants as part of the civil penalty.[82]

U.S. Customs acknowledges that diversion activity in the Far East area is on the rise. Although Chinese intelligence agents are not particularly proficient (despite being originally trained by the KGB), they do take advantage of the Hong Kong conduit. As a result, the Customs Service has placed a number of agents in its office in Hong Kong to halt diversion attempts. Stephen Walton at Customs considers the biggest concern for the United States the illegal munitions exports to China through Hong Kong; the military capability of the Chinese is antiquated, and "they feel that in the long run it is better to build a defense system based on U.S. weapons rather than on anybody else's because they will be friendly with the U.S. longer."[83]

Some munitions technology already reaches China legally through special arrangements with the U.S. government. According to former Secretary of Defense Weinberger, almost $1 billion worth of military-related technology traveled to China in 1984. More than $10 million passed from China to the United States for a satellite-tracking station. Furthermore, on the civilian side, the Department of Commerce spent $10 million in grants to study Chinese projects for ways the United States could invest in them. The United States is banking on the hope that China will never be tempted to use these advanced technologies against its neighbors—Japan, South Korea, and Taiwan—or the United States. China did, however, supply North Korea through illegal channels in Hong Kong with an American command, control, communications, and intelligence battle management system that originated in the United States.[84]

In 1985, the U.S. government agreed to sell new antisubmarine war-fare equipment to China.[85] Although the Chinese successfully obtained U.S. technology through the purchase, the United States did not give the Chinese the know-how to manufacture the equipment themselves. In another case, though, the United States gave the Chinese weapons-building know-how: By 1987, the United States was assisting China in the manufacture of ammunition for 105-mm howitzers.[86] The United States feels pressure akin to blackmail to continue these military technology sales, because the Chinese may turn to the Soviets if the United States ceases selling them arms. Military technology transfers have already had a tangible effect; some experts believe that they have helped the Chinese reduce the size of their military from 4 million personnel to 3 million.[87] These arms sales have clearly caused some embarrassment to the United States. Despite repeated denials, China has become Iran's largest arms supplier. By October 1987, it was evident that China was continuing to sell arms, specifically the Silkworm missiles, to Iran. U.S. government offi-cials stated that China had sold Iran $1 billion worth of weapons in 1987 alone.[88] As a result, the United States decided not to ease export restric-tions on high-technology products anymore.[89] And further underlining U.S. dissatisfaction with China's Silkworm missile sales, in January 1988, the United States added China to the Pentagon's list of nations hostile to the United States. As a result, the Defense Department denies security clearances for five years to naturalized American citizens from countries on that list.[90] And in December 1987, the United States expelled two Chinese diplomats for "commercial spying," although publicity was quelled in light of the delicate balancing of U.S.-Chinese interests. Still, with these rough spots in U.S.-China relations, the United States con-tinues to give the Chinese access to U.S. high technology. In March 1988, the Reagan administration removed restrictions imposed during the Silk-worm incident. China indicated its willingness to support a U.S.-sponsored arms embargo to Iran, giving the United States the assurances it needed to proceed with technology transfer to China.

Sending high technology to China is a risky affair. It cannot be assumed that Beijing will always remain friendly and open, or that the vast country is not a diversion route for goods on their way to the Soviets.

As a result, Japan and the West, ever mindful that the Chinese have smuggled high-technology goods in the past, employ some caution in their export dealings with China. In its role as a Cocom member, Japan polices restricted technology exports to China and other Asian communist countries. In November 1986 a smuggling ring for integrated chips lost its channel to China when Japanese police searched Tomei, a 43-year-old Japanese manufacturer of electronic scales. The scales contained integrated chips restricted by Cocom. In order to get the chips to China, members of the smuggling ring either removed them from the scales, stuffed their pockets with them, and carried them into China, or simply made fictitious customs declarations.[91]

NEW HOT SPOTS

During the early 1980s, Western countries—West Germany, Sweden, and Austria, to name three—were the major conduits for high-technology diversionary activities. Starting in 1985, illegal exports also began to occur with increasing frequency in the Far East, including Korea and Hong Kong. North Korea's embassy in East Berlin, always suspected of being an active conduit for restricted technology, appeared busy in the mid-1980s. In February 1986, four North Korean diplomats were expelled for illegally exporting military helicopter parts through East Berlin to Pyong Yang, North Korea. Later that year, in December 1986, three North Korean diplomats were barred from entering West Berlin for smuggling restricted U.S. high technology through East Berlin to North Korea.[92] In January 1987, Ronald and Monte Semler were indicted for selling eighty-five Hughes helicopters to North Korea through West Germany between 1983 and 1985. As of August 1987, they were awaiting trial in California.

Both the Department of Defense and the Department of Commerce see North Korea as a hot spot for illegal export of U.S. technology. Americans are not only concerned that the increased industrialization of South Korea will put advanced high technology nearer North Korea and perhaps make smuggling to the north easier; they also fear that it will continue to pose a threat to American competitiveness in several areas of high technology. North Korea, however, has had little success diverting the large quantities of high-technology goods now being manufactured by South Korea because of the latter's export controls aimed at keeping technology out of the North. The South Koreans avoid trade with countries to which Cocom restricts trade because those countries may be conduits for dual-use technology to North Korea. Other than that, South Korea places no controls on exports by its burgeoning high-technology industry.

Hong Kong, a major international trading and transshipment center, is an ideal environment for illegal shipments of high technology. Hong Kong cannot possibly monitor the millions of shipments that pass through its harbor and airport. Apparently, the majority of Hong Kong diversions originate in Western countries other than the United States. Both the Customs Service and the Department of Commerce closed in on one Hong Kong diverter, Tong Man-Chung, in San Francisco in February 1984. He was involved in illegal exports of almost twenty CRTs to Hong Kong and China through Vancouver, B.C. Customs seized the goods at the Canadian border in October 1983.[93]

Tong by no means dabbled in the profession of illegal high-technology exports. When he was arrested, Customs officials found in his possession a list of technology-related items worth more than $1 million, all of which he was planning to smuggle to Hong Kong and China. With an engineering background and a degree from Hong Kong Polytechnic, he had founded his own electronics company, Micro Data Systems, to market Tandy's TRS-80s in China and Alpha Micro Systems in Hong Kong. Tong was arraigned on Feb. 6, 1984, and granted bail of $350,000.[94] But, as of August 1987, he was listed by the U.S. Justice Department as a fugitive.

In another Hong Kong case in 1984, a federal grand jury in New York indicted Babeck Seroush, president of International Processing Systems GmbH, for smuggling semiconductors to North Korea through Hong Kong. He was charged with six counts of violating the U.S. Trading with the Enemy Act. Seroush, who conducted his business in West Germany, attempted to purchase 10,000 National Semiconductor and Texas Instrument chips, designed for night-vision goggles, without informing the manufacturing companies of their final destinations. A 38-year-old Iranian national, Seroush had homes in Connecticut, New York, and Germany. Not content to concentrate on only two U.S. suppliers for his illegal trade, he had also approached Analog Devices Inc., of Norwood, Mass., Kemet Capacitors of Union Carbide Corporation, Hauppage, N.Y., Schweber Electronics of Westbury, N.Y., and other chip suppliers. U.S. officials have been unable to extradite Seroush from West Germany. As of mid-1987, the case was still pending.[95]

The increasing international activity on both the espionage and diversion fronts creates several serious challenges for the United States. The first is the obvious one of trying to control people and events beyond the U.S. borders. This may be done in two ways, each of which has its limitations. The United States can ask its Cocom allies to operate within the guidelines of that organization and even expand those guidelines and further restrict the trade of high-technology products and information to the rest of the world. Many Cocom countries, however, have their own agendas that do not always conform with Cocom or the United States. Regarding nonaligned, non-Cocom nations, American trade officials may reach informal agreements with them on a country-by-country basis, requiring them to tighten high-technology exports to the Soviets in return for continued access to U.S. technology. Yet many of these countries are subject to the winds of political change; today's friend may be tomorrow's enemy, and any high-technology item that is shipped today may tomorrow find its way into Soviet hands.

Far more subtle is a second problem implicit in the restrictions on international technology transfer: that the very controls put forward by the United States to stanch Soviet acquisition of equipment and know-how critical to American national interests may be giving other nations an edge in the manufacture and marketing of certain high-technology products. And depending on the strength of these new competitors' connections to the United States, they could one day render the carefully conceived and administered export controls useless by selling equipment directly to the Soviets. Before they become a threat to U.S. national security, they will certainly invade the international markets of American high-technology firms. Therefore, the formulation of U.S. export controls must take into account both U.S. national security interests and international trade practices.

NOTES

1. Ted Agres, "Documents Unveil Soviet Methods of Obtaining Western Technology," *Research and Development,* June 1985, p. 48.

2. Paul Pilkauskas, deputy director of East-West trade, U.S. State Department, Washington, D.C.: Interview, Nov. 3, 1987.

3. Eduardo Lachica and E. S. Browning, "West Tightens Technology Export Rules but Shortens List of Controlled Products," *Wall Street Journal,* Jan. 29, 1988, p. 12.

4. Paul Freedenberg, assistant secretary for export administration, U.S. Department of Commerce, Washington, D.C.: Interview, Sept. 15, 1986.

5. U.S., Department of Justice, Criminal Division, Internal Security Section, Export Control Enforcement Unit, *Significant Export Control Cases, January 1, 1981 to August 6, 1987* (Washington, D.C.: 1987), p. 20.

6. Elizabeth Pond, "In Bonn, Schevardnadze Pushes Arms Cuts," *Christian Science Monitor,* Jan. 20, 1988, p. 7.

7. Angela E. Stent, "East-West Economic Relations and the Western Alliance," in Bruce Parrot, ed., *Trade, Technology, and Soviet-American Relations* (Bloomington, Ind.: Indiana University Press, for the Center for Strategic and International Studies, 1985), p. 297.

8. E. S. Browning, "France Apparently Is Nearing Rejection of Toshiba Charges of Illicit Sales by Firm," *Wall Street Journal,* Oct. 5, 1987, p. 26.

9. E. S. Browning, "Illicit Sales Made to Soviets by French Firm," *Wall Street Journal,* Oct. 19, 1987, p. 23.

10. E. S. Browning, "Four Executives in France Are Arrested for Exports of Technology to the Soviets," *Wall Street Journal,* Apr. 25, 1988, p. 22.

11. Edwy Plenel, "L'expérience positive de l'étranger," *Le Monde,* Mar. 30, 1985, p. 8.

12. "Tous les responsables du KGB dans la liste des 'rappelés,'" *Le Monde,* Mar. 30, 1985, p. 8.

13. Two others involved in the deal were Anatoly P. Troitsky, from the Soviet Industrial Machine Export-Import Corporation, and Vyacheslav A. Sedov, vice president of External Science and Technology Exchange Corporation. Previously, all three had been expelled from Western countries.

14. An axis enables the milling machine to twist and turn along a crossbar. The capability enables the machine to shape large, sophisticated propellers.

15. Senator Jesse Helms, "Toshiba/Kongsberg: A Chain of Conspiracy," *Congressional Record,* Aug. 6, 1987, S11454.

16. Eduardo Lachica and Robert S. Greenberger, "Norway Finds Allies Violated Cocom Controls," *Wall Street Journal,* Oct. 22, 1987, p. 30.

17. David Buchan and Nancy Dunne, "U.S. Seeks New Curbs on Sales to East Bloc," *Financial Times,* June 19, 1987, p. 2.

18. Helms, S11455.

19. *Television Digest,* "Consumer Electronics," Mar. 30, 1987, p. 12.

20. Andrew Pollack, "Japan's Growing Role in Chips Worrying U.S.," *New York Times,* Jan. 5, 1987, p. A1.

21. In 1987, the Semiconductor Industry Association proposed the formation of Sematech, a consortium of semiconductor companies dedicated to regaining American leadership in the semiconductor industry through research and development. The consortium has raised money from private industry ($100 million as of September 1987) and expects to receive a substantial sum from the federal government ($200 million a year). The objective of the U.S. government is to ensure that it continues to have an American supply of components such as semiconductors for military equipment.

22. Chiharu Ando, mergers and acquisitions analyst, Daiwa Securities America, New York: Interview, May 29, 1987.

23. Andrew Tanzer, "The Silicon Valley Greater Co-Prosperity Sphere," *Forbes*, Dec. 17, 1984, p. 32.

24. *Corporate Venturing News* (Wellesley Hills, Mass.), Venture Economics Inc., Oct. 13, 1987, p. 5.

25. "U.S., Japan Sign Pact on Patents, Resolving Sensitive Technology," *Wall Street Journal*, Apr. 18, 1988, p. 48.

26. Frederica M. Blinge, ed., *Japan, A Country Study*, 4th ed., Area Handbook Series (Washington, D.C.: Government Printing Office, 1983), p. 228.

27. Ibid., p. 328.

28. Stephen Sternheimer, *East-West Technology Transfer: Japan and the Communist Bloc*, (Washington, D.C.: University Press of America, for the Center for Strategic and International Studies, 1980), p. 12.

29. Ian Roger, "Soviet Machine Sale Rumpus Nears Clash," *Financial Times*, July 2, 1987, p. 6.

30. Daniel Sneider, "Soviets Seek Warmer Ties to a Skeptical Japan," *Christian Science Monitor*, Nov. 18, 1987, pp. 7 and 10.

31. Sternheimer, p. 14.

32. Ibid., pp. 43–47.

33. Bohdan O. Szuprowicz, "Japan's Push for Informatics Dominance," *Canadian Datasystems*, May 1985, p. 37.

34. Colonel Takashi Obata of the Japanese Self-Defense Force, visiting scholar at Stanford University, Stanford, Calif.: Interview, June 3, 1987.

35. John Mihalek, program administrator, Information Services Corporate Communications, IBM, Armonk, N.Y.: Interview, Oct. 26, 1987.

36. David Zielenziger, "Property Rights Principle Reaffirmed as IBM Wins Another Suit," *Electronic Engineering Times*, Jan. 16, 1984, pp. 1 and 13.

37. Clyde Haberman, "For Japanese, Anti-Spy Bill Raises Fears," *New York Times*, Mar. 8, 1987, p. A11.

38. A. E. Cullison "Soviets Take Fast Path to High-Tech Advances," *Journal of Commerce*, July 17, 1984, p. 2.

39. "Spies Allegedly Sold Radar Plane Data," *San Jose Mercury News*, May 26, 1987, p. 10A.

40. "Japanese Spy Gives Up Secrets," *Washington Times*, July 23, 1987, p. A7.

41. "Japan Announces It Will Participate in Research on SDI," *Wall Street Journal*, Sept. 9, 1986, p. 35.

42. "Three Japanese Executives Charged in Illegal Exports," *Wall Street Journal*, May 18, 1988, p. 27; Stephen Kreider Yoder, "Japan Intercepts Computer Exports to North Koreans," *Wall Street Journal*, Apr. 29, 1988, p. 18.

43. John J. Fialka, "U.S. Widening Probe of Alleged Spying by Israel," *Wall Street Journal*, June 5, 1986, p. 36.

44. Warren Richey, "Accused Spy's Leverage," *Christian Science Monitor*, June 5, 1986, p. 1.

45. Charlotte Saikowski, "Alleged Smuggling Latest in Series of U.S.-Israel Incidents," *Christian Science Monitor*, July 10, 1986, p. 1.

46. Ibid., p. 32.

47. "What's News," *Wall Street Journal*, Aug. 20, 1986, p. 1.

48. Richard Sale, "Israeli Spy Agency Compromised?" *San Francisco Examiner*, Dec. 14, 1987, p. B10.

49. Eduardo Lachica, "Neutral Nations Guard American Technology to Gain Import Rights," *Wall Street Journal*, Jan. 15, 1987, p. 16.

50. Ibid., p. 1.

51. Consent Decree, United States of America v. Datasaab Contracting, A.B., U.S. District Court for the District of Columbia, Apr. 27, 1984 (documents supplied by the U.S. Department of Commerce, January 1988).

52. "Sweden's Social Democrats Back Tighter Export Rules," *Wall Street Journal*, Sept. 22, 1987, p. 30.

53. U.S. District Court for the Central District of California, U.S. v. Marek Cieslak, Andrzej Stefan Stanislaw Schmidt, Indictment, May 29, 1987, pp. 1–15.

54. Eduardo Lachica, "Austria to Tighten Customs Law to Halt Illegal Shipping of Sensitive Technology, " *Wall Street Journal*, Nov. 12, 1986, p. 38.

55. Eduardo Lachica, "U.S. Takes Steps To Keep Goods From Soviets," *Wall Street Journal*, Aug. 13, 1986, p. 26.

56. Eduardo Lachica, "U.S. Uncovers Attempt to Ship Gear to Soviets," *Wall Street Journal*, July 28, 1986, p. 19.

57. Tim Carrington and Robert S. Greenberger, "Fight Over India's Bid for Computer Shows Disarray of U.S. Policy," *Wall Street Journal*, Feb. 24, 1987, p. 1.

58. Sheila Tefft, "Planned Sale of U.S. Computer to India Points Up Snags in Relations," *Christian Science Monitor*, Dec. 29, 1986, p. 8; Eduardo Lachica, "India Cleared for Cray Supercomputer After It Promises to Protect U.S. Secrets," *Wall Street Journal*, Oct. 12, 1987, p. 19.

59. Raju G. C. Thomas,"Thinking the 'Unthinkable'—Indo-U.S. Security Ties," *Christian Science Monitor*, Nov. 12, 1986, p. 26.

60. Condolezza Rice, professor of political science, specialist in Soviet military power, Stanford University, Stanford, Calif.: Interview, May 26, 1988.

61. "Soviet Military Power, An Assessment of the Threat, 1988," U.S. Department of Defense (Washington, D.C.: U.S. Government Printing Office) 1988, p. 26.

62. "Three Men Face Charges on Computer Sales to Cuba," *Wall Street Journal*, Apr. 6, 1987, p. 28.

63. Robert S. Greenberger, "U.S. Retaliates Against Chinese for Sales to Iran," *Wall Street Journal*, Oct. 22, 1987, p. 31.

64. Bob Goldberg, economics officer, China desk, U.S. State Department, Washington, D.C.: Interview, July 27, 1987.

65. "China's Bold New Program to Lure Foreign Investment," *Business Week*, Oct. 15, 1984, p. 183.

66. Amanda Bennett, "U.S., China Agree to Broad Terms of Nuclear Pact," *Wall Street Journal*, Apr. 30, 1984, p. 26.

67. "China Sets Laws Codifying Efforts to Reform Economy," *Wall Street Journal*, Apr. 1, 1988, p. 6.

68. "China Data," *China Business Review*, May–June 1987, p. 33.

69. A. J. Day, ed., Peter Jones and Sian Kevill, comp., *China and the Soviet Union 1949–84* (Harlow, Essex, England: Longman Group, 1985), pp. 186–87.

70. Jennifer Little, National Council for U.S.-China Trade, Washington, D.C.: Interview, May 29, 1987; Deborah Diamond-Kim, "Partners in Austerity," *China Business Review*, May–June 1987, pp. 12–13.

71. Nayan Chanda, "More Bytes for China," *Far Eastern Economic Review*, Aug. 6, 1987, p. 11.

72. *U.S.S.R. Facts & Figures Annual*, ed. John L. Sherer (Gulf Breeze, Fla.: Academic International Press, 1986), p. 31.

73. Adi Ignatius, "China Names Li Acting Premier as Shuffle Ends," *Wall Street Journal*, Nov. 25, 1987, p. 13.

74. Jim Abrams, "China's Li Becomes Premier," *San Francisco Examiner*, Nov. 24, 1987, p. A2.

75. Chanda, p. 11.

76. Ted Agres, "Do Accords with PRC Only Legitimize Technology Flow?" *Research and Development*, August 1984, p. 49.

77. Amanda Bennett, "Academic Exchange: China Trade Imbalance?" review of *A Relationship Restored* by David Lampton, with Joyce A. Madancy and Kristen M. Williams, *Wall Street Journal*, July 11, 1986, p. 26.

78. David Lampton, with Joyce A. Madancy and Kristen M. Williams, *A Relationship Restored: Trends in U.S.-China Educational Exchanges, 1978–1984* (Washington, D.C.: National Academy Press for the Committee on Scholarly Communication with the People's Republic of China, 1986), pp. 135–37.

79. Rich Mercier, U.S. Customs Service, Washington, D.C.: Interview, Feb. 12, 1988.

80. "U.S. Nets High-Tech Spies," *Asian Computer Monthly*, March 1984, p. 14.

81. Bruce Merrill, U.S. District Attorney, Newark, N.J., and Frank Ventura, U.S. Customs agent: Interview, June 3, 1987.

82. U.S., Department of Justice, "Significant Export Control Cases, January 1, 1981, through March 13, 1987," p. 15; and Jamie Trainter, U.S. Customs Service Special Agent, San Francisco: Interview, May 27, 1988.

83. Stephen Walton, director of strategic investigations, U.S. Customs Service, Washington, D.C.: Interview, Sept. 15, 1986.

84. Agres, p. 49.

85. Wayne Biddle, "U.S. Said to Plan to Sell Naval Weapons to China," *New York Times*, Jan. 13, 1985, p. 12.

86. David K. Shipler, "U.S. and China United by Antipathy to the Soviet Union," *New York Times*, Mar. 8, 1987, p. IV, e3.

87. Robert Grieves and Dave Griffiths, "Arming China: Washington Plays a Risky Hand," *Business Week*, Oct. 27, 1986, p. 63.

88. Robert S. Greenberger, "Chinese Appear to Have Sent Iran Improved Missiles," *Wall Street Journal*, Dec. 21, 1987, p. 2.

89. Ibid.

90. Charles Aldinger, "Pentagon Calls China 'Hostile,'" *San Francisco Examiner*, Jan. 26, 1988, p. B8.

91. "Japanese Police Cracks Smuggling of IC Chips to Red China," Central News Agency, Nov. 16, 1986.

92. "Western Allies Exclude North Koreans from West Berlin for Smuggling," Reuters North European News Service, Dec. 17, 1986, AM Cycle.

93. Joseph Russoniello, U.S. District Attorney, San Francisco: Interview, Feb. 5, 1988.

94. "U.S. Nets High-Tech Spies," *Asian Computer Monthly*, March 1984, p. 14.

95. Fred Varella, office of U.S. Attorney for the Southern District of New York: Interview, June 10, 1987.

7

THE U.S.
RESPONSE

Faced on the one hand with a growing number of high-technology spies, diverters, and thieves, and on the other with increasing foreign competition, the United States struggles to stop the illegal flight of its high technology while maintaining a healthy, favorable international trade environment for American companies. The United States responds to Soviet efforts to acquire its technology on several fronts, public and private, with varying success. First, it reacts with export-control legislation and related enforcement activities supported by foreign-policy maneuvers. Second, it elicits assistance from its intelligence community, which strives to uncover Soviet espionage activities and to locate technology smugglers. Last, American industry responds by instituting security and awareness programs that disrupt Soviet infiltration and intelligence-gathering efforts and by training employees not to ship unknowingly to companies that are fronts for export diversions to the Soviet Union. What follows is a summary of some of the most important legislation, enforcement efforts, and private initiatives designed to interrupt the flow of high technology to the Soviets.[1]

ILLEGAL EXPORTS: PLUGGING THE LEAK

Since 1949 and the passage of the first comprehensive export regulations, the United States has controlled the export of its technology to the Soviets. Before World War II, Washington had not yet fully realized the value of American high technology or the potential damage it could cause if it fell into the wrong hands. In addition to its other legacies, the war demonstrated the significance of technology in the building of a successful military machine. Time and again, the quantity and quality of Allied technology, embedded in its military equipment—aircraft, ships, rifles, radios—had made a crucial difference. Toward the end of the war, rumors of frightening German technological advances, especially in rocketry but also in germ and chemical warfare, suggested that the Nazis might possibly, through sheer technical wizardry, surmount the overwhelming odds they faced. Although Hitler fell before the new elements of his arsenal could be fully utilized, the message was clear: In modern war, technology could be as important as strategy and human resources. After the war, with the appearance of increasingly advanced technologies (especially the devastating new atomic bomb), the rise of the Soviet Union, and the polarization of East and West in the cold war, Washington decided it was high time to restrict the export of U.S. technology that had both civilian and military uses.

In 1949, Congress passed the Export Control Act, setting in place the complex rules restricting overseas trade of American technology that have guided U.S. exports ever since. It was a comprehensive embargo on technology going to the Soviet bloc. At the same time, the United States and its allies formed Cocom as a complement to NATO to regulate their own technology trade to the Soviet bloc. Although the specifics of the export controls have been altered periodically and their restrictions loosened by small degrees, especially in the Nixon years during détente, the law's framework has remained relatively the same since Congress's first statement of licensing procedures, penalties, and methods for determining which technologies are to be kept out of Soviet hands. Other laws, including the 1917 Trading with the Enemy Act, the Foreign Assistance Act of 1961, and related regulations, such as the Cuban Assets Control Regulations of 1963, have bolstered the legal basis for restricting trade.

Today, the specific document that restricts the export of critical high technology is the Export Administration Act (EAA) of 1979, as amended in 1985. The Commerce Department administers the act.[2] Much discussion and controversy surrounds the EAA each time it is mentioned in the House and Senate, and the controversy is bound to continue at least until September 1989, when the act comes up for renewal. The EAA and regula tions issued according to the act are amended in minor ways on a regular basis; a thorough understanding of export procedures thus requires constant monitoring of congressional activities.

The act restricts technology export for several reasons, primarily for national security, but also in support of foreign policy and nuclear nonproliferation or because of inadequate domestic supplies. High-technology equipment is restricted for national security reasons if its possession by a hostile nation would enhance that nation's military capability; similarly, information is not permitted to leave the country if a government review determines that it could weaken U.S. security were it obtained by the wrong party. For national security reasons, technologies with dual use—that is, both civilian and military—are generally not allowed to be exported except to allies. Some low-level, dual-use technologies are cautiously exported to the Soviets when it is clearly demonstrated that the products will have no bearing on U.S. national security. The act specifically restricts the export of equipment or know-how that contributes "significantly to the design, manufacture, or utilization of military hardware." For example, under the EAA, the export of certain very large scale integrated (VLSI) chips is restricted because they can be used as components in missile guidance systems.

Technology export controls are also applied to assist in negotiations and diplomatic efforts with other countries. This foreign-policy consideration was used to a great extent to diminish exports of nondual-use technology to the Soviets after the invasion of Afghanistan in 1979. Similarly, trade with Poland was all but stopped after the Polish government invoked martial law in 1981 in response to the Solidarity movement. Currently, foreign policy concerning South Africa, Namibia, and some Middle Eastern states, as well as the Eastern bloc, influences U.S. export restrictions. In addition to a nation's direct relations with the United States, its ties with those countries hostile or friendly to the United States is an issue in determining U.S. trade policy. Whether a country is communist or noncommunist is also a consideration; in general, trade with communist nations is tightly controlled.

An example of restrictions being levied because of inadequate domestic supplies was the quota imposed on the export of nickel and copper in the late 1960s.[3] During the 1980s, short-supply controls were also placed on unprocessed western red cedar and some petroleum products.

THE EXPORT LAWS: HOW THEY WORK

Companies that want to export high-technology goods, services, or information must obtain a license for each transaction from the Commerce Department. Commerce considers the license to export goods and services a privilege, not necessarily a right, and it has a licensing procedure that documents a company's use of the privilege. Laws restrict the export of both products and know-how—for example, superconductors and a scientist's notes on superconductor design. Exports leave the United States under one of two types of licenses: a general license or an individual, validated license. The first is a preexisting authorization to export certain products. It covers goods and information not restricted by the federal government. Companies shipping under a general license, called GL (General License) or G-DEST (General Destination), do not have to fill out a license application form, but they must document that they have thoroughly researched Commerce's list of controlled items to be sure that the one they wish to export is not restricted.

Most U.S. exports leave under general licenses. Low-technology items—toasters, watches, stereo equipment, even some elementary computers—are usually exported under GLs, but determining whether an item is controlled by Commerce can often be difficult. If a company has any doubt whether its exports are in the restricted category, the law requires it to check with the Commerce Department.

Before shipping any goods to a foreign country, a company is expected to classify its products, that is, a qualified engineer and export administrator must determine which classification on the Commerce Department's list of commodities best describes them. All products fall into a classification of some kind, and the company is wise to understand and document the rationale for determining their classification.

There are several types of general licenses, including GLV (General License for Limited Value) and GTF-US (General License for Trade Fair). A company uses a GLV to ship certain products, as long as their value does not exceed a specified amount. In the case of computer equipment exportable with a general license, the amount is a maximum of $5,000 to most non-Soviet bloc countries, except China and Afghanistan. GTF-US licenses cover shipments of products used in international trade fairs. New types of general licenses appear in revisions of the export regulations from time to time. G-COM (General License to Cocom), a general license announced in 1987, provides for certain exports to Cocom countries and some countries outside Cocom but considered friendly to the United States and supportive of U.S. export policies.

If a company finds that the product it wants to ship is on the restricted list, it must apply for an individual validated license. Applications can be submitted electronically or by mail. If the license is granted, the IVL (Individual License) allows the company to sell a specific product to a specific recipient in a specific country for a specified use. Individual licenses must be obtained before exporting the majority of high-technology products, including most computers, lasers, integrated circuits, software, telecommunications equipment, and scientific instruments.

Before granting an individual license, the Commerce Department considers the use to which the product will be put. If it is to be used for military purposes by an unfriendly nation, the license will usually not be approved. Theoretically, even low-technology exports with military end use can be denied. Moreover, if it appears that the export will aid a nonnuclear nation in developing nuclear capabilities, it is not permitted.

Even though the company is responsible for knowing the laws, in the past, companies accused of violating export laws have often cited their ignorance of regulations requiring licenses for exports. Locating pertinent information is not always easy. A company might think to seek advice from the local Chamber of Commerce, which would advise it to call the Department of Commerce. Or companies may learn of licensing requirements through industry associations, such as the American Electronics Association or the Semiconductor Industry Association. Many large companies engaging in high-technology export retain a lawyer in Washington to assist with the licensing process and to keep them informed about changes to the laws. Although this may seem extravagant, the loss of an export license (and with it, a foreign market) can inflict greater financial loss than retaining a lawyer. Other sources of information are freight forwarders, such as Emery Worldwide and DHL Worldwide Express, which must take responsibility for knowing export laws and can advise clients of compliance procedures and potential violations.

In addition, for an annual fee a company can subscribe to the *Export Administration Regulations* through the Government Printing Office. Subscribers receive a thick binder explaining all the regulations and containing pages of information aimed at making the licensing process easier to understand. They also receive periodic bulletins notifying them of changes in the regulations or suggesting ways of making the licensing process less burdensome. If a company is only investigating the procedure for exporting a product, it can go to a local library where the Commerce Department often places copies of the regulations. The publication contains the list of commodities that are restricted for exporting, called the Commodity Control List (CCL).

Someone in the company, preferably an export administrator, must become well versed in the export-licensing process and know when to seek information about the laws. Situations arise in which a company leaves export licensing to secretaries or low-level employees, who, while competent at their regular tasks, are unfamiliar with the licensing process. In one case, Columbus Instruments, a manufacturer of medical instruments, was accused of illegally shipping computer equipment to Moscow via Finland; the company president indicated that he had been exporting his products for many years and had his secretary handle the paperwork, although both of them were unaware of the licensing procedures and had never applied for an appropriate license. Simply stated, ignorance is no excuse.

To obtain an application for an individual license, a company contacts the Office of Export Licensing within the Export Administration of the Department of Commerce, in Washington, D.C. Many industrial regions, such as Silicon Valley or the Boston area, have their own regional Commerce Department offices that act as liaisons between Washington and local companies, but all license applications go through the Washington office.

After completing the application, often with the assistance of an export consultant, the company returns it to the Office of Export Licensing, which stamps it with a case number and sends an acknowledgment back to the company. The company can then follow the status of its application by using the case number as a reference.

The Department of Commerce has been making efforts to streamline the licensing process and shorten the time it takes to handle an application. Increased automation of licensing has made the process much smoother. In November 1986, Commerce first offered the System for Tracking Export License Applications (STELA). A company's export administrator can call a special phone number, input the case number using the telephone keypad, and receive a status report on that particular application. In some cases, the system can actually give a verbal O.K., enabling the company to proceed with the shipment before receiving the paperwork from Washington. In January 1988, Commerce further automated the licensing process when it introduced the Export License Application and Information Network (ELAIN), a computerized system that electronically issues export licenses. CompuServe links the Office of Export Licensing with companies that apply for licenses. Most applications take no more than three weeks to process unless they are subjected to review by agencies other than Commerce, usually the State and Defense departments, the Department of Energy, or the National Security Agency, and sometimes by Cocom. If an interagency review is to take place, the application acknowledgment sent by Commerce indicates which agencies will participate.

In addition to all the equipment covered by the regulations, the EAA
controls technical data about that equipment. Specifically, the act regu-
lates the export of "unclassified technical data related to industrial processes, including knowhow and computer software."[4] If the data have
been published and are, therefore, publicly available, they can be exported with a general license called a GTDA (General License for Technical Data). If an engineer wanted to send an unpublished set of drawings
of a high-speed semiconductor to his counterpart in a research institute in
a nation friendly to the United States, he would use a GTDR (General
License for Technical Data Under Restriction) license that covers shipment of restricted technical data. He would, however, also need
assurances from his counterpart that the material would not be reexported or used for purposes other than those designated. Even sales
and product literature is regulated, although it may be shipped abroad
under a general license, as is the vast majority of published material.
Also, academics traveling abroad need not obtain individual licenses to
participate in international conferences and symposiums, unless they
take with them technical data developed under a U.S. government contract. Most types of technical data can be sent to Cocom and neutral countries, but the Commerce Department requires assurances that the data
will not be reexported to the Soviet bloc, China, or Afghanistan.

The regulation of data export is broad and includes the transmission
of data orally or visually to foreign nationals. The export of technical data
can occur within the United States; if a company is visited by foreign nationals, it needs to be particularly careful to prevent the illegal transfer of
restricted technical information to its guests. The regulations also cover a
computer scientist visiting a foreign city to give a talk about computer-
aided design systems. He should do so only after checking the Commerce
Department list to see if his subject is restricted or whether it may be exported under a general license. If the information in his speech is publicly
available (say, published in a technical magazine), the regulations state
that he may export his speech using the GTDA. If his paper is unpublished and he has any doubts about whether it covers a restricted
topic, he must check with Commerce, which may allow him to export the
material under a GTDR or may require him to apply for an individual
license. The latter would most likely happen if Soviet scientists were to be

present at his speech. (The export laws are obviously of no help if a Soviet spy is present.) In some cases, Commerce may require the scientist to provide a letter from the sponsor of the foreign event assuring it that the information presented will not be given to proscribed countries.

THE LIST

The Commodity Control List (CCL), which is in the *Export Administration Regulations,* contains some 2,000 technology categories covering nearly 500,000 dual-use and nondual-use products organized into ten broad categories: metalworking machinery; chemical and petrochemical equipment; electric and power-generating equipment; general industrial equipment; transportation equipment; electronics and precision instruments; metals, minerals, and manufactures; chemicals, metalloids, petroleum products, and related materials; rubber and rubber products; and miscellaneous. (Most computer and electronics equipment is covered under the section electronics and precision instruments.) Each technology is described with performance characteristics; specific products are not listed. Entries are accompanied by a list of countries for which the United States requires that an individual license be obtained before a product may be exported to them. The list includes the reason each commodity is restricted; national security is the most common. In some cases, the entry lists a value limitation, specifying the dollars' worth of a product that can be shipped under a general license.

The Secretary of Commerce is responsible for maintaining the CCL, which is reviewed almost continuously by the Commerce Department's Office of Technology and Policy Analysis (OTPA), assisted by technical advisory committees (TACs) composed of industry and government representatives. The OTPA develops policies that form the bases of decisions in granting export licenses. It reviews certain sensitive license applications, and it is responsible for incorporating revisions into the export regulations. One of its most important functions is in communicating to foreign governments the U.S. position regarding export control. It does this in cooperation with the State Department, intent on convincing Third World nations of the need to cooperate with Cocom. OTPA also reviews the CCL and formulates U.S. position statements with the State Department for presentation to Cocom.[5]

A TAC provides industry with access to Commerce's export-control activities and a forum to air its opinions regarding the inclusion of a particular product on the CCL. Through the TACs, industry can inform Commerce about recent developments within different technical areas, such as computer communications or genetic engineering.

The Department of Defense contributes to decisions concerning the CCL, as does Cocom, which can be guaranteed to challenge the position taken by the U.S. government. (The Department of Energy also contributes from time to time.) The list is so large that it takes three or four years to review it completely. The computer products appearing on the list came up for review in 1986; they had been revised slightly in January 1985, but before then, no changes had been made to that category for six years. During the review process, far more items tend to be added to the list than taken away. Between October 1983 and September 1987, twenty-six items were added to the CCL and one was deleted.[6] Many items are also modified to reflect the evolution of technology and new products. Changes to the list appear in the *Federal Register* as well as in the *Export Administration Regulations*.

Items are added to the list for the basic reasons already mentioned, that is, national security, foreign policy, and shortages inside the United States. Similarly, they are decontrolled if they are no longer critical to national security, if they can no longer aid U.S. foreign policy, or if the shortage no longer exists. Decontrol also takes place if a given item can be proven to be available from non-Cocom suppliers. Commerce reasons that if the Soviets can get the product from another nation outside Cocom, which generally restricts the same technologies as those on the CCL, it would harm American trade to restrict trade of that product. Switzerland, for example, had been providing the Eastern bloc countries with automatic wafering saws used for cutting silicon ingots. As a result, the Office of Foreign Availability decontrolled them in March 1987; they had been on the CCL and Cocom's list. In mid-October 1987, IBM PC clones based on Intel's 8088 microprocessor were decontrolled because Finland, Taiwan, Korea, and Sweden also exported them.[7]

On the other hand, if a high-technology product available elsewhere is deemed vital to Western or U.S. security interests, the United States may try to convince the other country to restrict trade in it. The EAA allows the government six months from the time such a product is discovered to reach an agreement concerning the control or decontrol of the product; if, at the end of that period, the country still exports the article, Commerce will cease to restrict it as well. Six months, however, can be a long time for an American firm trying to open up a foreign market. Even after the six-month period, the president may decide to continue controls on the product if he deems that its export would threaten U.S. national security.

Commerce's Office of Foreign Availability exists to determine if a controlled item is being provided by other nations. U.S. firms may petition the office to have a high-technology product decontrolled. Usually, the company needs to show that the article is being produced in other countries and how it could be sold by them to the Soviet bloc. A sale to the Soviets may not have taken place, but if the company can demonstrate that such a sale *could* take place, a case can be made that continued control of the product by the U.S. will not keep it out of Soviet hands. The office considers the claim, consults with other government agencies, and then makes a decision, a process that can take years, because the office operates under no time limit.

A more efficient way to remove an item from the list is by working through one of the TACs. A chip manufacturer can contact the one for semiconductors and file a claim similar to that submitted directly to the Office of Foreign Availability. A decision may be reached more quickly, because the committees are bound by law to act within ninety days. Even if a product is decontrolled—for whatever reason—it is decontrolled only for West-West trade. For an item to be cleared for West-East trade, Cocom must remove it from its list. Cocom reviews its list continually through the Commerce Department's Office of Technology and Policy Analysis and at its meetings in Paris.

DESTINATIONS AND END USES

In deciding whether to allow an export, Commerce considers its destination as carefully as it does the product. For this purpose, it groups the world's nations according to their status for receiving exports. Each item on the list is then annotated with the letters of countries to which export of that item is restricted. Nations that in general are not permitted to receive exports of dual-use and other vital U.S. high technology fall into three groups. The category Q, W, Y, and Afghanistan includes the U.S.S.R., Afghanistan, Albania, Bulgaria, Estonia, Czechoslovakia, the German Democratic Republic (including East Berlin), Hungary, Laos, the Mongolian People's Republic, Poland, and Romania; group Z includes North Korea, Vietnam, Kampuchea, and Cuba; and group S has its lone member, Libya. Other than Afghanistan, which occasionally can receive restricted high technology if it is needed by the civilian population, countries in these groups are the targets of the high-technology export controls. Exports to groups Z and S are, as of this writing, even more tightly controlled than those to the other nations, the United States having embargoed all high-tech and some low-tech shipments to countries in those two groups. Libya can receive certain types of seeds, food, and gifts to families in accordance with a carefully worded general license for gifts.

The Soviet invasion of Afghanistan caused the Commerce Department to restrict trade to most nations in group Q, W, Y, and Afghanistan even further. Before that time, Commerce had relaxed controls to a few of the countries. For example, Poland liberalized its communist regime somewhat in 1956 and was therefore dealt with more leniently until martial law was declared there in 1981. With the Polish government's clampdown, the United States again restricted exports as a way of putting pressure on the Soviet Union.

The United States does not control exports to Canada. U.S. companies can ship all products, except for munitions and nuclear devices, to the northern neighbor without applying for export licenses. Only when an export is destined to pass through Canada to another destination is a license required.

Group T comprises nations in North, Central, and South America (including Bermuda and the Caribbean, but not Canada and Cuba). These countries receive a wide range of exports for which the Commerce Department does not require supporting documentation. Group V contains all the countries not included in the other groups. China, a newcomer to Group V, enjoys access to a variety of U.S. technology, even though it is a communist country. Commerce approves most exports to countries in groups T and V unless an export is covered by nuclear proliferation- or foreign policy-based controls.

Nations that carry out or support terrorism are generally not allowed to receive U.S. high technology, even though many of them are included in group V. For example, exports to Iran, a group V nation, have been restricted since the Ayatollah Khomeini came to power in 1979. On Oct. 26, 1987, those restrictions were tightened in response to the Iranian attacks against tankers in the Persian Gulf. The EAA requires that Congress be notified before any technology worth more than $1 million is sold to a country supporting international terrorism. There are exceptions; the president can allow technology to be sold to a nation if it has not engaged in terrorist acts for six months and promises to restrain itself in the future.

In addition to its list of nations, Commerce keeps a file on companies and individuals that have been known in the past to divert high technology to the Soviets or in some other ways abuse the U.S. export system. Such well-known diverters as Richard Müller, Charles McVey, and Brian Möller-Butcher and firms such as Datasaab appeared on the list in January 1987, along with about 100 others. The list, updated every month, appears in the *Export Administration Regulations*, and high-tech exporters should know its contents well, because any attempt to ship to people or firms on the list will result in, at least, a denied license and, at worst, a fine and revoking of other export privileges.

On top of that, sellers must be careful to verify that exported products are not simply reexported to other destinations. If the purchaser is discovered reshipping the goods to another country without a U.S. license for the reexport, the original U.S. seller can be held responsible and fined or denied further exports.

THE PLAYERS:
ADMINISTRATORS AND ENFORCERS

To understand fully the U.S. response to Soviet high-technology acquisition and diversion efforts, it is necessary to see how U.S. agencies— the Commerce, Defense, and State departments, the Customs Service, and the FBI, to name the principal players—and the international body called Cocom work together to interrupt illegal access to U.S. high technology.

THE COMMERCE DEPARTMENT: INDUSTRY'S CHAMPION

The Commerce Department is the main government agency charged with overseeing the Export Administration Act and its regulations. Within a separate Commerce bureau called Export Administration,[8] the Office of Export Enforcement enforces the EEA. In addition to administering the export-control regulations, Commerce plays an important role in the enforcement of the law. The Office of Export Enforcement investigates both criminal and administrative cases. The difference between the two types of cases may rest with the evidence alone: If it points to an intent to break the law, it may turn an illegal export into a criminal offense.

In many cases, Commerce enforcement agents respond to tip-offs from industry. As a result of Enforcement's Outreach program, instigated in 1985 by the Commerce office in Silicon Valley, the number of tip-offs has been on the rise. By helping industry identify potential illegal transactions, enforcement officials receive notification when an employee spots a "red flag" or a characteristic of an illegal purchase. (These "red flag" indicators are listed on pp. 233–34.) Although it is difficult to measure the effectiveness of any preventive program, the tip-off statistics point to an improved awareness throughout industry. During its first year, the Enforcement office in San Jose, Calif., received only three tip-offs. In 1987, eleven out of eighty-eight industry tip-offs led to enforcement cases.

Other forms of preventive work also occupy Commerce's enforcement agents. Not only do they screen licenses to check for known diverters or suspicious shipping activities, they also follow up on a shipment after it reaches a consignee to verify that the end use and end user are those indicated on the export license.

The Office of Export Enforcement has been growing and receiving additional support for its investigative activities. From 1980 to 1986, the staff grew from 39 to 160. Further budgetary increases appear to have continued this trend, with the consequent addition of even more investigators. In 1980, $1.7 million was allocated to enforcement; in 1986,

$4.9 million.[9] Enforcement investigators now operate from field offices in New York, Springfield (Va.), Miami, Boston, Chicago, Dallas, Burbank (Calif.), and San Jose. Two investigators serve in Europe.

Commerce has to maintain a delicate balance between enforcing the law and promoting international trade and finds itself in the position of playing "bad cop" and "good cop" simultaneously, sometimes stopping even the most marginally improper shipments but also trying to help industry understand and work within the laws. Although the department's officials do everything in their power to enforce the letter of the EAA, as amended, Commerce's pro-business stance has often caused it to argue for simplifying, and even loosening, the trade restrictions. Because of these conflicts of interest, Senator Jake Garn (R-Utah) promoted legislation in the early 1980s to remove export-law administration from the Commerce Department and to establish an independent Office of Strategic Trade. Former Secretary of Commerce Malcolm Baldrige, killed in July 1987 in a rodeo accident, sided with many chiefs of American industry in believing that the laws diminished U.S. high-technology firms' ability to expand internationally. His successor, C. William Verity, Jr., feels even more strongly that the laws harm U.S. competitiveness while doing little to stop the Soviets from acquiring high technology. He once remarked that the United States was "shooting itself in the foot" with the controls. In 1984, while cochairing the U.S.-U.S.S.R. Trade and Economic Council, he concluded that in most cases the U.S.S.R. was able to obtain restricted U.S. technology elsewhere.

Commerce is also responsible for educating industry about the export regulations. Large companies tend to be eager to learn the law; for them, a denied license almost certainly means serious financial loss. Also, they have sufficient resources to hire a staff dedicated to export-law compliance. But many midsize and small companies have often been too occupied with survival and "get-the-job-done" procedures to be patient and persistent enough to achieve export-law compliance. Seminars sponsored by consultants, industry associations, and the Commerce Department are helping industry executives become more savvy about the exporting business.

THE DEPARTMENT OF DEFENSE: THE TOUGH GUYS?

An assortment of Defense Department programs, offices, agencies, and committees support the protection of U.S. technology against acquisition by the Soviet bloc. The Defense Technology Security Administration (DTSA) consolidates all Defense work with export controls and protection of defense-related technology. The DTSA's Strategic Trade Directorate works closely with the Commerce Department to administer the export laws; its analysts process dual-use technology export license applications sent them by the Commerce Department. The directorate also communicates with the Department of State's Political Military Bureau and its Office of East-West Trade. The Munitions Directorate of DTSA works with the State Department to administer the Arms Export Control Act and license reviews for technologies controlled by the International Traffic in Arms Regulations (ITAR).

A broad assortment of committees and offices support the DTSA, ranging from the office of the under secretary of defense for development research and engineering to the Advisory Committee on Export Policy. The under secretary of defense for acquisition is responsible for the Militarily Critical Technologies List (or MCTL, Defense's list of strategic technology), adding and deleting items as the department evaluates new technologies. The Defense Intelligence Agency (DIA) supports the department's efforts to monitor technology trade. It studies illegal technology transfers, checks end users of technology to verify that the products are being put to the use stated on export licenses, reviews foreign availability of the technology, provides intelligence concerning the impact of Soviet technology acquisitions, and collaborates with Customs and Commerce.

When a company applies to the Commerce Department for a license to export a product that employs dual-use technology, the application is passed on to the Defense Department for review. Cocom also submits licenses for Defense review via its U.S. delegation, which operates under the State Department. The DTSA reviews the case and prepares a statement of its position, which in turn is presented at an interagency group that formulates the U.S. position finally put forth at Cocom.

Of the 160,000 licenses processed by Commerce in 1987, some 7,000 were reviewed by the Defense Department for trade between the U.S. and Eastern bloc countries. By law, Defense has twenty days to review a license with an optional twenty days in addition if necessary. In 1987, Defense took an average of only eight days to review licenses, down from an average of thirty to thirty-five days in 1983.[10] In the future, direct links with Commerce computers may enable the department to cut another day from its review process. Defense also has a computerized telephone inquiry system similar to Commerce's STELA. Companies interested in knowing the status of licenses being reviewed by Defense can call the Export License Status Advisor (ELISA).[11]

The Department of Defense maintains its own technology list to help its staff review export-license applications referred to it by Commerce—the Militarily Critical Technologies List (MCTL). The 800-page, 2,500-item document was classified until 1984, when portions of it were declassified. Most commodities on the MCTL appear on the Commerce list. Dan Hoydysh, acting director of Commerce's OTPA, describes it as being "so broad that, basically, it is a laundry list of all modern-day technology."[12] The document describes each technology and explains why it is critical and what it contributes to national security. It also includes background, development, and manufacturing information. Not legally binding, the MCTL is nonetheless influential, because Defense uses it to advise Commerce on whether to include a technology on the CCL; Commerce rarely ignores Defense's advice. The Commerce Department also consults the MCTL to review its own CCL and to help prepare proposals on how to control new technologies.[13]

The criteria Defense uses to evaluate an item for inclusion on the MCTL seem so broad that few high-technology products would not be included. Entered on the list are "arrays of design and manufacturing knowhow, keystone manufacturing, inspection, and test equipment, goods accompanied by sophisticated operation, applications or maintenance knowhow, and keystone equipment which would reveal or give insight into the design and manufacture of a United States military system." These broad categories subject a major segment of the electronics industry to potential control. Foreign availability of a product often influences a decision to exclude an item from the MCTL. Defense reviews the list annually. Each year, about 15 percent of the items are removed, and about 15 percent are added. The updated list is officially reissued within the Defense Department every two to three years.

Defense analysts utilize two computerized information systems to review license applications for exports to Eastern bloc nations or to Western nations such as Austria, Switzerland, and Japan that have proven unreliable in keeping high-technology products out of the Soviet Union (usually by tolerating diversion activities by companies inside their borders). For West to East exports, Defense uses the Foreign Disclosure and Technical Information System (FORDTIS) to evaluate the impact of a product's export on national security. For West to West exports, it uses the Defense Automated Cases Review System (DACRS), which processes information about the product to be exported, its CCL status, the history of the end user, and the end user's country of residence. DACRS is linked to the Commerce Department's license-reviewing system and enables Defense to review license applications electronically.

The Defense Investigative Service (DIS), another organization within the Defense Department, helps disrupt Soviet technology-espionage efforts. The DIS was formed in 1972, primarily to investigate personnel for security clearances. In essence, it secures clearances for personnel in private industry under government contract. The DIS investigates security clearances for the military, although the armed forces actually grant their own clearances. DIS employees check the police, IRS, credit bureau, military, FBI, and other records of about 900,000 people each year to clear them to work on confidential, secret, and top secret projects.[14]

DIS runs an Industrial Security Program, which investigated nearly 19,000 facilities during fiscal year 1987. About 15 percent of these investigations are not announced to the facility in advance. About 500 DIS investigators visit government contractors to monitor their compliance with the DIS-produced *Industrial Security Manual*, a detailed guide to protecting classified information. They check companies working on classified government projects about every six months and those using confidential information about every nine months.[15]

Well-researched security clearances can help protect U.S. technology. Several espionage cases that broke in the mid-1980s involved personnel with security clearances who had access to classified technical information. In several cases, the government might have been able to prevent espionage by reacting to telltale behavioral changes and financial situations. For example, John Walker's obvious financial problems induced him to succumb to the monetary rewards of spying. If the government had been aware of his money troubles, it might have revoked Walker's security clearance. In addition, some suspect that too many government employees and government contractors hold security clearances. Millions of Americans have some level of clearance, but for financial and staffing reasons, few of them are reviewed with any regularity. As a result, many employees with no current need hold clearances issued years ago. With only subtle life-style changes, such individuals could become prime recruitment targets for the Soviets. The Pentagon, though, is committed to tightening the procedures for granting and retaining security clearances. Between 1985 and 1988, it reinvestigated more than 175,000 individuals with TOP SECRET clearances and access to sensitive information. By September 1988, the Defense Department had reduced clearances by 35 percent.[16]

American industry often makes the Department of Defense the "bad guy" among government agencies charged with upholding the trade laws. The reason for the unpopular image is its conservative position regarding the control of high-technology exports and the fervor with which it pursues its position. Under the diligent former Defense Secretary Caspar W. Weinberger, it took an especially hard-line approach to export controls with an eye toward protecting national security. When the National Academy of Sciences published its 1987 report, *Balancing the National Interest,* claiming the negative impact of export controls on industry, then Assistant Defense Secretary Richard N. Perle called the report "rich in assertion" and the statistics it used "complete rubbish."[17] Perle and Dr. Stephen D. Bryen, deputy under secretary of defense for trade security policy, both of whom would point out that Defense is not *anti*trade but rather *pro*-nonstrategic trade, advocated tighter controls of dual-use, strategic high technology during the Reagan Administration.

The advent of the Strategic Defense Initiative only hardened the Defense Department's position and its concern that SDI-related technologies will find their way into the Soviet space-based defense system.

THE STATE DEPARTMENT: TRADE AND DIPLOMACY

The State Department's most important contribution to the control of high-technology flow to the Soviets is making the underlying foreign policy. It answers Soviet political moves with U.S. policies to tighten or loosen access to U.S. high technology. While Defense occupies itself with national security, the State Department wrestles with issues ranging from embargoes on other nations' goods to the potential for Soviet military invasions into the Third World.

The State Department also administers the Arms Export Control Act through its Office of Munitions Control. The act, passed in 1976, limits the export of military equipment—ammunition, firearms, explosives, naval vessels, tanks and other vehicles, aircraft (including spacecraft), military training equipment, protective personnel equipment, and military and space electronics. This last category covers some items included on the CCL and the MCTL, for example, very high-speed integrated circuits (VHSIC) with military applications.

Prepared in conjunction with the Defense Department, the Munitions Control List appears in the International Traffic in Arms Regulations (ITAR), which also contains guidelines for executing the Arms Export Control Act. Control of these items is far stricter than of those on the CCL. No sales of products on the Munitions Control List are allowed to countries hostile to the United States. General licenses for these items are not issued; before any munitions are exported, both Defense and State must provide written authorization. They also closely watch the export to ensure that the items are not reexported to a country that is either hostile to the United States or involved in terrorist activities.

Weapons incorporating sophisticated technology can pass into Soviet hands via intermediary countries. U.S. arms sold to Afghan rebels have sometimes landed in the Soviet camp. When items on both the CCL and Munitions Control List are diverted, the smugglers are often convicted under the Arms Export Control Act rather than the Export Administration Act.

The State Department also manages U.S. representation in Cocom and almost all bilateral discussions relating to export controls. Because American Cocom activities are viewed as a diplomatic function, the State Department provides the U.S. representative to the group, who, along with an assistant, operates out of the U.S. embassy in Paris. The State Department's Office of East-West Trade manages the hands-on U.S.-Cocom relationship. Commerce works with this office to formulate positions to be presented by the U.S. representative and to smooth the group's review of license applications from U.S. companies. It also works with Commerce to review license applications for which foreign policy is the reason for the export restriction. Other bureaus within the State Department make policy that affects technology flow to the Soviets. For example, one group manages the travel of Soviet citizens within the United States. Another reviews visa applications of Soviet bloc citizens who want to study at U.S. universities.

THE U.S. CUSTOMS SERVICE: OPERATION EXODUS

Inspectors and agents of the U.S. Customs Service, which is part of the U.S. Department of the Treasury, join Commerce in enforcing export laws. Although Commerce emphasizes industry compliance with licensing procedures, the Customs Service actively investigates, pursues, and catches high-technology smugglers. Inspectors check baggage for items leaving the U.S. illegally; at major entry points to European countries, they check incoming U.S. goods. Customs investigators follow up tips about potential illegal shipments, track known smugglers, and seize suspected or known illegal cargo, essentially combing the world in an attempt to capture high-technology smugglers and their booty. Although Commerce administers fines and denies licenses, the Customs Service actually discovers the illegally shipped computer terminals hidden in a remote warehouse in Austria. When a major electronics shipment to the Soviet Union is seized in West Germany, the Customs Service is often at the center of the sting. It is also assisted by the Department of Commerce, the FBI, and the CIA and by local law enforcement agencies.

The U.S. Customs Service has been in the enforcement business since 1789, the year the U.S. Constitution became effective. At least forty other government agencies look to Customs to enforce the laws. Bolstered with increased power by the Export Administration Amendment Act of 1985, the agency has developed new counter-smuggling programs, such as one directed at interrupting the illegal export of technology through Canada. William von Raab, the Customs Service commissioner, states with pride that Customs continues to increase its export seizures, arrests, and convictions. This is due in part to the general increase in trade but also to the increased efficiency of the service.

Stephen Walton is director of the Strategic Investigations Division of the Customs Service, another way of saying that he is head of Operation Exodus, the Customs program initiated in October 1981 to disrupt sales of American high technology (including munitions) restricted by the Commerce and State departments. An independent Mainer, he has a polished link of heavy chain looped casually around the pen set on his desk. His voice drops to a tone of shaded intrigue when he describes how it arrived there. As an agent in Germany, working on the case of the notorious diverter Richard Müller, he was involved in the seizure of computers illegally shipped to East Germany. The chain came off one of the crates containing the computers as the Customs agents opened them with bolt cutters. The glistening chain link reminds Walton of action in the field and the gritty reality of Soviet efforts to get U.S. technology.

Although Customs officials do not like to talk about the numbers of agents and support personnel (Walton confirmed Customs' unwillingness to divulge its inner workings: "We don't talk about how we're set up here. The very titles of personnel and branches sometimes give away too much"[18]), they make it clear that Operation Exodus is continuing to expand, particularly by placing more agents in the field. The Exodus command center is in a quiet area in the Customs building in Washington, D.C. It acts as a clearinghouse for agents who need to verify licenses or check company or individual names by using the computerized data base. There, inspectors and program analysts hover over computer terminals to support enforcement agents in the field.

Two hypothetical examples show how the command center operates. In one, an inspector in San Francisco examines an outgoing shipment of computer disk drives on their way to China. He reviews the export-license paperwork issued by the Department of Commerce and telephones the command center to verify the license. There, an inspector searches the data base; or if the product has been cleared under the Munitions Control Act, the State Department data base is accessed. The company's licensing history appears on the screen, and the inspector is assured that the company has complied with all requirements. The disk drives travel over the Pacific unhindered. In the second example, an agent in Germany learns from an informant of a possible diversion of IBM 3031 computers. He finds out the name of the firm in Cologne that is handling the shipment in that city and calls the command center. The inspectors tell the agent that the firm was involved in several diversion schemes in 1984 but was never caught. The agent receives further background information from the inspectors, such as the names of known diverters associated with the firm, and seizes the equipment in Cologne.

In its brief existence, Operation Exodus has built an impressive record. In January 1986, John Martin, chief of the Internal Security Section, Criminal Division, of the Justice Department, observed that during the late 1970s and early 1980s, only two or three technology theft cases were prosecuted; in January 1986 alone, however, the department was prosecuting more than 100 such cases, all brought in by Exodus. Between 1982 and 1987, it participated in 584 convictions, 1,171 indictments, and 910 arrests. Operation Exodus spearheaded 6,204 seizures worth $428.8 million and detained 11,729 shipments. High technology accounted for $141,963,548 worth of the seizures.[19] When Operation Exodus began, only about 10 percent of detained shipments were seized, suggesting that agents were still learning how to look for illegal technology shipments. By 1987, 85 percent of detentions had turned into seizures. The technology caseload continues to rise, and Customs Service personnel and budget have been increased in response to the increased activity.

During its first year, Operation Exodus focused on inspecting cargo and export documents at ports of exit. From then on, these activities were augmented, and part of the operation's money was spent on developing intelligence data bases, industry information and contacts, and cooperative links with other agencies, such as the Department of Defense. Today, Exodus investigators also monitor illegal shipping patterns and hot spots such as Hong Kong and Vienna.

The operation's narrow focus and clearly defined mission have helped improve the rate of seizures per shipments detained, Customs' own measure of effectiveness. Exodus concentrates only on dual-use and strategic electronics technology and items on the Munitions and Commodity control lists. Its officers usually know what to look for and have an efficient network of investigators in cities throughout Europe, including London, Bonn, and Rome, as well as in Hong Kong, Japan, and Panama.

Operation Exodus enables Customs to act aggressively and use the information it gathers and analyzes to arrest those who are already moving technology out of the country illegally. As a further refinement, Customs has used its data bases to pinpoint companies and technologies that are likely targets for illegal diverters. By doing so, its agents can anticipate diversion schemes and propose preventive measures.

The greatest difficulty that Customs has with convicting illegal diverters lies in getting solid evidence. In some cases, the alleged lawbreaker is in a foreign country that is unwilling to cooperate in extradition, or the suspects are fugitives, and Customs simply cannot track them down.

Customs' seizures of high-technology exports can alarm firms trying to sell goods abroad because Operation Exodus agents are usually certain that a shipment is improper before they seize it. A company would first know about a seizure of its equipment when a Customs agent notified it that a shipment was being temporarily detained and that license verification was in process in Washington. Sometimes shipments are detained because the shipper is on a list of companies denied export licenses, because the shipping documents do not appear to be in order, or perhaps because the recipient in Europe has been a known way station for goods bound for the Soviet Union. In other cases, Customs has been tipped off that an illegal shipment is destined for an Eastern bloc country.

Goods are usually detained for a day, and if everything is determined to be legitimate (an increasingly rare event with detained merchandise), the shipment proceeds toward its destination. If Customs finds that the export is improper, it notifies the exporting company, with the help of the Commerce Department, that it will be fined or that the shipment will be seized and forfeited. If the Customs Service suspects that the exporting company has intentionally broken the law, it may notify its Office of Enforcement, which sends investigators to the company to determine if there is any criminal culpability.

The 1985 EAA amendments strengthened Customs' powers by permitting agents to investigate outside as well as inside the United States. The Customs Service can also search suspected carriers of illegally shipped goods without warrants, and it can seize suspect shipments. To ensure that these powers don't make Customs agents too zealous in chasing suspected diverters, Congress limits how much can be spent on enforcement: In 1986, it was $14 million.

Operation Exodus also educates industry about how to spot an illegal shipment of high technology and to detect a shipment headed to a diverter or to some other questionable destination. Customs feels that each employee has a responsibility to assist in preventing illegal shipments and by so doing lessen the possibility of the company's losing its export privileges. A series of business advisories issued by Customs keeps computer and electronics companies advised of methods, characteristics, and successes of those who divert or steal technology from private companies. The Customs Service has also determined that a significant number of illegal technology exports could have been stopped if employees and management had known what to look for. It thus publishes a list of customer traits that could tip off exporters that a shipment is headed toward a diverter. The indicators are revealing and, if nothing else, contribute to a company's ability to operate efficiently. The "red flag" indicators are:

1. A customer's willingness to pay cash for high-value orders or an unusual or extremely generous financial compensation for the product.
2. The purchaser's reluctance to provide end use or end user information and an end use incompatible with the customary purpose for which the product is designed.
3. Instructions given by the customer to ship directly to trading companies, freight forwarders, export companies, or companies with no apparent connection to him or her.

4. Packaging requirements inconsistent with the shipping mode and/or destination.

5. Products or options ordered that appear incompatible with the customer's environment or line of business.

6. Circuitous or economically illogical routing, particularly through Canada to a non-Canadian destination.

7. A customer's apparent unfamiliarity with the product or its application, support equipment, or performance.

8. Customer refusal of a normal service and installation contract.

9. An order placed by a firm or individual from a foreign country other than that of the end user shown on the license.

Employees can use a Customs "hot line" (202-566-9464) to report events that they suspect contribute to illegal technology export. Posters inside corporations announce the hot line and its purpose. In some large multinational companies, such as IBM, Customs inspectors work full-time on the premises to ensure that shipment contents and documentation comply with licensing procedures and with export laws. Companies accept such an intrusion because a simple oversight could cost the company its export license(s).

In 1987, Customs began to zero in on diversions from defense contractors in reaction to the publicity surrounding the Walker and Pelton trials. Walton explains that defense contractors require more hand-holding to understand the complexities and nature of illegal technology transfer. Because defense contractors must agree to government security procedures and conditions before they are awarded a government contract, most feel that their environments are controlled and fairly well protected. But once a product leaves a defense contractor's buildings, it is just as susceptible to diversion as the products of nongovernment contractors.

Another area concerning the Customs Service is the illegal acquisition of technology by countries that represent themselves as friendly to the United States, such as Japan. The Toshiba case, publicized in 1987, emphasized concerns of this nature, causing those in Customs, as well as the Commerce, State, and Defense departments, to scratch their heads for diplomatic and effective ways to solve the problem.

Walton realizes that Operation Exodus functions at levels of intensity determined by the direction of the political winds on Capitol Hill. When a dramatic spy case related to technology theft hits the headlines, lawmakers become worked up, worried, and willing to allocate the funds to keep the program running at full force.

Over the years, Customs has developed a series of programs to try to be more clever than the culprits it snares. Some, like Operation Exodus, have succeeded; others have passed away quietly. Project Ramparts was an electrifying, innovative project that silently disappeared. The idea was to place electronic bugs inside computer equipment before it left the United States. An electronic device, such as a satellite, would track the equipment. The satellite would detect any diversion attempt and reveal it to Customs agents. But the tracking devices often lost the bugs' signals. Such techniques may still be used today. Information about them is classified, however, so their existence is difficult to confirm.

The Customs Service makes an effort to improve its ties with industry with speeches in public forums and with distribution of information through a project called Gemini. Started in May 1983, Gemini has helped Customs initiate and improve industry contacts while increasing its understanding of the high-technology industry. As of February 1988, Customs agents had contacted 3,700 companies.[20] Through these contacts, investigators keep informed of changes in technology that might affect export restrictions. During the period that Gemini has been operating, export-license applications have been increasing, a trend that Exodus chief Walton feels is related to the improved communications. This trend may be further fed by the team effort developing among Customs and Commerce, State, and Defense agencies. Operation Exodus also initiated an internal program to educate its personnel about the high-tech industry.

CRACKS IN THE ARMOR

Unfortunately, the Commerce Department and the Customs Service had difficulty cooperating on the enforcement of export controls in the 1970s and early 1980s. Walton described the conflict as "bureaucratic bloodletting."[21] It stemmed from the two agencies' overlapping responsibilities.

Although Commerce's Office of Export Enforcement is charged with enforcing export laws, Customs saw the department's sole purpose as promoting trade. Customs officials viewed Commerce's enforcement activity with disdain because its personnel lacked law enforcement training; they felt they were being underutilized, if not ignored, by an agency that seemed to be ill-prepared for the enforcement business. On the other hand, Commerce officials thought they were being intentionally shown up by Customs, which had the advantage in enforcement because of its agents' training and their tradition of strong investigative work.

At the peak of the conflict, in 1983, it was not unknown for Customs agents and Commerce employees to scream at each other on the telephone or spitefully withhold information. Congress was worried that the discord had gone so far that export controls were suffering and that money was being wasted. With the bureaucratic air crackling between the two buildings, it would not have taken much to get Bill Rudman, the head of Customs' Operation Exodus in 1983, and Theodore Wai Wu, then chief of Commerce's export enforcement, out on the Washington Mall for hand-to-hand combat. Customs agents and Commerce officials were victims of the turmoil, with headquarters more absorbed in the next best way to retaliate than in better ways to detect illegal shipments.

The 1985 amendments to the export law zeroed in on this situation by requiring that the agencies inform each other and share data whenever possible—and matters have gradually improved. The legislators who wrote the amendments realized that the law had to include a reprimand and a reminder to both groups that they would have to put aside their bickering. By 1987, relations between the two had calmed, although disagreements continued to pierce the increasingly cooperative atmosphere. As personnel have turned over in each agency, old grudges have been replaced by new hope. One of the hopefuls, Walton, says, "I think it is going to take a lot of time." But he feels that some tension in the agencies' relations can be beneficial. "There should be healthy competition to stimulate both agencies; it is not good to have a one-agency responsibility."

Commerce has also tussled with Defense. Commerce, which feels that it carefully balances considerations of the foreign availability of high technology and the impact of trade restrictions on U.S. competitiveness and the trade deficit, sometimes regards the Defense Department attitude toward export controls as one-sided, from only the point of view of national security. Although Commerce supports Defense's efforts to protect national security, that issue can often be the most controversial in export-license decisions. Tensions also arise out of one agency's frustration concerning the other's enforcement of the export laws. In one 1987 case, Defense protested the export of an IBM mainframe to a 51-percent Soviet-owned shipping firm in Hamburg, West Germany. The Commerce Department delayed the shipment while it argued with Defense; in the meantime, Commerce authorized the shipment of a Hitachi computer containing U.S.-manufactured components to the Soviet-owned firm, Transnautic Shipping Company. The Pentagon also protested that shipment, made without consulting the Defense Department. In June 1987, the review by the Defense Department of license applications to communist-controlled companies in nonsocialist countries was waived in response to complaints from U.S. industry and important traders with the Soviets, such as West Germany. After the Transnautic episode, the review was reinstituted in September 1987 in spite of IDM assertions that its shipment only upgraded an existing IBM mainframe at Transnautic used to track shipments to the Soviet Union.[22]

Again in 1987, an oversight in the Commerce Department almost led to the shipment of an IBM minicomputer to Singapore Soviet Shipping, a Soviet shipping company in Singapore. A Defense review of the license application turned up the company's name, not clearly identified on the filled-out form.[23] Some industry observers feel that the adversarial relationship between Commerce and Defense, which takes time from both departments that could be used to hasten license reviews, has no prospect of improving. Dan Hoydysh elaborates: "We just spend a lot of staff time dueling with Defense over issues that should be decided at a much higher level."

THE SPY CATCHERS

Espionage is defined by the U.S. Espionage Act of 1917 as the theft of material "for the purpose of obtaining information respecting the national defense with intent or reason to believe that the information to be obtained is to be used to the injury of the United States, or to the advantage of any foreign nation."[24] Because espionage is the target of the U.S. intelligence services, information on specific counterespionage operations and tactics is usually classified and cannot be discussed here.

Local law enforcement agencies often provide a link between high-technology companies and the federal government. And companies themselves attempt to thwart the theft of technology secrets, including those that are unclassified, by employing private security companies and instituting procedures to safeguard their latest technical breakthroughs.

Federal legislation may increase the efficiency of the U.S. spy-catching net. For example, senators William V. Roth, Jr. (R-Del.) and Robert J. Dole (R-Kans.) introduced two bills in 1986 (and reintroduced them in 1987) intended to deter Soviet espionage. One broadens the Foreign Missions Act, supporting the State Department's effort to further restrict the movements of Soviet diplomats. The Roth bill (S947) would extend those limitations to the Eastern bloc diplomatic corps. Because the CIA has determined that the Soviets ask the Eastern bloc intelligence services to acquire much of the needed U.S. technology through espionage, this bill would inhibit their ability to visit Silicon Valley and other similarly sensitive areas. Another bill, also introduced by Roth and Dole (S946), would impose the death penalty as an optional sentence for spying to gather information about cryptanalysis, communications, counterintelligence operations, nuclear weapons, and war plans. Because a case can be made that millions of U.S. lives may be lost as a result of the receipt of key U.S. technology by the Soviets, some legislators see the death penalty as the only one serious enough to deter a potential recruit from giving away U.S. technology.[25]

The Espionage Act, along with these bills (if enacted), along with ongoing counterespionage efforts, provide the legal basis for disrupting Soviet espionage as a means of capturing U.S. high-technology secrets.

FBI: COUNTERESPIONAGE, COUNTERINTELLIGENCE, AND DECA

As part of its effort to enforce the U.S. espionage statute, the FBI investigates those espionage-related activities within the United States that are connected to the transfer of restricted technology. Its main tools are counterintelligence (CI) and counterespionage (CE). (If a case requires investigations overseas, the CIA becomes the key player.) At the core of all the publicized technology spy cases are FBI agents who ferreted out the facts, the culprits, and the stolen booty. They are frequently called in by Customs. Customs and the FBI commonly work shoulder to shoulder on technology-smuggling cases. The FBI's focus is hostile intelligence service (HOIS) involvement. A simple diversion of computers masterminded by two California engineers and an Austrian freight forwarder, for example, would receive FBI attention if it appeared that an HOIS were involved. Even though the bureau does not directly enforce the Export Administration Act, its agents investigate violations of U.S. espionage statutes and activities of foreign intelligence services. Their foreign counterintelligence (FCI) activities seek to identify HOISs, monitor their activities, and disrupt their efforts. Although the defendant in a diversion case may be charged with violating the EAA, the case may be investigated by the FBI if it involves violations of other federal laws.

In their foreign counterintelligence role, FBI agents interview contacts in private industry, conduct electronic surveillance, and closely observe both known and suspected Soviet and Soviet bloc agents in the United States. In most successful espionage investigations, an informer has supplied information that enabled the FBI to launch an investigation and eventually gather enough evidence to make an arrest.[26]

Government agencies can be wary of working with the FBI, according to Walton, because its agents tend to go it alone rather than work closely with others. The FBI, however, emphasizes its commitment to working with other federal agencies whenever the circumstances require its expertise. The Commerce Department uses intelligence provided by the FBI in investigations of its diversion and smuggling cases.

The FBI sponsors a program called Development of Counterintelligence Awareness (DECA), which educates high-technology companies, particularly government contractors, about Soviet and Soviet bloc efforts to acquire high technology through technical espionage. DECA representatives visit defense contractors and provide them with information about government security procedures and HOIS activities. FBI personnel speak with executives and security officers, provide support for company security programs, and often make presentations to those closely involved in the companies' technology. Discussions center on KGB recruiting techniques and possible scenarios for technical espionage. Larger government contractors receive visits from DECA once or twice a year. In Northern California alone, more than 600 defense contractors are visited by DECA representatives. Smaller companies may receive only a phone call and literature describing Soviet techniques. But high-technology companies not involved in classified work, even though they work in state-of-the-art areas, can fall through the cracks. The FBI does not have the personnel to cover them, even though the companies do not have tight security or a great deal of awareness of KGB recruiting methods. Much advanced high technology is not yet classified by the Defense Department.

The FBI is aware that a program such as DECA does not stop espionage but that it can make life more difficult for the Soviets. The bureau feels that an awareness of hostile intelligence services allows a company to protect its secrets in a proactive manner rather than "locking the barn door after the horses have been stolen" and simply patching leaks only to lose critical government contracts.

Project DECA is the first FBI program to direct preventive measures against espionage, an effort that industry generally welcomes and supports. Many would agree with John O'Loughlin, manager of security for Intel Corporation, that "companies themselves have to be the first in line of defense—and many are now beginning to wake up to their vulnerability."[27]

PENALTIES: PAYING THE PRICE?

Whether caught by Commerce, Customs, or the FBI, those arrested for high-technology diversion or espionage can be prosecuted under the Export Administration Act and under a host of other laws. The Arms Export Control Act, the International Emergency Economic Powers Act, and the Trading with the Enemy Act, as well as laws against conspiring to transport stolen property, interstate transportation of stolen property, violating any foreign country sanctions or embargoes, wire fraud, or making a false statement, also provide bases for prosecution. Sometimes high-technology export-control cases are prosecuted under both the EAA and the Arms Export Control Act. Despite this armament of laws, however, the price high-technology thieves and export-regulation violators pay is likely insufficient to prevent them and others from continuing their actions.

As it is in most areas of U.S. law, intent is key in determining the extent of punishment. Both civil and criminal charges are sometimes levied against violators. Most trespassers of the EAA unknowingly violate the regulations, mistakenly omitting or putting incorrect information on a license application or shipping equipment to a company that is denied access to U.S. exports. Those committing unwitting violations receive civil penalties, or administrative sanctions as they are sometimes called. If an American citizen intentionally violates the export law, however, he or she may feel the full weight of punishment resulting from criminal prosecution under the federal statutes. For example, intentional violators under criminal charges can be fined five times the value of the export or $50,000, whichever is greater, plus a prison term of a maximum of five years. An individual who deliberately violates the EAA (with knowledge that the exports would be used by countries covered by export controls for national-security or foreign-policy purposes) can be fined as much as $250,000 and serve a maximum of ten years in prison; a corporation can be fined as much as $1 million. In most cases, goods seized are also forfeited. Other criminal violations include possessing CCL items with the intent to export them illegally and evading the EAA.

Civil penalties take the form of fines (as much as $100,000 if the export is controlled for national-security reasons and as much as $10,000 if it is controlled for short-supply or foreign-policy reasons). Even though a company is convicted of civil violations of the EAA, the firm's executives are not treated as criminals and usually are not prosecuted. Penalties for companies range from the denial of a license to those that put a firm on probation and call for a specified number of hours of charitable work.

But the penalties generally sound far worse than they really are. Almost all export violations involving high technology are viewed as white-collar crimes and result in either administrative or criminal fines of less than $50,000. For example, Jong Hee Park of United Compudata Corporation was fined only $10,000 for illegally shipping $232,000 worth of Perkin-Elmer computer equipment in 1984. Although a 1985 *Electronics Week* article said that D. Frank Bazzarre, convicted of diverting $6.5 million worth of semiconductor fabrication and test equipment, faced a maximum $5 million fine and as many as fifteen years in prison, he actually received a one-year prison sentence, a $110,000 fine, and 700 hours of compulsory community service. The only prison sentences of five or more years for export-law violations handed down since 1981 (except for that given Werner Bruchhausen, who received a fifteen-year prison term) have been for illegal exports of arms. As a result, both companies and individuals that export illegal material know that they are unlikely to pay the stiff penalties outlined in the EAA, even if they are apprehended. Anyone caught for intentionally breaking the export laws cannot apply for an export license for ten years. An illegal exporter may, however, start a new company and have its new president (another individual) apply for a license. The Commerce Department may eventually figure out the ruse, but by then the new enterprise may have sold millions of dollars of equipment to the Soviets.

Smugglers found guilty of their crimes are often free in a few years, still flush with funds garnered from their illegal enterprise and able to commit the same crimes again under different names or with different front companies and personnel. Barrett Liebe, convicted in New York in 1985 for thirty-six illegal shipments of microcomputers worth more than $350,000, landed a five-year sentence and a $10,000 fine and was required to perform 300 hours of community service.[28] These penalties are hardly equal to the value of the illegally exported equipment.

Plea bargaining sometimes replaces a stiff penalty. In 1982, Paul Carlson pleaded guilty to fifteen counts of violation of U.S. export laws but agreed to assist federal law enforcement officials by testifying against his former business partner and smuggling-ring leader, Brian Möller-Butcher. Carlson had shipped computer and electronic test equipment to Möller-Butcher in England in late 1979 and 1980; Möller-Butcher then shipped it to the Soviet bloc.[29] After plea bargaining, Carlson was fined

$5,000 and given a one-year suspended sentence and two years' proba-
tion. Möller-Butcher remains a fugitive.

Anstruther Davidson, acting director of Commerce's Office of Export Enforcement, believes that the penalties meted out to those who
violate export laws are sufficient to deter other potential technology
diverters. He says: "The administrative sanctions we have available to
us, the fines, the denial of export privileges, I guarantee, get the attention
of any businessman in the United States who wants to continue in business." But Davidson feels the frustration of trying to catch seasoned, successful technology diverters, such as Richard Müller and Werner
Bruchhausen, and of preventing others from following them. He thinks
the criminal penalties are too light to stop them and to discourage future master diverters. The problem, he points out, is that these criminal
cases are often difficult to prove, the facts are unclear, and foreign countries uncooperative. Often, an illegal diverter will get a stiff sentence
only if the prosecutor sensationalizes a case so that the media become
interested in it.

Each government agency has its own view of how to deter technology-export crimes and what enforcement means, but Dan Hoydysh of
Commerce points out that "largely, our enforcement is voluntary. Like in
come tax laws, if you get away with it, you get away with it....So compliance is to a large degree voluntary."

CORPORATE AMERICA:
RISING TO THE CHALLENGE

Without the cooperation and active participation of private industry, all
the laws, enforcement activities, and penalties can do little to make life
difficult for technobandits. Individual companies can often respond to
Soviet technology-espionage efforts faster than the government. In general, corporate America is patriotic and interested in protecting its high
technology from acquisition by hostile countries. Even those companies
committed to joint ventures with the Soviets feel that they should not
jeopardize U.S. national security in any way. Arthur M. Dula of the Space
Commerce Corporation in Houston, Tex., expresses his exuberant

patriotism when he says he plans to "put up a flagpole and run up an American flag as soon as we land our freighters on the airfield at Leninsk."[30] His company is doing a commercial cooperative space venture with the Soviets.

Many high-technology companies, particularly government contractors, use their own internal security programs to prevent technology theft. These programs are supported by the FBI's DECA program as well as by the Defense Investigative Service. DIS agents have traditionally monitored security inside government contractors, rewarding extraordinary diligence with monetary bonuses.[31] If the company does not have a security program, they will assist it in developing one; if a company's program does not meet DIS standards, they make recommendations for achieving compliance. In late 1986, President Reagan announced proposals for additional spending to strengthen security for government contractors, including assigning DIS agents permanently to large defense contractor plants. In May 1987, Thomas J. O'Brien, Director of DIS, indicated that eighteen companies had been targeted for potential placement of DIS personnel, although he did not say which ones.

Most companies have some type of security program, if only to protect their secrets from competitors, but they rarely discuss security procedures with outsiders for the obvious reason: If outsiders know what precautions a company takes, they can work around them. Companies with security programs will indicate, however, that they do have them. Hewlett-Packard, in Palo Alto, Calif., follows the standard practice of providing badges for its employees, and its R&D staff sends only previously published materials overseas. Ford Aerospace, also in Palo Alto, carefully follows the DIS manual for security guidelines and the State Department's International Traffic in Arms Regulations for pointers on classified information. SRI International in Menlo Park, Calif., another DIS manual user, is visited every six months by a DIS inspector who sees that all security requirements for government-classified projects are being followed. The inspectors talk to employees to assess their knowledge of security procedures.

Most major high-technology exporters carefully comply with the export laws. Usually, a company employs an in-house export administrator, sometimes with a staff, and retains a lawyer to assist that staff with compliance issues. The export administrator needs to develop a compliance program along with a means for anticipating licensing problems. He or she must be alert to changes in the law by reviewing the *Export Administration Regulations* and all other Commerce Department bulletins pertaining to export controls, in addition to maintaining close contact with the licensing staff in Washington, D.C. Management must be involved in export compliance issues because an oversight could result in the loss of valuable exporting privileges, not to mention adverse publicity. Finally, a company should know the behavioral characteristics of diverters so that they can spot a potentially illegal shipment before it is sent.

THE U.S. ELECTRONICS INDUSTRY: CAUGHT IN THE MIDDLE?

The laws' complexities, however, can make compliance difficult, if not onerous, especially for small and midsize companies with few resources to spend on export staff and consultants. Many companies argue that compliance with the law is so costly and time-consuming that it inhibits their export activities and makes it difficult to compete with foreign high-technology firms in the international marketplace. The experience of one company shows the kind of difficulty compliance can create for high-technology exporters. Columbus Instruments, a $1.7 million company founded in 1970, sells laboratory machines linked with personal computers to measure respiration of laboratory animals. Until June 1, 1985, nearly one-half of its annual sales were to foreign customers, including some in Eastern bloc countries. At that time, Customs agents, suspecting the company of shipping restricted technology, confiscated sixty-nine boxes ($228,812 worth) of its equipment at J. F. Kennedy International Airport in New York. The shipment, including the IBM PC clones that are used in Columbus' Oxymax-85 rat oxygen monitor and five Apple IIes, was headed for a biotechnology conference in Moscow.[32] In 1987, two years after the seizure, Columbus Instruments was still awaiting a decision on whether it could export the confiscated items, and the company's president, Jan Czekajewski, still faced possible grand jury investigation for intentionally violating the EAA.[33] Charges were eventually dropped in 1987 because of "insufficient evidence."

Czekajewski and his company were caught between Customs and the Commerce and Defense departments. Customs, convinced it was stopping an illegal export to the Soviets, seized the equipment because it was addressed to Finland instead of its destination in the Soviet Union, indicating that the company might be concealing the shipment's ultimate destination and not complying with requirements to obtain a reexport license. The Commerce Department then took months to determine if one of the confiscated personal computers had a high enough processing data rate to require that it be exported only with an approved license.[34] When Commerce decided that the computer did not fall within the controls, the Defense Department launched its own study of the computer's processing speed. The final decision awaited a ruling on export laws proposed in early 1987 and still not decided by the year's end. By fall 1987, Commerce found no fault with the company. Customs, on the other hand, still held $50,000 worth of the company's equipment from the seizure and continued to keep the case open. In October 1987, Customs was to have auctioned off the equipment, but as of June 1988 it was still in storage in New York.

The Columbus Instruments experience illustrates weaknesses on both sides of the industry/government relationship. On the one hand, the government bureaucracy in some cases seems to handicap a company's ability to compete in world markets and may absorb an unnecessary amount of company resources in the export compliance process, both problems that the controversial 1987 National Academy of Sciences study found to be rampant. On the other hand, the Columbus Instruments experience reveals the devastating effects of a poorly organized, actually nonexistent, in-house export compliance program. The company's staff was simply unaware of export-licensing procedures. When initiating the shipment, the company contacted an airline for instructions on completing the paperwork. Columbus contends that the airline told it to put Finland on the shipping label rather than Moscow, the final destination.

Some companies complain about the time it takes to get their export license approved, while others are content to go along with the system and feel they experience minimal delays. Industry also complains about detention times for shipments that Customs inspects, the complex license application forms, the technical competence of Commerce and Customs officials, and the broad scope of the CCL. Even Dan Hoydysh of the Commerce Department admits that the CCL "sweeps into it more than it has to."

On the other side, a company sometimes gets a signed purchase agreement from a foreign buyer and then demands that the Commerce Department issue an export license at the last minute, even though the company likely had the opportunity to prepare some of the paperwork ahead of time, explaining angrily that it will lose the contract if the license is not issued within 24 hours.

The 1987 National Academy of Sciences study looked at actual license-processing times, that is, the time between the delivery of a license application and the receipt of a notice of action. In 1986, it took an average of twenty-one days to process an export license to all countries in the Free World, fourteen days for exports to Cocom countries, sixty-four days for those to the People's Republic of China, and seventy-five days for applications to export to the Soviet bloc.

Disgruntled industry executives and associated members of Congress confirm the NAS findings. On Apr. 16, 1987, Congressman Norman Y. Mineta (D-Calif.), and Congressman Don Edwards (D-Calif.), both of whom view export control as a hindrance to U.S. high-tech companies, held a public hearing on the subject in Silicon Valley. On that occasion, several companies, including Ultratech Stepper, Hewlett-Packard, Sun Microsystems, and Finnegan Corporation, expressed their frustrations with the export laws. One by one, the high-tech companies testifying at the hearings lamented lost sales and vented their impatience with the export laws. Adaptec, a five-year-old company with 20 percent of its sales overseas, makes application-specific integrated circuits and controller boards for mass-storage devices. At least three foreign companies manufacture the same products, but Adaptec feels its resources are inadequate to make a case for foreign availability, that is, that its goods were available from foreign sources and therefore should not have been restricted by the CCL. Furthermore, its foreign sales were inhibited by four- to five-month delays in the licensing process. Hardtimes, a company of only five employees, lost almost $1 million in sales of 5 MB hard disks when it was denied an export license. The company argued futilely that the same disk was practically obsolete (5 MB disk drives were first produced in 1983) and furthermore was available from companies in Japan, Singapore, Taiwan, and Great Britain.

Another firm, E-MU Systems Incorporated, a manufacturer of electronic musical instruments, spoke of trying to sell its digital sampling keyboard abroad. When the company enhanced one of its instruments with a half-height 20 MB hard-disk drive, the product fell into the same export category as high-speed digital computers. E-MU applied to Commerce for a clarification of the classification and waited seven months— only to find out that the instrument did not require an export license. The delay and the time and effort taken from other important projects in the company made the overseas sale of its product a costly proposition.

The companies concluded by arguing strongly for a liberalization of the law so that they could export more high-tech products to restricted countries without the many problems brought on by current regulations: filling out complicated forms, waiting an unreasonably long time for license approvals, and losing contracts because of foreign availability. The hearing took place at a time when the U.S. trade deficit made new headlines every week and was on the lips of every lawmaker in Washington. As a result, interest was high in what these high-tech companies had to say. Their comments illustrate some classic objections to the current U.S. response to the Soviet threat. Mineta summed up industry's plight by saying: "When high-tech companies try to compete in world markets, we do so with one hand tied behind our back. The worst part is that we are doing the tying ourselves. The present system of excessive and inefficient export barriers unnecessarily raises the price of doing business with U.S. businesses."

Licensing delays and other export-control problems appear to be on the road toward resolution, with current law calling for a reduction in the time it takes to process a license. But at the same time, incidents such as the Toshiba case pressure lawmakers to tighten controls and scrutinize exports more closely. As U.S. foreign policy moves between open and closed relations between the two superpowers, the legal flow of U.S. technology to the Soviet bloc will grow and diminish in direct response. The United States will rely on a mixture of individual awareness, corporate internal security measures, and government export controls, depending on the political climate. For the time being, the one constant is the Soviet commitment to acquiring and depending on U.S. high technology.

In concert with this commitment, the United States applauds Gorbachev's effort in improving individual rights, applying democratic concepts to the Soviet political system, and exercising capitalist principles. Few pundits know the extent to which Gorbachev's initiatives will penetrate Soviet society and politics, and, as of this writing, *perestroika*'s future is tentative. Despite Soviet interest in improving relations with the United States, recurring cycles of hot and cold relations linked with overt and covert efforts to acquire U.S. technology are bound to continue.

The issues are complex and the solutions depend on careful compromises, but a greater awareness of the issues enables individuals and the private sector to take a greater and more promising role in safeguarding America's investment in technology research and development. The role of the government has its limits in protecting critical technology, many of them apparent in this chapter. It is therefore the responsibility of those in the high-technology industry to know why the Soviets want U.S. technology, how they illegally and legally acquire it, and the options available and utilized for controlling the flow to the Soviets.

NOTES

1. The many specific acts, penalties, and private industry efforts are far too numerous and complex to detail here; such a discussion could easily fill a volume three times this size, and would not reflect the ongoing changes in legislation.

2. The United States also restricts the export of "defense articles" (for example, arms and ammunition) through the International Traffic in Arms Regulations (ITAR). The State Department administers these regulations through its Office of Munitions Control with guidance from the Defense Department. The Iran-contra arms affair, exposed during intensive public hearings in 1987, involved illegal sales of arms to hostile countries, a violation of ITAR.

3. Rodney Joseph, Industrial Resources Division, U.S. Department of Commerce, Washington, D.C.: Interview, Jan. 11, 1988.

4. U.S. Department of Commerce, *A Summary of U.S. Export Administration Regulations*, (Washington, D.C.: 1985), p. 13.

5. John Black, Export Licensing Office, U.S. Department of Commerce, Washington, D.C.: Interview, Jan. 8, 1988.

6. Ibid. Also, U.S. Department of Commerce, Export Administration, Annual reports, 1984–87.

7. Toli Welihozkiy, division director for assessments, Office of Foreign Availability, U.S. Department of Commerce, Washington, D.C.: Interview, Dec. 22, 1987.

8. As of October 1987, the Department of Commerce was reorganized to create the Export Administration with the objective of elevating licensing activities. Previously, they had been handled by the International Trade Administration. Now, the head of the EA, the under secretary of Export Administration, reports directly to the secretary of commerce. Activities relating to imports remain under the ITA. Congress and industry are hoping that this reorganization will expedite the licensing process and draw attention to the issues surrounding export controls.

9. U.S. Department of Commerce, *Commerce Enforcement of U.S. Export Controls: The Challenge and the Response*, (Washington, D.C.: 1986), p. 7.

10. John Konfala, director, Defense Technology Security Administration, U.S. Department of Defense, Washington, D.C.: Interview, Nov. 4, 1987.

11. U.S. Department of Defense, Technology Security Program, Caspar W. Weinberger, A Report to the 99th Cong., 2d sess., 1986, p. 34–53.

12. Dan Hoydysh, acting director of the Office of Technology and Policy Analysis, U.S. Department of Commerce, Washington, D.C.: Interview, Sept. 18, 1987.

13. Oles Lomacky, office of the deputy under secretary of defense for international programs and technology, U.S. Department of Defense: Interview, Nov. 3, 1987.

14. The Defense Department defines confidential, secret, and top secret as follows: "CONFIDENTIAL" is the designation that shall be applied to information or material, the unauthorized disclosure of which could be reasonably expected to cause damage to the national security. Examples of "damage" include the compromise of information that indicates strength of ground, air, and naval forces in the United States and overseas areas; disclosure of technical information used for training, maintenance, and inspection of classified munitions of war; and revelation of performance characteristics, test data, design, and production data on munitions of war. "SECRET" is the designation that shall be applied only to information or material, the unauthorized disclosure of which reasonably could be expected to cause serious damage to the national security. Examples of "serious damage" include disruption of foreign relations significantly affecting the national security, significant impairment of a program or policy directly related to the national security, revelation of significant military plans or intelligence operations, compromise of significant military plans or intelligence operations, and

compromise of significant scientific or technological developments relating to national security. "TOP SECRET" is the designation that shall be applied only to information or material, the unauthorized disclosure of which reasonably could be expected to cause exceptionally grave damage to the national security. Examples of "exceptionally grave damage" include armed hostilities against the United States or its allies, disruption of foreign relations vitally affecting the national security, the compromise of vital national defense plans or complex cryptologic and communications intelligence systems, the revelation of sensitive intelligence operations, and the disclosure of scientific or technological developments vital to national security. (Source: *Industrial Security Manual for Safeguarding Classified Information* [Washington, D.C.: U.S. Department of Defense, 1986], pp. 6, 13, and 15.)

15. Dale Hartig, public affairs official, Defense Investigative Service, San Francisco: Interview, Jan. 20, 1988.

16. Bettie Sprigg, deputy chief of broadcast pictorial, U.S. Department of Defense: Letter to the author, Feb. 24, 1988.

17. David Willman, "Official Denies Cost of High-Tech Export Limits, "*San Jose Mercury News*, Feb. 10, 1987.

18. Stephen Walton, director of strategic investigations, U.S. Customs Service, Washington, D.C.: Interview, Apr. 1, 1987.

19. David Hoover, U.S. Customs Service, Washington, D.C.: Interview, Feb. 11, 1988.

20. David Hoover: Interview, Feb. 16, 1988.

21. Stephen Walton: Interview, Sept. 15, 1986.

22. Eduardo Lachica, "U.S. Reimposes Tight Review on Exports to Companies Controlled by Communists," *Wall Street Journal*, Sept. 28, 1987, p. 62.

23. Stephen Koepp, "Shoot Out at Tech Gap," *Time*, Oct. 12, 1987, pp. 50 51.

24. U.S., *Statutes at Large*, vol. 40, p. I, Ch. 30, p. 217.

25. Senator William V. Roth, "Comprehensive Counterespionage Efforts," *Congressional Record*, Apr. 8, 1987, S4773–S4776.

26. Remarks by William H. Webster, then director of the FBI, before the National Association of Former U.S. Attorneys in Orlando, Fla., Mar. 22, 1986, pp. 11–14.

27. "Kremlin Spies Target U.S. Electronic Knowhow," *Business Week*, Sept. 20, 1982, p. 77.

28. U.S. Department of the Treasury, U.S Customs Service, *Department of the Treasury News*, Dec. 31, 1985, p. 3.

29. "Man Pleads Guilty in Export Case," *Computerworld*, July 25, 1983, p. 9.

30. Arthur M. Dula, partner, Dula, Shields & Egbert, Houston, Tex.: Letter to the author, Jan. 5, 1988.

31. Michael J. Sniffen, "Counterintelligence," Washington Press, Associated Press, Nov. 30, 1986 (data base).

32. Michael Wels Hirschorn, "Ohio Firm Is Entangled in Confusion over U.S. Policy in High-Tech Exports, *Wall Street Journal*, Feb. 10, 1987, p. 16.

33. Ibid.

34. Jan Czekajewski, president of Columbus Instruments, Columbus, Ohio: Interview, Feb. 23, 1987.

INDEX

A

A. J. Brandt 50
academic community
    security in the 159–62
    Soviet connection to 154–57
Academy of Sciences 103
acquisitions, methods of Soviet
    76–77, 107–34
administrative agencies 221–35
Aeroflot 120
Afghanistan, invasion of 61, 220
Agat personal computer 90
agencies, U.S. 221–35
agents, Soviet high-technology
    110, 116
Akademset 93
Aksyonov, V. B. 185
Albert Kahn Inc. 50
Alexis, Tsar 44
allies
    access to U.S. 169–209
    export laws of the 174–77
American Semiconductor Inc. 198
American Trade Consortium 33
Amtorg Trading Corporation 30,
    48, 126–27
Analogue und Digital Technik 5
Anderson, Kevin Eric 12
Andropov, Yuri 61
anti-Semitism 47
Apple Computer, sales to the
    Soviets 149
Arkhipov, Ivan 195
Arms Export Control Act 4, 228
    penalties under 241

Arthur G. McKee Company 50
ASEA AB 188
Asia, export controls and 193–201
Association for Computing
    Machinery 163
Austria, export controls and
    190–92
automobiles 57

B

Baker, Dr. Lara 163
Baldrige, Malcolm 223
Balzer, Harley D. 75
Bank of Tokyo 182
banks, attempted acquisition of
    California 128–29
Barr, Joel 81–84
Batinic, Ivan Pierre 12
Batinic, Stevan 13
Bay of Pigs 56
Bazzarre, D. Frank 191, 242
Belousov, Igor S. 113
Belyakov, Oleg 113
Berg, Yosef Venyaminovich 81–84
Beria, Lavrenti P. 54
Berlin blockade 171
Berlin Wall 56
BESM computer 81
Betriebs & Fianzierungs
    Beratungs GmbH 191
Bhoge, Keakh 120
BK-0010 personal computers 86
blackboard rule 75
blackmail, use of 122
Bollinger GmbH 191
Bolshevik Revolution 46–50

Robyn Shotwell Metcalfe

Robyn Shotwell Metcalfe has been involved in the computer industry since the late 1970s as both a writer and a consultant. Her work with Arthur D. Little as a management consultant specializing in electronic publishing and information systems included projects with a number of high-tech companies. Metcalfe is the author of several books and the former "Computer Update" columnist for *Publishers Weekly* magazine. She lives in Woodside, California.

Other Tempus™ Books

THE TOMORROW MAKERS
A Brave New World of Living-Brain Machines
Grant Fjermedal

"Talespinners have nothing on the hard-core science freaks. This nonfiction book has enough new ideas for 16 Star Trek sequels. And better dialogue."
Rudy Rucker, San Francisco Chronicle

Award-winning science writer Grant Fjermedal paints a richly human picture of the lives and work of the brilliant and sometimes eccentric robotics researchers at Stanford, MIT, and Carnegie–Mellon. Through Fjermedal's keen journalistic eye, you will see the world of artificial intelligence and robotics and witness the breakneck speeds at which these technologies are evolving. He also provides the most astounding account of all—the process of downloading individual human minds into computerized robots that never die. An enthralling portrait of world-class computer scientists and intense hackers who all possess unmatched passion and ability for "making tomorrow."

288 pages, 6¹/₈ x 9, softcover $8.95   Order Code: 86-96247

THURSDAY'S UNIVERSE
A Report from the Frontier on the Origin, Nature, and Destiny of the Universe
Marcia Bartusiak

"Marcia Bartusiak entered the universe of research at the frontiers of astronomy and cosmology and returned with a gem of a book. I recommend it."
Heinz Pagels, author of The Cosmic Code

Cited by *The New York Times* as one of the best science books of 1987, and named a 1987 Astronomy Book of the Year by the Astronomical Society of the Pacific, THURSDAY'S UNIVERSE takes you on a tantalizing journey of discovery to the outer reaches of the cosmos. How did the universe begin? How will it end? What populates the endless expanse of space? Through THURSDAY'S UNIVERSE you will explore current ideas about the moment of creation; the birth and death of stars, quasars, and galaxies; the composition of black holes and neutrinos, and the still-unanswered questions about the cosmos. Bartusiak will introduce you to the brilliant astronomers, astrophysicists, and researchers behind today's theories about the universe.

336 pages, 6 x 9, softcover $8.95   Order Code: 86-96627

INVISIBLE FRONTIERS
The Race to Synthesize a Human Gene
Stephen S. Hall

"An important and pioneering book, dealing with events of high scientific and economic consequence...[Hall] succeeds marvelously in making the science accessible to the general reader."
The New York Times Book Review

In 1976 scientists realized that synthesizing, or cloning, a human gene was imminently possible. INVISIBLE FRONTIERS weaves you through the intense and dramatic race to clone a human gene and then to engineer the mass production of the life-sustaining hormone insulin. Stephen Hall takes you through the developments of this high-stakes race, which resulted in the birth of the biotechnology revolution, a Nobel Prize, and the founding of the first genetic engineering company. INVISIBLE FRONTIERS, based on interviews with both major and minor participants, is an authentic and vivid account and rivals the importance and excitement of *The Double Helix*.

360 pages, 6 x 9, softcover $8.95   Order Code: 86-96817

NOBEL DREAMS
Power, Deceit and the Ultimate Experience
Gary Taubes

"...a rare inside look at particle physics."
Time magazine

Follow Carlo Rubbia and his ambitious and ultimately successful quest to confirm experimentally the existence of hitherto undiscovered subatomic particles and garner the 1985 Nobel Prize in Physics. His is a saga of big science, big ego, frenetic competition, and hardball politics. A modern day adventure story that illustrates the chaotic and chancy nature of scientific discovery.

288 pages, 6¹/₈ x 9, softcover $8.95   Order Code: 86-96239

INVENTORS AT WORK
Interviews with 16 Notable American Inventors, by Kenneth A. Brown
Foreword by James Burke

INVENTORS AT WORK is a colorful collection of 16 engaging and illuminating interviews with the most notable inventors of our time, from professional R&D specialists like NASA's Maxime Faget to independent tinkerers like inventor/artist Nat Wyeth. Their accomplishments—the laser, the microprocessor, the man-powered airplane, the Apple II computer, the plastic soda pop bottle, the implantable pacemaker, and many others—represent both the boldly significant and the subtly brilliant. These are the innovators, the risk-takers in high technology and science today. INVENTORS AT WORK is revealing, surprising, and informative.

408 pages, 6¹/₈ x 9, softcover $9.95   Order Code: 86-96080
hardcover $17.95   Order Code: 86-96312

THE WORLD OF MATHEMATICS
A Small Library of the Literature of Mathematics from A'h-mosé the Scribe to Albert Einstein, Presented with Commentaries and Notes by James R. Newman
Foreword by Philip and Phylis Morrison

"Newman writes with unfailing wit, tinted with irony and never dulled by cliché. But good writing would not be enough. He is able to make these 133 selections, chosen with great success to allow access by the nonspecialist, more accessible still by a brilliant page or two of his own introduction."
Philip and Phylis Morrison, from the Foreword

"...the most amazing selection of articles about mathematics yet unpublished...a delight to readers with a wide range of backgrounds."
The New York Times

First published in 1956 to wide acclaim, THE WORLD OF MATHEMATICS is now available again. Out of print for many years, this four-volume anthology is a rich and spirited collection of 133 articles from the literature of mathematics. You'll read intriguing essays that provide windows on the history and concepts of pure mathematics, the laws of probability and statistics, puzzles and paradoxes, and the role of mathematics in economics, art, music, and literature. The selections range from hard-to-find classical pieces by Archimedes, Galileo, and Mendel to works of twentieth-century thinkers, including John Maynard Keynes, Bertrand Russell, and A. M. Turing. This new Tempus edition is completely recomposed, reindexed, and printed on high-quality acid-free paper. Historical and biographical details are updated where appropriate.

2784 pages in four volumes, 6 x 9 boxed set, softcover $50.00   Order Code: 86-96544
hardcover $99.95 Order Code: 86-96593

Microsoft Press books are available wherever fine books are sold, or credit card orders can be placed by calling 1-800-638-3030 (in Maryland call collect 824-7300).

The manuscript for this book was prepared and submitted to Microsoft Press in electronic form. Text files were processed and formatted using Microsoft Word.

Cover art by David Shannon
Interior text design by Darcie S. Furlan

Text composition by Microsoft Press in Times Roman with display in Times Roman Bold, using the Magna composition system and the Linotronic 300 laser imagesetter.

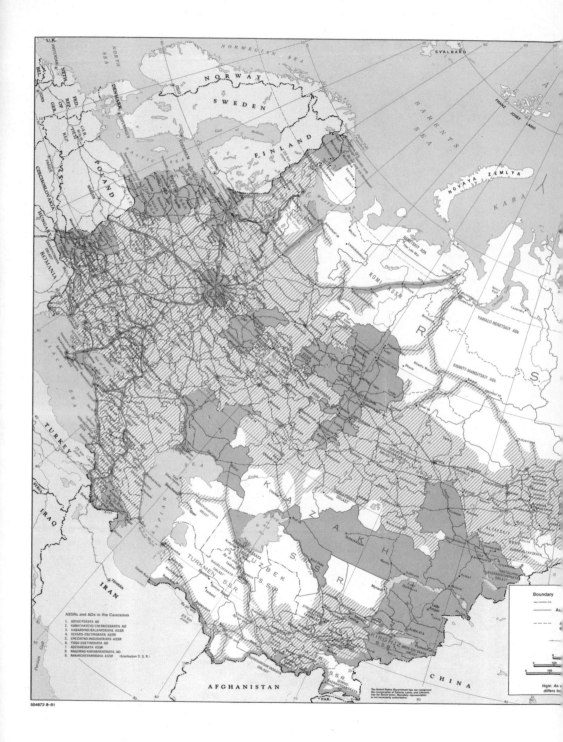

ASSRs and AOs in the Caucasus

1. ADIGEYSKAYA AO
2. KARACHAYEVO-CHERKESSKAYA AO
3. KABARDINO-BALKARSKAYA ASSR
4. SEVERO-OSETINSKAYA ASSR
5. CHECHENO-INGUSHSKAYA ASSR
6. YUGO-OSETINSKAYA AO
7. ADZHARSKAYA ASSR
8. NAGORNO-KARABAKHSKAYA AO
9. NAKHICHEVANSKAYA ASSR   (Azerbaijan S.S.R.)

Boundary

The United States Government has not recognized
the incorporation of Estonia, Latvia, and Lithuania
into the Soviet Union. Boundary representation
is not necessarily authoritative.

Note: An
differs fr